ESSENTIALS
OF
RISK
MANAGEMENT
AND
INSURANCE

John J. Hampton

amacom

American Management Association

New York • Atlanta • Boston • Chicago • Kansas City • San Francisco • Washington, D.C.
Brussels • Toronto • Mexico City

This publication is designed to provide accurate and authoritative information in regard to the subject matter covered. It is sold with the understanding that the publisher is not engaged in rendering legal, accounting, or other professional service. If legal advice or other expert assistance is required, the services of a competent professional person should be sought.

Library of Congress Cataloging-in-Publication Data

Hampton, John J., 1942–
    Essentials of risk management and insurance / John J. Hampton.
        p.   cm.
    Includes index.
    ISBN 0-8144-7782-8
    1. Risk (Insurance)—United States. 2. Risk management—United
States. I. Title.
    HG8054.5.H36   1993
    368'.00973—dc20   92-31935
                                                                    CIP

Printing number

10   9   8   7   6   5   4   3   2   1

To Richard Ognibene, David Bossman, and Others Who Know the Importance of Friendship

Contents

Preface

The world of insurance and risk management has changed dramatically in the past twenty years. Individuals and organizations have been forced to confront a wide range of new and increasingly complex exposures that threaten their financial viability. For families, their health and property are at risk. For organizations, survival itself may be at stake.

This book shows how to manage exposures by identifying risks and developing techniques to deal with them. The text provides explanations of the important points and shows examples and applications. The chapters provide an overview of each topic and serve as a source of information. However, this is primarily a book of exercises. To benefit the most, you must complete them. The exercises provide opportunities to analyze, interpret, and apply the lessons of the text. The emphasis is on thinking and problem solving. The exercises will also help you to fully integrate the language of insurance and risk management into your working vocabulary.

You may think that insurance is dull. Nothing could be farther from the truth. You may be bored at the thought of gaining a better understanding of the homeowners policy. This could change when you complete the exercise where the family dog chases a deer through a window. If you do not know what protection you have against financial loss, you could be unpleasantly surprised.

This book can be used for two purposes. You can gain a better understanding of your insurance protection. Coverage for your life, car, home, and exposure to the threat of lawsuits is important. Everyone should know the risks and exposures of life. The second purpose is to help you assess whether the world of insurance and risk management might be attractive as a career field. It truly is an interesting area that needs bright and dedicated professionals.

As you read this book and complete the exercises, you will discover the exciting field of insurance and risk management. Have a pleasant journey.

Acknowledgments

A number of people have provided helpful comments and reviews of this book. Particular thanks go to Craig Gass for his excellent suggestions for structure and content. Thanks also to Professors Laurie Bilik, Judy LaMonica, Ken Mead, and Jack Nelson at The College of Insurance.

1

The Nature of Risk

Any investment of money for the purpose of earning a return involves decisions related to risk and return. To be acceptable, any investment opportunity must offer a level of return that is appropriate to the level of risk involved. Thus a higher-risk situation must offer a higher expected return than another situation with a lower risk level.

In this chapter, we deal with the nature of risk as it is defined in different areas of the organization. In making distinctions among various categories of risk, we establish the foundation for covering risk in the context of insurance and risk management.

The Conceptual Foundation

Individuals and organizations conduct their activities in a risky world. Intuitively, all people understand that risk refers to uncertainty of the future. Still, different people have varying understandings of the term. In this section, we examine some of the concepts related to risk.

Elements of Risk

A dictionary definition of *risk* refers to the chance of injury, damage, or loss. An economist might define it as "the dispersion of actual from expected results." A statistician might define it as "the probability of any undesirable outcome." With any of these definitions, risk must involve three elements:

1. *Uncertainty of an Event.* Risk can exist only when two or more future outcomes are possible. A fire can occur, causing damage to a house, or not occur. The price of common stock can rise or fall. Both examples involve an uncertainty of future outcomes.

2. *Loss.* One of the outcomes must be undesirable or negative. A

fire destroys a house. A decline in common stock prices causes a financial loss.

3. *Linkage.* The risk must affect an individual or organization. A fire causes a loss to the owner, occupants, or possibly the neighbors of a house. A decline in stock price causes a financial loss to an owner of the stock.

Speculative Risks

A number of different kinds of risk can be identified. One category covers *speculative risk,* defined as any chance where both loss and gain are possible. Individuals and organizations deal with many speculative risks, including:

1. *Operating Risk*—The possibility of failure to succeed as a viable organization. A company may fail to sell goods or services at a profit. A nonprofit organization may fail to collect adequate donations to support its activities. A government may be unable to collect taxes. In its operations, an organization can be highly successful or can fail. Thus operations reflect a speculative risk.

2. *Financial Risk*—The chance that an individual or organization may lose money on its investment in assets. It can occur when money is lent to a third party who later is unable to make interest payments and principal repayments. It can occur with the purchase of common stock, real estate, or other investments. Since assets can involve either profit or loss, the purchase of assets involves speculative risk.

3. *Purchasing Power Risk*—The chance of a change in the amount of goods or services that can be purchased with money being held by an individual or organization. Inflation erodes the value of money being held as savings or due to be paid at a future date. Deflation occurs when prices decline in an economic system. Individuals and organizations who hold money realize an increase in their ability to buy goods. Even though inflation is more common, this risk is speculative because prices can rise or fall.

4. *Foreign Exchange Risk*—The chance that a currency will change in value compared to other currencies. If a currency rises in value, it can purchase more goods. If it declines, goods become more expensive. Individuals or firms who hold or owe foreign currencies undertake a speculative risk.

Pure Risk

A *pure risk* is defined as the chance of an unexpected or unplanned loss without the accompanying chance of a gain. This is the risk that is properly the domain of insurance and risk management. Three characteristics may be identified with a pure risk:

1. *Expected and Unfavorable Outcomes.* A pure risk involves a likely outcome that may not materialize. A house is not expected to burn down. A person is not expected to die in the near term. Yet, the house may catch on fire, and the person may die. These are both unfavorable and unexpected outcomes.

2. *Objective Possibility.* A pure risk exists when an unfavorable outcome is possible as a condition of the real world. It is not necessary that it be known to the individual or organization. This situation has two implications: (a) Dangers can exist that are not recognized in advance. A meteorite crashing into a home is such a risk. It is a pure risk. (b) An individual can believe that danger exists when it does not. An individual can believe that her coffee pot is emitting radioactive particles that will kill her. Most of the time, this is an imagined risk.

3. *Not Necessarily Measurable.* The extent of the pure risk may not be measurable. Hence, no one may be able to predict the likelihood of loss. This does not matter. A meteorite hitting the house is a pure risk whether or not we can predict or measure the frequency of occurrences.

Degree of Pure Risk

The *degree of risk* refers to the magnitude of the pure risk facing the individual or organization. A situation with a high degree of risk is called very risky. With a low degree of risk, it is called not too risky.

The degree of risk can be measured objectively or subjectively. An objective measure provides historical or other data to determine the level of past losses and the likelihood that such loss levels will continue. A subjective measure may use intuition or judgment to assess the degree of pure risk. Individuals and organizations commonly make objective or subjective evaluations of the degree of pure risk in their lives and operating environments.

However measured, we can identify two dimensions that determine the degree of pure risk:

1. *Likelihood of Loss.* A high probability of loss may be viewed as having a high degree of risk.

2. *Size of Loss.* A potential loss that is large compared to the resources of the individual or organization may be viewed as having a high degree of risk.

The total degree of risk involves a combination of both likelihood and size of potential losses.

Insurable Risks

Insurance and risk management are disciplines that deal specifically with those pure risks that meet two tests, as follows:

1. *Contingent Loss*—A loss that is not certain to occur. A house built in a forest faces pure risk from a forest fire. If the fire is set on purpose by the owner of the house in order to destroy it, the loss is not based on a contingency. Thus it is not insurable. Similarly, if the fire has already begun and is moving toward the house, the loss is not insurable.

2. *Financial Loss*—A decrease in money or the disappearance of monetary value. Only a potential loss that has a financial impact meets the standards for insurability. Some risks clearly involve losses but no money: A student who fails to study for an examination may fail a course; a person who is late for dinner may not get fed. These actions may have financial or physical consequences, but are not financial losses.

Categories of Insurable Risk

Insurable risk may be broken down into four distinct categories:

1. *Personal Risk*—The possibility of economic or emotional losses that might be suffered by individuals as they live their daily lives. Examples are the possibility of death, injury, disability, illness, and unemployment.

2. *Property Risk*—The possibility of economic losses that would result if tangible property were to be damaged, destroyed, or stolen. Such losses can be direct, as when a building is destroyed by a hurricane. They can be indirect, as when a company loses sales because its factory has been shut down by a fire.

3. *Liability Risk*—The economic losses that could occur if someone accuses another person or organization of causing a loss or damage and then pursues reimbursement through various legal means.

4. *Performance Risk*—The possible economic losses that would occur if a person or organization failed to provide goods or services as promised. Examples are the failure to pay a debt according to the terms of a loan agreement or allegations that a contractor failed to construct a house according to the blueprint specifications.

Calculation of a Loss

Indemnity is defined as a reimbursement that compensates exactly for a loss. It is, in effect, the payment of an amount of money that restores an individual or organization to the position that existed prior to the loss. For example, an individual sustains a $1,000 loss. If he is reimbursed $1,100, he receives indemnification of $1,000 plus an extra $100. If he receives $900, he is not fully indemnified for the loss.

The magnitude of a loss involves a recognition of obvious and less obvious financial consequences. The calculation of a loss must include three components:

1. *Direct Costs*—Reflecting the damage in its most primary and visible form. For a personal loss, direct costs may be funeral or medical expenses. For a property loss, direct costs may involve money spent to repair or replace the property.

2. *Indirect Costs*—Reflecting damages not so obvious or visible. For a personal loss, indirect costs may compensate individuals for inconvenience, pain, or suffering. For a personal property loss, indirect costs may recognize the loss of the use of an item until it is fixed or replaced. A homeowner may, for example, have to pay for a motel room until her house is repaired after a fire. An organization may suffer a loss of income that would have accrued in the absence of property damage.

3. *Additional Expenses*—Covering monies that must be spent as a consequence of a loss. For a personal loss, additional expenses may be incurred to provide psychological counseling for a traumatized victim. For a property loss, expenses may cover renting a temporary substitute for a damaged item, sometimes referred to as *consequential expenses*.

Exposures, Perils, and Hazards

We earlier defined a pure risk as the chance of an unexpected or unplanned loss without the accompanying chance of a gain. Here, we distinguish among the three terms that provide a framework for pure risks:

1. *Exposure*—A condition where risk could cause a loss. Alternatively, in this situation an individual or organization is vulnerable to loss. Simple examples are a person who could be injured or killed or property that could be damaged. Once an organization signs a contract to purchase a building, it has an exposure. Similarly, the birth of a baby is an exposure to a parent. The hiring of an employee presents an exposure to a company. Without an exposure, there is no possibility of loss.

2. *Peril*—The immediate cause of a loss, such as death, fire, an accident, a flood, and theft.

3. *Hazard*—Any condition that increases the likelihood of a loss

from a peril, such as a can of gasoline stored in a garage. It increases the chance of a fire.

Conceptually, it is important to distinguish between a peril and hazard. This allows us to take every possible step to reduce hazards that increase the chance of a loss. At the same time, some overlap can occur. For example, a can of gasoline stored in a garage is a hazard that increases the chance of fire, which is a peril. At the same time, the possibility of fire is a hazard that increases the chance of the peril of death to an individual.

Categories of Hazards

Individuals and organizations can take steps to reduce the hazards that increase the chance of future loss. In this context, the task is to identify the hazards, which are not always apparent. These three categories of hazard should be noted:

1. *Physical Hazard*—A physical condition or behavior that increases the chance of loss. An individual who commutes to work on a motorcycle increases the chance of loss from the peril of an accident. A company that manufactures chemicals has physical hazards that may increase the chance of cancer in its employees. A government agency located in an old wooden building may have electrical wiring that increases the chance of fire.

2. *Moral Hazard*—Any tendency of an individual to be dishonest or otherwise lack integrity. An automobile mechanic who installs faulty parts in an automobile increases the chance of an accident. A dishonest employee might steal office supplies, take kickbacks from suppliers, or file a fraudulent accident claim.

3. *Morale or Behavioral Hazard*—Any tendency of individuals to be careless. A homeowner may leave tools blocking a doorway, increasing the chance of someone tripping and falling down. A driver may improperly load his truck, increasing the chance of an accident. A night security guard may fail to check the locks on all entrances to a museum, increasing the chance of theft.

Dealing With Risk

It is not possible for individuals or organizations to escape entirely from situations of pure risk. Thus strategies must be identified and steps taken to handle the major risks that can cause serious financial and emotional losses. Basically, we can identify a number of major approaches to dealing with risk.

Risk Retention

Worldwide, the most common approach to dealing with pure risk is to retain it. We face so many potential risks that it is not possible to avoid or control all of them. In this context, we identify two categories of retention:

1. *Involuntary Retention*—Occurs when the individual or organization is not aware of the existence of the pure risk. An individual retains a risk without realizing the exposure or financial consequences. A person who works outdoors in the sun may be exposed to an increased chance of skin cancer. A company may face future lawsuits as a result of a design change in its products, yet may not have insurance to cover future damages that may be awarded by the courts. If the company is unaware of the defect and lack of coverage, a situation of involuntary retention exists.

2. *Voluntary Retention*—Occurs when the individual or organization is aware of the pure risk and decides to assume the financial impact of any future losses. A family with safe drivers may not purchase insurance that would pay the cost of repairs on their cars after an automobile accident. In effect, the family retains the collision risk on its automobiles. A university may not insure the chairs and desks in its classrooms.

Retention is a logical and cost-effective approach to dealing with many risks. The family of safe drivers would pay insurance premiums priced high enough to cover losses from some unsafe drivers. As long as the family is financially able to repair or replace a damaged vehicle, insurance may not be cost-effective. Similarly, the university may experience a certain level of damaged or stolen classroom furniture. Still, insurance requires the payment of premiums, and filing claims for losses may involve expensive procedures for maintaining inventories and proving losses. It may be cheaper to retain the pure risk and simply buy new furniture each year.

Risk Avoidance

The risk avoidance strategy involves an individual's or organization's refusal to accept the exposure that can cause a future loss. An individual can avoid the risk of an airplane crash simply by refusing to fly. A company can avoid the pure risks of a manufacturing facility by purchasing its components from other manufacturers. A hospital can avoid some malpractice lawsuits in high-risk areas by refusing to accept patients with certain illnesses or injuries.

As a general rule, avoidance is not a widely used technique for dealing with risk. In many instances, it has greater negative than positive aspects. The quality of life and ability of a society to improve itself involve the acceptance of risks. Excessive reliance on avoidance would undermine many of the advances and benefits of technology, economics, and social activity.

Risk Control

If pure risk cannot be avoided in total, it may be possible to reduce the likelihood of loss. Four loss reduction techniques are commonly used:

1. *Loss Prevention*—Averting a loss before it occurs. Removing oily rags from manufacturing premises may prevent the start of a fire. Regular maintenance and checkups of the major systems in an automobile increase the odds of preventing an accident that might otherwise result from a mechanical failure. Hiring a security guard to work in a warehouse may prevent theft or burglary.

2. *Loss Reduction*—Reducing the severity of a loss if it does happen. Installing a home security alarm system connected to the police department may reduce the allowable time for a burglary while a homeowner is on vacation. Placing fire extinguishers in the workplace facilitates a rapid response to small fires and may limit the damage they inflict. Investigating the work history of potential employees for signs of dishonesty or careless behavior may reduce the number of future thefts.

3. *Segregation*—Any practices undertaken to reduce the extent of loss from a single event. An organization can stipulate that senior executives travel on different modes of transportation. A single accident cannot kill all the members of the management group. A company can store its inventory in several warehouses that are physically separated. A fire at one location will not destroy all the inventory.

4. *Duplication*—The maintenance of multiple systems or assets to reduce the impact of a loss on primary systems or assets. An extra set of accounting records and computer disks can be stored in a bank vault. Key medications can be purchased by a hospital from multiple suppliers. Arrangements can be made for a backup telephone system in case of damage to the firm's switchboard.

Transfer

Transfer refers to the shifting of pure risk from one individual or organization to another. Basically, two mechanisms are common:

1. *Noninsurance Contractual Transfer*—An agreement between two

parties where one party accepts the risk that normally would be borne by the other party. A tenant can agree to indemnify a landlord for any lawsuits that arise out of the tenant's use of property. Similarly, a manufacturing company could agree to assume risks that otherwise would be the responsibility of the owners of the trucks that carry its goods.

2. *Insurance Contractual Transfer*—Far and away, the largest transfer mechanism. An insurance policy is a contract between two parties where one party pays a premium and the other party assumes financial responsibility for a pure risk. An insurance contract is a business arrangement designed specifically to transfer risk from a party that cannot bear the full exposure to another party, an insurance company, that can bear a possible loss.

Hierarchy of Insurable Risk

This chapter introduces several risk concepts. A hierarchy of insurable risk can be used to express the relationship of insurable risk to other kinds of risk noted in the chapter. In a sense, we are viewing risk sequentially from the broadest to the most specific definitions. This hierarchy may be expressed as follows:

1. *Risk.* This broadest risk concept involves the chance of injury, damage, or loss. Some of these risks are insurable; some are not.

2. *Pure vs. Speculative Risk.* The first subdivision recognizes pure and speculative risks within the broader category of all risks. Normally, only pure risks are insurable.

3. *Economic vs. Noneconomic Risk.* Pure risk can be divided into economic and noneconomic risks. Only those risks that qualify as having potential economic losses are insurable.

4. *Insurable vs. Noninsurable Risk.* Economic risk can be divided into insurable and noninsurable risks. Insurable risks are properly the subject matter for a book on insurance and risk management.

5. *Personal, Property, Liability, and Performance Risks.* Insurable risk can be broken down into personal, property, liability, and performance areas. As we see later, the discipline of insurance is quite varied in order to deal with each of the four kinds of insurable risk.

Exercises

1. Wallace Corporation manufactures interconnect modems that are used to convert telephone company software into special applications for per-

sonal computers. The company has a one-year contract to provide 18,000 modems to National Computer Corporation. At its manufacturing plant in Alabama, Wallace is experiencing difficulty meeting the quality control standards for the contract. Then, a fire destroys the area of the factory where quality control tests are made. Fifteen months later, the contract is cancelled by National Computer after only 1,100 modems are delivered. Two months later, Wallace declares bankruptcy. What kinds of risk are involved in this situation? What kinds of losses?

2. Sunshine Travel sells vacation packages to wealthy individuals. The overhead for its operations has been causing the company to lose money for almost a year. Then, the company incurs three problems. (a) Money that was being held in a bank account for future cruises is not adequate to pay for the cruises because the shipping company raised the price of deluxe accommodations. Sunshine had guaranteed the price of the voyages and has to make up the difference. (b) The Italian lira has risen in value since the start of the year. Once again, the company has to make up a difference on promised hotel reservations in Rome, Florence, and Venice. (c) Three of its offices have failed to attract wealthy people as clientele. Those offices will soon have to be closed. Also, the manager of one of the offices has lied to clients about trip conditions and costs. Three lawsuits have been filed against the company alleging fraud and criminal behavior. What kinds of risks are involved in this situation?

3. Danforth Corporation manufactures and sells small electric heaters. Because of rising electric rates and new government regulations, the product can no longer be sold in sufficient numbers to cover overhead. If the company fails to develop some new products, it will soon be out of business. Danforth wants to manufacture automatic gourmet coffee makers using the heating element technology that it knows. Banks are reluctant to provide enough money to finance the project. If money cannot be found in six months, the company will probably declare bankruptcy. What kinds of risks are involved in this situation?

4. John Jacobs smokes a cigarette while pumping gasoline in a gas station. A spark ignites an explosion that kills a customer. It also injures a fellow worker who is disabled for six months. The explosion causes $16,000 of damage to a car and the station itself. Three lawsuits are filed against John and the station. The station is closed for three months, and the owner defaults on his bank loan because he has no revenues. What risks are involved in this situation? What are the exposure(s) and peril(s)? What kind of hazards are present?

5. A new employee at Carlson Corporation uses his key to enter the company garage at night. He takes a truck without permission to move some household furniture for a friend. This violates company policy. The regular driver never checked the brake fluid in the truck. While the employee drives down the highway, the brakes fail and the truck hits a

car from behind. The truck and car are damaged. The employee and his friend go to the hospital. The driver of the car sues Carlson. What risks are involved? What are the exposure and peril? What kinds of hazards are involved?

6. Delan Company refuses to purchase fire insurance coverage on its main manufacturing plant. The cost of insurance is simply too high in the view of management. To reduce the chance of fire, the company has hired a full-time employee who is a former Cleveland firefighter. The individual inspects all property regularly and removes fire hazards. The company does have a liability insurance policy to pay for damages awarded in lawsuits. The policy states that Delan must pay for any damages awarded under $25,000. Insurance covers larger awards. What approaches are followed by Delan to deal with risk? What approach is not identified?

7. Ann Allen is the risk manager for Mackey Products. She is looking at the following list of proposed company actions:
   a. Investing employee health care funds in common stock until needed
   b. Insuring the headquarters against the theft of office supplies
   c. Insuring the plant against the theft of inventory
   d. Providing disability benefits to employees
   e. Hiring an attorney as a full-time employee to handle lawsuits
   f. Protecting a refinery from a civil disturbance
   g. Enhancing the image of the company as a responsible citizen of its various communities
   h. Purchasing insurance to provide reimbursement if the company treasurer steals or embezzles funds

   Place each of these actions in its proper place in the hierarchy of insurable risks.

2

The Nature of Insurance

Insurance is defined as a financial device that redistributes the costs of unexpected losses from pure risks. It does this by combining the risks of many individuals or organizations into a group and then using funds contributed by the group members to cover the losses. It is both a social and economic device that is used to pay the costs of economic losses from illness, injury, accidents, or natural causes. It is the primary tool used by individuals and organizations to transfer pure risks.

In spite of this simple definition, insurance is a highly developed academic discipline and practical field of activity. In this chapter, we examine the nature of insurance.

Characteristics of Insurance

Insurance can be examined from different viewpoints. In this section, we cover some of the characteristics of insurance.

Definitions of Insurance

Insurance is viewed differently depending upon whether we are dealing with an economic, legal, or social viewpoint. Three common definitions are:

1. *Economic Viewpoint.* Insurance is a mechanism that reduces uncertainty in an economic system by transferring or financing risk.

2. *Legal Viewpoint.* Insurance is a legal device that permits the transfer of risk from one party to another through the use of a contract of indemnity.

3. *Social Viewpoint.* Insurance is a device that permits the combining of the risks of many individuals or organizations into a large group, thus allowing the statistical prediction of losses and the use of small payments by many people to pay for large losses.

Purpose of Insurance

The purpose of insurance is to reduce uncertainty and some of the economic consequences of unexpected loss. Insurance provides a means to transfer or share the risk of large uncertain losses. Although it provides funds to cover losses, insurance specifically does not prevent loss.

Benefits of Insurance

As a social and economic device, insurance provides four major benefits to society:

1. *Security for Individuals and Organizations.* Because insurance provides a source of funding to cover a portion of economic loss, it provides a certain measure of security and peace of mind to individuals and managers.

2. *Resources to Cover Losses.* When accidents or other harmful events cause economic losses, society must have devices to cover them. A worker injured in a factory will have hospital bills. A building destroyed by fire will have to be replaced. Insurance provides resources to cover such losses.

3. *Encouragement of Safety Consciousness.* Because insurance focuses on possible losses and the cost of insurance is related to the hazards that increase the chance of losses, the purchase of insurance encourages safety consciousness of employees and other individuals. Hazards are sought out and eliminated where possible. Such loss prevention efforts can reduce the number of accidents and injuries.

4. *Capital Formation.* Insurance companies collect money and invest it until it is needed to pay for losses. Large sums of money are collected and invested in financial securities, real estate, and other assets. The insurance activity thus provides capital for a country and assists in financing economic growth.

General Characteristics of Insurance

Several broad characteristics may be matched with the insurance device.

1. *Transfers of Risk to a Group.* Insurance brings together many individual exposures and combines them in a group. Thus the funds from the group are available to pay for individual losses.

2. *Pooling of Losses.* Each of the individual policyholders pays a small sum of money in return for coverage in the event of a large loss. Thus large losses are shared by many individuals.

3. *Indemnification of Economic Losses.* Since money is collected in advance of losses, insurance companies have available funds to pay for economic losses when they occur.

Law of Large Numbers

One of the benefits of insurance is that it makes losses more predictable. As an example, we may know that one accident will occur each year for every 500 automobiles. In spite of having this information, one person cannot know whether he or she will have an automobile accident in any given year. The situation is different for an insurance company that provides insurance for 100,000 automobiles. The company can expect 200 accidents, more or less, during the year. Although it does not know which cars will be involved, the insurance company can predict with some accuracy the number of accidents that will take place.

The reason an insurance company can predict losses more accurately than an individual involves a law of mathematics. The *law of large numbers* is a statistical theorem stating that as a sample becomes larger, the outcome will be closer to the predicted probability. For example, if we flip a coin six times, the most likely outcome for heads is three times, or 50 percent. Yet, nearly half the time we will have either two heads or four heads, a percentage of 33 or 67 percent. These are large deviations from the 50 percent probability of a head or a tail.

What happens if we increase the number of coin flips to 10,000? The answer is that the deviation will become smaller. We can be reasonably certain that in 10,000 coin tosses we will not deviate from 50 percent by very much. The phenomenon of increasing predictive accuracy with many outcomes is also called the *law of averages*.

Insurance vs. Gambling

Insurance is fundamentally different from gambling in three important ways:

1. *Existing vs. New Risk.* Insurance is used only for risks that currently exist in the real world. For example, by its very existence a house is exposed to the peril of fire. Since this is an existing risk, fire insurance can be purchased to repair or replace the house after a fire. Gambling, in contrast, creates a new risk. When one dollar is used to purchase a lottery ticket, the risk of losing the dollar is created at the moment the ticket is purchased.

2. *Social Role.* Insurance plays a different social role than gambling. Insurance meets the needs of society for a device to pay for losses from

pure risks. Gambling, in contrast, has nothing to do with pure risks. Gambling may meet some individual needs for excitement. In some cases, taxes on lotteries or race tracks provide funds for social purposes. However, gambling plays only a minor social role compared to insurance.

3. *Gambling Reduction.* If a homeowner takes no steps to purchase insurance to pay for damage from fire, he or she is, in effect, gambling that fire will not occur. The purchase of insurance does not eliminate the chance of fire, but it can overcome much of the negative financial impact. Thus insurance is a way of reducing the gambling on uncertain events by individuals or organizations.

Insurable Risks

All pure risks do not qualify for loss reduction through the mechanism of insurance. For a risk to be insurable, it usually must meet seven requirements:

1. *The loss must not be trivial.* Creating an insurance policy requires payments for administrative costs, including the writing of the policy, examining whether the exposure is insurable, and investigating any claim that a loss has occurred. Thus insurance would be prohibitively expensive if it were purchased to cover trivial losses.

2. *The loss must not be catastrophic to the insurer.* An insurance company can cover large losses from the viewpoint of the insured. It cannot cover such losses if they would exceed the insurer's ability to cover them. Insurance is provided in a system whereby insurance companies often reinsure their large exposures. Still, losses such as those that would occur from a nuclear war between nations could be catastrophic from the viewpoint of the insurer and reinsurer. Thus it is difficult to purchase insurance to cover these risks.

3. *Premiums must be affordable.* A *premium* is the payment made for insurance coverage. Insurance will not be available if a reasonable premium cannot be charged. Normally, this means that the chance of loss must be reasonably low. As an example, a man may be able to purchase $100,000 of life insurance for a premium payment of $2,000 per year. If he learns that he will shortly undergo open heart surgery, the required premium might jump to $25,000 per year. The individual would probably not be able to afford the high premium. Thus in most cases insurance is not available when premiums are not likely to be affordable.

4. *Large Number of Exposures.* Most lines of insurance involve many individuals or organizations who face pure risks. Two kinds of exposures are insurable:

a. *Similar Exposures.* A large number of similar exposures allows the operation of the law of large numbers to predict losses. This assists the insurer in establishing premiums to be paid for policies.

b. *Unique Exposures.* In some cases, the identical nature of exposures is waived. An example would be insurance to cover an opera star against losing her singing voice. Although it is not possible to use the law of averages to predict losses, a large number of unique exposures operates similarly to the law of averages. This is the case when an insurer accepts large numbers of different kinds of risks. Even though individual losses cannot be predicted accurately, the distribution of exposures among many different risks diversifies the coverages and permits the unique exposures to be insurable.

5. *The loss must be calculable or diversifiable.* It is possible to have many exposures and still not be able to apply the law of large numbers. Similarly, it is possible to have a unique exposure that can be averaged among many other unique risks. The first situation occurs when loss data have not been collected or are unavailable. The second occurs when a single exposure is too large to be handled by the insurer. For a risk to be insurable, the insurance company must have a way to estimate losses or diversify them. In the United States, actuarial data are available and frequently shared by insurance companies to facilitate calculating the likelihood of losses. For unique risks, Lloyd's of London specializes in insurance policies for unique exposures. It does this by diversifying the risk among many individuals willing to provide a percentage of the coverage.

6. *The loss must be accidental.* A *fortuitous loss* is accidental or one that happens by chance. Insurance is designed to cover such losses. It must certainly be accidental or unintentional from the viewpoint of the insured. If the chance of loss is under the control of the insured, a policy will not be written. Similarly, if an insured person deliberately causes a loss, benefits will not be paid under a policy.

7. *The loss must be definite.* An insurable risk can exist only when losses are definite as to the cause, time, and location and the extent of the damage. In situations where it is difficult or impossible to determine whether a loss occurred and to measure its extent, an insurance company would not be willing to offer coverage. For example, it is not possible to purchase insurance to provide financial benefits in the event of severe psychological depression on the part of an individual. An individual may feel bad at times, but it may be impossible to agree on a definition of severe depression. This exposure is not insurable.

The Insurance Device

Insurance is available to cover many of the risks and uncertainties in society. In this section, we examine some of the common features of the various insurance mechanisms available to individuals and organizations.

The Insurance Contract

Insurance is provided in a contractual agreement between two parties. Some of the important terms in the contract are:

1. *Parties to the Contract*—The *insured*, which is the individual or organization that has purchased insurance, and the *insurer*, the insurance company that provides insurance.

2. *Insurance Policy*—A written agreement that states in detail the rights and obligations of the insured and insurer.

3. *Premium*—The money paid by the insured to obtain coverage against a loss.

4. *Loss*—The decline in value that occurs as a result of an accident, illness, or other unexpected event.

5. *Claim*—A statement that a loss has occurred and a demand for the payment of benefits under an insurance policy.

6. *Policy Limit*—The maximum benefit or indemnification of loss covered by an insurance policy.

7. *Deductible*—A policy provision that requires the insured to pay for losses up to a specified sum. If a policy contains a $5,000 deductible, the insurance company is responsible only for losses above $5,000.

Categories of Insurance Coverage

Insurance is designed to provide coverage against losses from a variety of perils. Thus we do not have total agreement on how to categorize the coverages. One approach uses broad categories that match the four areas of insurable risk:

1. *Personal Insurance*—Coverages that indemnify individuals against the economic and emotional losses that occur in daily life. Examples are life, health, and unemployment insurance.

2. *Property Insurance*—Coverages that indemnify losses when tangible property is damaged, destroyed, or lost. Payments can be received when property is directly damaged, as by fire, or indirect losses can be

covered. An example is the loss of sales when a hurricane destroys a warehouse.

3. *Liability Insurance*—Coverages that indemnify the losses and expenses of defending lawsuits alleging negligence by a person or organization.

4. *Surety Insurance.* These coverages indemnify losses when one party defaults on an obligation and thus causes damage to another party. An example is coverage to pay for losses if a contractor fails to construct a building in time for sales during the busy Christmas season.

The Lines of Insurance

Separately from categories, insurance may be identified by the purchaser. A *line of insurance* is defined as a grouping of related coverages. Lines of insurance may be identified in two broad categories:

1. *Personal Lines*—Includes policies purchased by individuals and families that cover nonbusiness exposures. Some of the policies cover the lives or health of individuals. Others cover property owned by one or more persons. Examples are life, health, automobile, homeowners, and boat insurance.

2. *Commercial Lines*—Purchased by businesses and other organizations and cover exposures faced by employers, companies, other private institutions, and governments. Commercial coverages indemnify organizations against personal, property, liability, and performance losses.

Property, Casualty, and Liability Insurance

The terms *property, casualty,* and *liability* insurance overlap and can be confusing. Without trying to resolve the specific problems with definitions of these terms, we instead note some of the problems.

1. *All-Inclusive Use of Property Insurance.* In some cases, the term *property insurance* is used to identify all coverages involving tangible property. Thus someone may discuss automobile liability insurance as a property coverage even though it is generally regarded as a casualty area.

2. *Definition of Casualty Insurance.* A term that has developed historically and is defined by exclusion, it refers to insurance against losses or liabilities arising from accidents or mishaps that are not defined by law or custom as noncasualty lines. Fire and marine insurance, for example, involve casualties but are not lines of casualty insurance. Examples of

casualty insurance are workers compensation, automobile liability, and burglary.

3. *Overlap of Liability Insurance.* With respect to losses of property, accidents, and mishaps, liability insurance overlaps property and casualty. The phrases *property and casualty* and *property and liability* are used interchangeably to describe insurance companies that offer a range of property, casualty, and liability coverages.

In this book, we use the terms *property/casualty* and *property/liability* to refer to insurance companies that offer a wide range of property, casualty, and liability coverages.

Personal Exposures

Personal insurance, not personal lines, is designed to cover four primary exposures facing individuals:

1. *Loss of Life.* Life insurance provides a death benefit to cover the cost of burial or cremation and provides funds for beneficiaries and dependents.

2. *Injury and Illness.* Health insurance provides funds to cover the cost of hospitals, doctors, and therapy to restore individuals to full health or reduce the negative consequences of injuries or illness.

3. *Old Age.* Insurance offered or required by private companies or the government is designed to provide living expenses and other funds for older individuals who are not working or who have retired from their jobs.

4. *Inability to Earn a Living.* Disability and unemployment insurance can be used to provide living expenses for individuals who are unable to earn a living, either temporarily or on a permanent basis.

Nonliability Exposures

Property/casualty or property/liability insurance covers the following four categories of exposure that do not deal with liabilities:

1. *Direct Accidental Damage*—Covers damage or destruction of tangible property. Examples are collision coverage on automobiles and damage to the roof of a building as a result of a storm.

2. *Direct Intentional Damage*—Covers theft and vandalism that are caused intentionally. If such damage is inflicted by the insured party, it is not covered.

3. *Indirect Loss of Income*—Covers losses of profits because an insured cannot use damaged property until it is repaired or replaced. An example is the loss of income from carrying cargoes because a ship has been damaged in a collision at sea.

4. *Indirect Extra Costs*—Covers higher expenses incurred because an insured no longer can use the damaged property. An example is higher living costs in a hotel and restaurants when a family cannot occupy a home damaged by fire.

Liability Exposures

Property/casualty or property/liability insurance covers three categories of liability exposures:

1. *Third Parties*—Individuals or organizations that do not have a contractual or prearranged legal relationship that deals with losses caused by an insured. Third-party liability covers lawsuits and claims by customers, suppliers, strangers, or others who allege that an individual or organization has caused them a loss.

2. *Employees*—Covers claims by employees who allege that the organization has been responsible for injuries, illnesses, or wrongful actions. These are not third-party liabilities because employers and employees have legal responsibilities prescribed by law.

3. *Legal Fees*—Covers the costs of investigating claims and defending them in court.

Insurance Functions

The providing of insurance to cover a specific risk involves a number of functions performed by different individuals. In this section, we examine the functional areas of insurance.

Marketing

Insurance is sold in different ways, depending upon the nature of the product and the needs of the market. Some of the common approaches to marketing are:

1. *General or Independent Agent*—An independent businessperson who represents an insurance company in the selling of insurance and servicing the customer. Most insurance in the United States is sold by

independent agents whose commissions are based on the volume of sales. Agents may work primarily either for the insured or the insurer.

2. *Salaried Representatives*—Insurance sold through employees who receive a salary and bonus. A salaried representative, called a *direct writer* in the property-liability field, works for the insurance company.

3. *Brokers*—Deals with agents or companies to arrange for the purchase of insurance by a customer. Brokers are commonly involved in purchasing insurance for large companies or where specialized knowledge is needed by the insured. The broker works for the buyer of insurance.

Underwriting

Underwriting is the process of determining whether to issue an insurance policy. An *underwriter* is the person who makes this determination. The tasks of the underwriter are:

1. *Evaluate the Exposure.* The underwriter evaluates the perils presented by the application for insurance and examines the hazards that can increase the chance of loss.

2. *Compare the Exposure Against Company Guidelines.* An insurance company has specific guidelines for accepting risks. The company may prohibit certain exposures, restrict the acceptance of others, limit the geographic area of coverage, or otherwise impose restrictions before writing policies.

3. *Recommend or Deny Coverage.* After assessing the dimension of the risk, the underwriter recommends or denies coverage.

Ratemaking

A *rate* is the price charged for each unit of insurance protection and varies with the kind of insurance. In life insurance, a rate might be established for each $1,000 of protection for an individual of a certain age and health. In automobile insurance, a rate might be established for each $100 of liability coverage.

An *actuary* is a mathematician trained in probability theory, calculus, and other areas of mathematics. One of an actuary's duties is to determine the rates for insurance coverage.

The rate charged for coverage is usually based on historical data dealing with losses. The actuary considers the likelihood and severity of loss and develops rates that compensate the insurance company for accepting exposures. Five basic approaches to ratemaking are:

1. *Class Rating.* A single rate is applied to all applicants with a given set of characteristics. The rate is generally based on historical loss data and is the most common method of establishing the price of insurance products.

2. *Schedule Rating.* A list of adjustments is applied to a class rating system. If an individual exposure is less risky than the average, the premium is adjusted downward. Higher-risk situations have increases to the class rate.

3. *Experience Rating.* The prior accident history of the insured is considered in the rate paid for coverage.

4. *Judgment Rating.* When statistical data is missing, the actuary may have to make a subjective estimate of the degree of exposure. Judgment rating allows this approach.

5. *Retrospective Rating.* The actual losses during a policy period are the basis for the rate. A *deposit premium* is defined as an estimated premium paid in advance for insurance coverage. At the end of the period, the premium is adjusted to reflect actual losses. If the insured experiences large losses, additional monies must be paid. With small losses, the insured receives a refund.

Adjusting

Adjusting is the process of investigating an alleged loss and determining whether a claim should be paid. The task is handled by a *claims adjuster*. Basically, the adjusting process involves six steps:

1. *Notice of Loss.* An insurance policy generally provides that an insured must notify the insurance company of a loss that may be covered by the policy. The notification is normally required on a timely basis and may have to be in writing.

2. *Coverage Determination.* When the company is notified of an alleged loss, the adjuster must evaluate whether such a loss is covered by the policy. Four elements must be considered:
   a. Was the policy in effect? The policy may not yet be issued or may have expired.
   b. Does the policy cover this kind of loss?
   c. Did the insured meet all policy conditions? The insured may have intentionally caused the damage or otherwise may have violated the policy.
   d. Is the insured entitled to payment? For example, if the insured sold property prior to the occurrence of the loss, the insurance coverage may no longer be valid.

3. *Investigation.* The adjuster gathers relevant facts, opinions, and

other data to develop a scenario of the events surrounding the alleged loss.

4. *Loss Determination.* If it is determined that the loss is likely to be covered by the policy, the adjuster must decide whether an actual loss occurred. In many cases, people file fraudulent claims seeking insurance payments for an accident or property damage that did not actually occur.

5. *Calculation of the Loss Coverage.* The task of determining the amount to be paid under a policy ranges from relatively easy to highly complex. A life insurance policy of $100,000 can be paid directly at the completion of an investigation. Damages from an industrial accident can involve a complex process of calculation.

6. *Payment of the Claim.* The final step is to pay the claim.

Supporting Functions

Underwriting, ratemaking, and adjusting are the direct functions involved with providing insurance coverage. In addition, the following supporting tasks are performed:

1. *Investing Assets.* Insurance companies collect premiums in advance of losses. While holding the money, the company can invest it to earn a return. This provides additional funds to cover losses and operating expenses.

2. *Regulatory Compliance.* Insurance is a highly regulated business, with considerable interaction between state regulators and insurance companies. Lawyers, accountants, and other individuals ensure compliance with the laws of a state and the requirements of insurance regulators.

3. *Loss Prevention.* Insurance companies are quite active in programs to reduce accidents, illness, and injury. By reducing the number of losses, insurance can be made more affordable. Life insurance companies may have staffers whose primary concern is improving the health of insureds. Property insurance companies may have engineers and other specialists who assist organizations in avoiding accidents.

4. *Administration.* Insurance companies tend to have large staffs to perform administrative tasks. Policies must be printed, checks must be received and distributed, computerized records must be kept, and reports must be prepared.

Insurance Finances

Building upon the functions and activities of insurance, it is important to understand how an insurance company works financially. This topic is covered in this section.

GAAP vs. Statutory Accounting

Generally Accepted Accounting Principles (GAAP) refers to the rules and procedures developed by accountants so that financial records and statements accurately reflect the financial status of a business. To receive an unqualified auditor's opinion, businesses are required to make use of GAAP accounting. *Statutory accounting* refers to the rules and procedures required by state laws or regulatory authorities. The goal of such regulation is to ensure solvency of the insurance entity. Hence, statutory accounting is more conservative than GAAP accounting.

Private insurance companies are required to prepare reports using both GAAP and statutory accounting. The GAAP reports are prepared for shareholders and other parties interested in the financial performance as compared to noninsurance companies. Statutory reports are prepared for regulators interested in the solvency of the company.

Public insurance providers prepare a variety of financial statements that meet the requirements of regulators or interested parties. Aside from the form of the statements, these providers must have sufficient financial resources to meet all claims.

Income Statement Accounts

Whatever the form of insurance provided, a basic relationship must exist between money flowing in and out if an insurance organization is to be financially stable. The relationship involves five accounts:

1. *Premiums*—All monies received or due from premiums on insurance policies.

2. *Investment Income*—Interest, dividends, or other receipts on securities and investments, plus gains on the sale of assets held by insurance organizations.

3. *Losses*—Covers the monies paid or owed to policyholders as a result of claims, plus any adjusting or legal expenses.

4. *Administrative Expenses*—Covers all operating expenses to conduct business and sell, process, and support the company's activities.

5. *Increase to Capital*—In effect, the excess of revenues compared to losses and expenses. For a profit-making company, it is a profit. For a nonprofit insurer, it is an increase to capital.

The basic relationship of these accounts is that all insurance operations must achieve sufficient premiums and investment income to cover losses and expenses, plus provide a margin of safety. This margin is expressed as a profit or an increase to capital.

Balance Sheet

A stable insurance organization also has to be concerned with the relationship between assets and the sources of assets. The relationship involves four accounts:

1. *Admitted Assets*—Highly liquid investments that also meet certain standards of safety. These assets are readily available to pay claims. Assets that are not liquid or are otherwise not available to pay claims are not counted as admitted assets. Examples of nonadmitted assets are furniture, equipment, and overdue premiums.

2. *Reserves*—Liabilities recognizing that the insurance company must set aside funds to pay claims. Reserves are also established for premiums that have not yet been earned.

3. *Other Liabilities*—The other debts of an insurance company in addition to reserves.

4. *Capital*—An equity account on the balance sheet. A portion of the equity is called *policyholders' surplus*, an account similar to retained earnings in a noninsurance organization.

The basic relationship of these accounts is that insurance operations must set aside sufficient funds to pay future losses. Thus, regulators carefully examine the level of reserve adequacy. The insurance organization must have sufficient assets to pay likely future claims.

Exercises

1. A South American country provides medical coverage for its population. It has authorized the formation of an insurance company to collect premiums and pay medical bills for individuals injured in automobile accidents. The company would also be expected to invest its funds in economic projects that will benefit the country. Which viewpoint of insurance best reflects this action? Which benefits are sought? not sought?
2. A coin is flipped 3,000 times and turns up heads 1,900 times. Does this support the law of large numbers?
3. A company is concerned with fire burning down the homes of employees, who then will not be productive at work. It is also concerned with the accidental death of skilled workers. It worries about individuals who spend too much of their money on lottery tickets. And it worries about losing its customers to competitors. Which of these are insurable risks?
4. A company has an explosion in a chemical plant; $200,000 of damage

is caused to the facility, 11 people are hospitalized, and 3 people die. One individual is permanently disabled. The plant closes for six weeks causing a loss of $60,000 in profits. A customer visiting the plant is injured and files a lawsuit. She wins $15,000 in damages. The company spends $8,000 defending the lawsuit. The owner of the company is so angry about the explosion that he smashes a computer with a hammer on a visit to the site. Name each exposure and the area of insurance that covers it.

5. ENTEC Corporation accepts the first $5 million of annual losses and pays for them as an operating expense. Losses from $5 million to $15 million are insured by an insurance company owned by ENTEC. Losses from $15 million to $25 million are insured by Commercial Lines Insurance Company. Losses above $25 million have been passed on by Commercial Lines to Lloyd's of London. Name the risk financing mechanisms used in this situation.

6. Dacron Company can purchase $2 million of insurance coverage for $140,000. It expects losses of only $200,000. Alternatively, it can self-insure for the exposures. What would be its motive to self-insure? to purchase the insurance?

7. Anna Garcia works for Larkin and Jones and helps large corporations purchase insurance to cover machinery. Charlie Andrews is offering insurance underwritten by either Martell Insurance or Continental Insurance. Joe Johnson offers insurance only for Commercial Auto Insurance Company. In terms of marketing, what role is played by each person?

8. Safe Property Insurance sells machinery insurance based on the past losses of a company. It offers workers compensation insurance with a deposit premium paid in advance and either additional premiums or a refund after losses are known. It sells fire insurance on the basis of the past losses of categories of companies. Thus travel agents have different rates from gas stations. Burglary insurance is also sold by category, but the existence of burglarproof locks and size of vaults and safes are considered. The company also offers to insure fine art, but limits the policy to $300,000 per item. Which approach to ratemaking is used for each line of business?

9. Selma White is a claims adjuster. A bakery files a claim under Policy #104665 for a fire loss. Damage is estimated at $3,500. What questions must Selma answer?

10. A company collects $6 million during the year from policyholders. It owns financial securities worth $11 million. It has losses during the year of $5 million. Its reserve for covering losses is $7 million. Its administrative expenses total $2 million. Its capital is $3 million. Which of these items will be recorded on the company's balance sheet? on the income statement?

Each of the following proposals is being evaluated by an insurance company. For each, tell whether it represents a viable policy. Why or why not?

11. If a person dies before age 60, a death benefit will be provided in the amount of $100,000. If the person lives to be age 60, the individual will be given $200,000 plus a $3,000 monthly income for the rest of his natural life. The policy will be offered to individuals below the age of 58.

12. If any financial officer of a company speculates in the stock market with the company's funds and loses more than $1 million, the insurance policy will cover the losses.

13. If an overseas factory is confiscated by the local government for no valid reason, the insurance policy will pay for the loss.

14. If a homeowner snaps under pressure and sets fire to her house, the damages will be covered by insurance if a court-appointed psychiatrist certifies that the person suffered from temporary insanity at the time the fire occurred.

15. If a child loses a favorite toy, the insurance policy will pay for the damages if the toy does not cost more than $100.

16. In the event an employee suffers serious depression for a considerable period of time, the insurance policy will provide monies for travel to a restful resort and will cover expenses during the visit.

17. In the event of the destruction of a factory as a result of the meltdown of a nuclear power plant that generates electricity, 80 percent of the damages will be covered by insurance.

18. In the event a new drug for treating cancer does not receive the approval of the Food and Drug Administration, insurance will reimburse all expenses for developing the drug.

19. In the event of the loss of professional singing quality, the voices of opera singers and rock stars will be insured in an amount equal to the individual's likely earnings over the next five years.

20. In the event of the loss of a person's wallet or purse, insurance will pay for the loss of cash up to a limit of $10,000.

21. In the event of a child losing her belief in the religion of the parents, the parents' pain and suffering will be reimbursed in the amount of $20,000.

3

Insurance in the United States

The U.S. insurance industry is large and varied. It contains a number of private and public insurers with different approaches to selling policies and managing their operations. Insurance is regulated at the state rather than federal level.

In this chapter, we cover the structure and regulation of the U.S. insurance industry.

Types of Insurers

Insurance companies are classified by the kind of insurance products they offer, by the legal form of their organization, or by whether they are private or public. In this section, we examine the structure of the U.S. insurance industry in terms of these different categories.

Classification by Underwriting Categories

Insurance companies are categorized by the nature of the business they undertake. The major underwriting categories are:

1. *Life Insurance.* More than 2,300 companies identify their primary lines of business in the areas of life and health insurance. These companies also issue annuity contracts that provide retirement benefits to policyholders.

2. *Property Casualty Insurance.* More than 3,800 companies provide insurance in the property, casualty, and liability areas. In many cases, these companies also provide health and accident insurance.

3. *Health and Accident Insurance.* Blue Cross, Blue Shield, and independent organizations are organized throughout the United States to

provide hospital and medical expense coverage. These organizations are major providers of health insurance with more than 100 million covered persons.

Classification by Legal Form

A second approach to categorizing the U.S. insurance industry makes use of the following legal forms:

1. *Stock Companies.* A *capital stock company* is privately owned by its shareholders. These companies operate with the goal of earning a profit. Stock companies may operate in life, health, and property-casualty areas.

2. *Mutual Insurance Companies.* These private companies do not seek a profit to be distributed to shareholders. In effect, they are owned by their policyholders or members. They operate at a level that covers losses and expenses and positively contributes to capital. The United States has a wide variety of mutual insurance companies, including:

   a. *Life Insurance.* Even though there are fewer than 125 mutual life companies, they provide almost half of the nation's life insurance coverage. Some of the largest providers of life and health policies are mutuals.

   b. *Fraternals.* A *fraternal society* is a voluntary social organization. These nonprofit organizations often provide life and health insurance to their members.

   c. *Reciprocals.* A *reciprocal exchange* is an unincorporated association organized to provide insurance for its members. Each member is both an insured and an insurer. If a member, called a subscriber, has a loss, the other members provide funds to indemnify the loss.

3. *Health Care Organizations.* Health care insurance is provided by both profit and not-for-profit organizations. These include Blue Cross, Blue Shield, and independent plans discussed earlier.

4. *Government Insurance. Social insurance* may be defined as a government insurance program designed to provide economic security for citizens of a country. In the United States, a number of state and federal programs provide unemployment, disability, and retirement insurance and workers compensation. These programs operate on a nonprofit basis.

5. *Lloyd's Associations.* Groups of individuals agree to provide insurance coverage in specified areas with losses covered up to certain limits. Some thirty such associations make a profit for the individuals underwriting the risks.

Classification by Company Organization

A third approach to classifying the insurance industry is by the structure of the company. The categories are:

1. *Monoline Company*—An organization that specializes in providing a single line of insurance coverage, for example, a company that provides only homeowners insurance.

2. *Multiple Line Company*—A company that provides coverage in more than one area. In most cases, the coverage is provided by separately incorporated subsidiaries. Originally, multiple line companies tended to restrict their activities to either the life-health or property-casualty areas. Today, these companies may offer all forms of insurance coverage.

3. *Financial Services Company*—An organization that has insurance and noninsurance operations in the same corporate structure or group of companies. Generally, the various companies are all involved in providing financial services for customers. In some cases, nonfinancial operations are undertaken. Financial services are offered by either a capital stock or mutual parent company. The subsidiary companies normally are separately incorporated along the lines of the various business enterprises.

Size of the Industry

The insurance industry in the United States is an important part of the overall economy. In this section, we examine some indicators of industry size and importance.

Size of Life Insurance

Insurance in force refers to the face amount of insurance provided under issued policies. In 1988, life insurance in force in the United States exceeded $8 trillion, an average of $87,000 per household. During the same year, companies collected $229 billion in life premiums and paid out $74 billion in policy benefits.

In 1990, some 2,300 companies were in the business of selling life insurance, up from 611 companies in 1950. They employed 800,000 individuals, up from 500,000 employees in 1950. These numbers do not include the hundreds of thousands of agents, brokers, and independent personnel who support the industry.

In 1990, 3,900 property-casualty companies operated in the United States. Their policies covered 95 percent of owned homes and 23 percent of rented apartments and houses. The companies wrote automobile insurance with premiums of $90 billion and covered 164 million drivers of 184 million vehicles. The companies employed 550,000 individuals, not counting agents, brokers, and independent claims adjusters.

Size of Health Care Insurance

Insurance companies and private hospital and medical expense organizations paid benefits in 1990 of over $200 billion for various health care services. Private insurers accounted for $69 billion, Blue Cross and Blue Shield organizations paid $45 billion, and other organizations paid $47 billion. In addition, government benefits for health care totalled $125 billion.

Public and private insurance benefits accounted for over 50 percent of the $600 billion total expenditures for health care in the United States in 1990. The benefits were paid to 6,800 hospitals, 5,000 mental health facilities, and 575,000 physicians. The average cost for a hospital stay of one day was over $600. The average stay per patient was seven days.

Size of Property-Casualty Insurance

Property-casualty insurance activities are highly developed in the United States. Some $202 billion of premiums were received in 1988, and companies earned $28 billion in investment income for total revenues of $232 billion. They incurred losses and adjusting expenses of $157 billion, underwriting expenses of $55 billion, and paid taxes of $4 billion. This left $16 billion in after-tax income for the total industry.

Marketing of U.S. Insurance

Insurance products are distributed in the United States using several marketing systems. In this section, we examine the marketing of U.S. insurance.

The Law of Agency

An *agent* is a person or organization authorized to act on behalf of another person. A *principal* is the person or organization who makes use of the agent. An insurance company is the principal and another party is the agent with respect to the sale of insurance.

The marketing of insurance in the United States is closely tied to the use of agents. Two characteristics of the agent-principal relationship are important in the sale of insurance products:

1. *Express Powers.* The insurance company authorizes certain actions in a written contract or agreement. These include the right to represent the company with potential clients and other rights and limitations on those rights.

2. *Implied Powers.* In addition to express powers, courts have ruled that agents have powers based on the appearance of an agent-principal relationship. As an example, an agent is authorized to sell automobile insurance for a company. If the agent also sells a homeowners policy, the company is bound by any loss that occurs.

Agents and Brokers

Insurance is marketed by both agents and brokers in the United States. As already noted, an agent is a representative of the insurance company. A *broker* is a person who sells insurance without representing an insurance company. Basically, the broker places orders for coverage either with a company designated by the insured or selected by the broker. In either case, the broker is a representative of the insured, not the insurer, and seeks to get the best possible coverage at the lowest price.

Life Insurance Marketing

Life insurance is generally sold in the United States through one of the following systems:

1. *Branch Office*—An insurance company office that conducts various operations including selling life insurance. It is staffed by employees of the life insurer rather than by independent agents. The branch system is a major approach to marketing life insurance.

2. *General Agent*—An independent businessperson empowered to sell life insurance by the company. Varying degrees of control are exercised by the underwriter over the activities of the general agent. The independent or general agent system is a major vehicle for selling life insurance policies.

3. *Direct Mail*—Information on life insurance policies mailed directly to potential customers. The selection of individuals may be based on specific criteria such as income level. They may also be members of an identifiable grouping, such as a trade association or holders of a specific credit card. This is a less important but growing approach to marketing life insurance.

4. *Group Life*—Life insurance programs connected to fringe benefits packages offered by employers. All employees may receive life insurance tied to their salary levels. The employer and employee may both contrib-

ute to premium payments. This insurance is marketed directly to employers.

Property-Casualty Insurance Marketing

Property-casualty insurance is generally sold in the United States through one of the following systems:

1. *Direct Writer*—An insurance company that sells its policies through salaried employees who may also receive a sales commission. This is similar to the life insurance branch system.

2. *Exclusive Agent*—Also called a *captive agent*, selling only for a single underwriter. A large commission is normally paid to the agent when the policy is issued. A much smaller commission is paid when the policy is renewed.

3. *American Agency System*—Sales through independent agents who represent more than one underwriter. The major difference with independent agents involves renewals of policies. The underwriter must pay a large commission on renewals as well as on a first policy. Otherwise, the independent agent could switch the policy to another company.

Providers of Insurance

The various kinds of insurance available in the United States come from a number of sources. In this section, we examine the underwriting structure.

Private Voluntary Insurance

The thousands of stock and mutual companies and other private associations are the primary providers of life, accident, health, automobile, and homeowners insurance. This is the largest component of insurance in the United States.

Private Compulsory Insurance

Some insurance is mandatory but is provided by private underwriters. These include:

1. *Automobile Insurance.* Most states require individuals to purchase liability insurance if they register or drive automobiles. Most of the compulsory auto insurance is provided by private companies.

2. *Workers Compensation.* Most states require employers to purchase insurance to pay the costs of injuries suffered at work. The payments cover medical care, loss of income due to disability, and rehabilitation expenses. This insurance is commonly provided by private insurance carriers.

Social Insurance

Social insurance is essentially compulsory insurance that covers certain benefits or indemnifies specified losses. The social insurance programs in the United States cover retirement, medical expenses, disability, unemployment, and workers compensation. Some of these coverages are optional in different states.

Social insurance is viewed as necessary by the government or society. Its characteristics differ from voluntary insurance. The major features are:

1. *Compulsory.* Social insurance is always required by law.

2. *Contributions and Benefits Established by Law.* The methods of funding the programs and level of benefits are defined by law. They are not related to whether an individual has paid sufficient monies to be eligible or whether the individual has a financial need for the monies.

3. *Long-Term Financing Plan.* Social insurance is funded by a long-term plan of contributions from covered persons, their employers, or both. The plan is administered or supervised by the government.

Public Guaranty Insurance

Some public insurance programs in the United States closely resemble social insurance. They are designed to achieve a public good. Some examples are:

1. *Financial Institution Deposit Insurance.* Money deposited in banks and other financial institutions is protected against loss up to specified limits. In 1990, the limit was $100,000 per depositor. Financial institutions pay a premium to a government agency to guarantee the coverage.

2. *Pension Guaranties.* The Pension Benefit Guaranty Corporation (PBGC) provides insurance guaranteeing the payment of benefits by private pension plans. The funding is provided by employers who pay premiums for the coverage.

3. *Financial Securities Coverage.* The Securities Investor Protection Corporation (SIPC) provides insurance guaranteeing the safety of monies and securities owned by investors but held by licensed securities broker-

age firms. Brokers pay fees for the coverage. In 1990, SIPC provided coverage up to $500,000 per investor.

Regulation of U.S. Insurance

The insurance industry in the United States is highly regulated compared to other industries. In this section, we examine insurance regulation.

Rationale for Insurance Regulation

The conceptual foundation for the regulation of insurance in the United States is as follows:

1. *Affected With the Public Interest.* In 1914 the U.S. Supreme Court ruled that insurance is a business that is "affected with the public interest." This means that a failure of a company causes losses to individuals and organizations outside the insurance company itself. The purchasers of insurance seek to protect themselves against financial losses in the future. It is important to public security and welfare that these purchasers be indemnified when losses occur. This is a public interest that justifies regulation.

2. *Complexity of Issues.* A second conceptual basis for insurance regulation lies in the complexity of policies that provide coverage. A consumer may lack the skill to read and understand insurance contracts. To ensure fair contracts at reasonable prices, government regulation is needed.

3. *Solvency of Companies.* Insurance companies collect funds today to cover losses in the future. A *solvent insurance company* has the resources to meet its future obligations. Regulation of the pricing of policies and investment of assets assists in ensuring the solvency of companies.

4. *Avoidance of Excessive Competition.* Competition is widely viewed as a positive feature of insurance activity. However, excessive competition can cause companies to operate dangerously close to the line of bankruptcy. Regulation avoids such destructive competition.

The Regulators

The U.S. insurance industry is regulated by three distinct authorities:

1. *State Legislatures.* Insurance is regulated at the state rather than federal level. Although laws vary by state, they provide broad guidelines to ensure fair treatment of consumers and solvency of insurance companies.

2. *State Insurance Commissioner.* Every state has an official charged with interpreting the state's insurance laws and enforcing regulations and guidelines. The title is usually the *commissioner* or *superintendent* of insurance. This individual investigates company activities or complaints by consumers to ensure compliance with the law and court decisions.

3. *The Courts.* A portion of insurance regulation occurs as a result of lawsuits filed by insured persons who feel that they were not treated fairly by insurance companies. *Stare decisis,* a Latin term meaning "to stand by decisions," is a legal doctrine whereby current court decisions should be consistent with past decisions in similar circumstances. Since prior decisions set precedents under this doctrine, insurance companies are effectively regulated by rulings of the courts.

Regulated Areas

Insurance companies are regulated with respect to specific activities and actions. These include:

1. *Licensing of Insurers.* A *license* is a formal authorization by law to engage in some activity. The office of the commissioner of insurance has the authority to grant or deny licenses to companies to sell insurance. To qualify for a license, a company must meet certain requirements. It must have sufficient capital to be financially sound. It must have personnel who are competent and experienced in selling insurance products. And the incorporators must be persons who are honest and reliable.

2. *Auditing of Companies.* Insurance companies must submit annual reports to the insurance commissioner. The reports contain information on revenues, expenses, losses, assets, liabilities, and capital. Using this report as a starting point, the state insurance department may examine or audit all or a portion of a company's operations or financial records. Corrective actions are taken when discrepancies or improper practices are uncovered.

3. *Approving Rates.* For some lines of insurance, the premium rates must be approved or accepted by the insurance commissioner. Three objectives are sought by the regulator:
   a. *Adequacy of the Rate.* The premium must be sufficiently high to pay for losses as they occur and expenses of the company. In determining adequacy, the regulators factor in the earnings from investments.
   b. *Nonexcessive Rate.* The premium must not be so high as to produce an unreasonable return for the company.
   c. *Nondiscriminatory Rate.* The premium must not be unfair to some policyholders as compared to others. The company

cannot charge a markedly different rate to two policyholders with essentially the same risk.

4. *Authorizing Reserve Levels.* A *reserve* is a liability of an insurance company created to recognize future benefits or losses that must be paid. The state insurance department is concerned about the adequacy of reserves and regulates the levels established for many lines of business.

5. *Investment Guidelines.* While holding funds to pay future benefits or losses, an insurance company invests the money in securities or other assets. State regulators provide guidelines to ensure that only sound investments are undertaken by a company.

6. *Policy Forms.* New policy forms must commonly be submitted to state regulators before they are distributed to customers. In many cases, the insurance commissioner must actually approve the form before it can be used, particularly so for policies sold to individuals and families.

7. *Licensing of Agents and Brokers.* Many states require insurance agents and brokers to be licensed before they can sell insurance. Normally, this means passing an examination demonstrating that the applicant understands the policies he or she will be selling. In some cases, states investigate the background of the applicant to ensure that the person is a respected and responsible citizen.

Exercises

1. The national sisterhood of Alpha Alpha Alpha offers life and health insurance to the 26,000 members and alumnae of its 170 college chapters. A group of 145 doctors has incorporated to offer medical care under a health plan purchased by 15 municipal governments in two counties of New York. An unincorporated membership association has 1,500 members who have agreed to share any collision losses involving their off-the-road campers. What organizations are each of the above?

2. A company owns three insurance companies that sell different lines of insurance, a small bank, and a real estate mortgage subsidiary. A second company offers only fire insurance on oil storage depots. A third company offers life, health, and homeowners insurance. What kind of company is each?

3. At a cocktail party, a man states that "Japan is the world's largest insurance market." A woman disagrees. Who is right?

4. Delton and Company is a general agent selling life insurance for the Greater General Insurance Company and five other firms. An employee of the company sells 300 disability policies and keeps the premiums. Neither Delton nor Greater General authorized the sale of the policies.

Five claims are filed for disability payments with Greater General. Must these claims be honored?

5. Tulsa Agency sells 300 three-year policies and earns commissions of $75,000. Altward Agency sells 320 three-year policies and earns commissions of $85,000. Ninety percent of each agent's policies are renewed. Tulsa earns $7,000 and Altward earns $80,000 on the renewals. What kind of agent is each agency?

6. In one state, workers compensation insurance is required of all employers and can be purchased from private insurers. In another state, it is encouraged but not required. In a third state, it is required and must be purchased from a state agency. What category of insurance is represented by each state?

7. A state court of appeals upholds a ruling that an insurance company must refund 85 percent of unearned premiums within 30 days of cancellation of a policy. The president of an insurance company does not believe that the ruling applies to her company. Is this likely?

8. A company offers a policy that costs 35 percent more for an unmarried policyholder as opposed to a married policyholder. There is no actuarial basis for the difference. Rather, it reflects a belief by the board of directors that married persons make greater contributions to society and should receive a break in their insurance premiums. Is this a legal policy?

4

Legal Environment of Insurance

The purchase of insurance involves a transfer of risk under the terms of a contract. Such contracts are drawn in a legal environment that shapes the rights and responsibilities of parties. Other legal principles and obligations affect the creation of risk and the need for insurance.

In this chapter, we examine the legal environment in the United States as it affects insurance transactions. We look at the nature of contracts, then, examine the concepts of legal liability and negligence. Finally, we cover major legal principles affecting contracts that transfer risk.

The Nature of Contracts

A *contract* may be defined as an agreement between two or more parties that is enforceable by law. An example is an insurance policy. In this section, we examine the nature of insurance contracts.

Requirements for a Legal Contract

For a contract to be legally binding in the United States, it must have these essential elements:

1. *Unqualified Offer.* One party must make a definite, unqualified offer to another party. Test the following statements:

"I will drive you home for $10; also, you must give me some other things."

"I will buy your car for $3,000 if you will replace the battery."

The first statement does not qualify as an offer because the "other things" are not definite. The second statement is an offer. If the second party replaces the battery, the first party will buy the car.

2. *Unqualified Acceptance.* A second party must accept the definite offer without conditions or modifications. Test the following responses to the offer to buy the car:

"I accept your offer, but I will not replace the battery."

"I accept your offer, but only if you pay me $3,200 for the car."

The first statement is a rejection of the offer because it is not an unqualified acceptance. The second statement is a counteroffer, not an acceptance.

3. *Consideration.* Something of value is given in order to make a binding contract. For a contract to be enforceable, each party must supply consideration. Consider the following:

"On behalf of the church, I accept your offer of $10,000 as a donation to our building fund."

"On behalf of the church, I accept your offer of $500 to use the church hall for a social club meeting."

In the first statement, the offer of money is a gift. It would be difficult to prove a binding contract because the recipient gave back no visible consideration. In the second example, money is given for the rental of facilities. Both sides put up consideration.

4. *Competent Parties.* The parties to an agreement must be competent in the eyes of the law to enter into a contract, that is, they must be capable of understanding the terms of the contract. As a general rule, minors, very elderly people, or others whose mental or emotional capacity may be questioned may be excluded as competent parties by courts of law.

5. *Legal Purpose.* A contract must be an agreement that does not violate any laws. Thus contracts involving criminal activities are usually not enforceable.

6. *Legal Form.* A contract must follow the form required by law for its category of business. Many contracts are oral. Other contracts are written. In insurance, some contracts must follow specific legal forms approved by state authorities. If an agreement does not follow the form prescribed by law, it may not be enforced in court.

Aleatory Contract

The term *aleatory* refers to any situation that depends upon chance, luck, or random occurrence. It is often applied to gambling, as when a person buys a lottery ticket or places a bet on a roulette wheel.

The term has been borrowed and is now applied to insurance agreements. An *aleatory contract* is an agreement where the apparent values are not equal in pure dollars. A small but certain premium is exchanged for an uncertain large benefit should a loss occur. This is a characteristic of insurance agreements.

The aleatory contract appears different than most other agreements where each party gives up something of roughly equal value. These are called *commutative contracts*. An example is a contract to purchase a new car worth $10,000 at a price of $10,000.

Although insurance contracts are aleatory in nature, they are not unfair. In fact, both parties give up approximately an equal value. The small certain premium has a mathematical value close to the uncertain benefit when probabilities of loss are taken into account. As a highly simplified example, consider a $100 premium for $100,000 of protection when the odds of a loss are 1,000 to one. The equation linking the value provided by the insurance company and shareholder can be expressed as

$$\text{Premium} \times \text{Probability} = \text{Benefit} \times \text{Probability}$$
$$\$100 \times 100\% = \$100,000 \times 1/1,000$$

or

$$\$100 = \$100$$

This formula indicates that the value on each side of the equation will be approximately the same. Of course, selling and administrative expenses must also be considered in setting the actual premium for an insurance policy.

Contract of Adhesion

A *contract of adhesion* refers to any agreement prepared by one party and accepted or rejected by another without modification. The agreement is not reached by negotiation, where each party engages in a process of give and take.

For individuals and most organizations, insurance contracts are almost always contracts of adhesion. The insurance company provides a detailed contractual form and the applicant can accept or reject it. If insurance coverage does not meet an applicant's needs, he can search for other insurers who will write a policy that is more acceptable. Still, the final policy is likely to be a contract of adhesion.

Increasingly, large companies seek coverage where the contract is negotiated. Although this is not always possible, such contracts can be tailored to meet the exact needs of each corporation. In these cases, the final document is not a contract of adhesion.

Personal Contract

Under the law, *assignment* is the right of an individual or company to transfer a claim, right, or piece of property to another individual or company. *Consent* is the permission or approval to make an assignment. In some legal contracts, rights are assigned without the permission of both parties. In others, the attempt to assign a right voids the contract.

An insurance contract is *personal in nature*, which means that the insurance coverage matches the two parties who initially signed the agreement. This affects the assignment of rights under the policy. Such assignment differs from the two major categories of insurance contracts, as follows:

1. *Property-Casualty Insurance.* Neither party can assign any rights without the permission of the other party. If the property is sold by the insured, coverage ceases unless the insurance company specifically consents to continuing the coverage. An example is fire insurance on a commercial building. The new owner may have a poor record for safety, which will affect whether the insurance company will write a policy. When the building is sold, the new owner can request assignment of the policy or a new policy. If neither is done, the building is no longer covered because the insurance policy is personal in nature and does not transfer with the change in title on the property.

2. *Life Insurance.* Once again, the contract is personal. A life insurance policy covers one individual and cannot be transferred from one life to another. At the same time, the beneficiary of a life insurance policy may be changed without the permission of the insurance company. In effect, the personal nature of the policy involves the insured and insurer but not the beneficiary. As long as the policy premiums are paid, the insurance company only requires written notice of any assignment of benefits to a new beneficiary. This helps the company avoid a situation in which two individuals claim the proceeds of the policy after the death of an individual.

Conditional Contract

A *conditional contract* refers to any agreement where one of the parties must perform only if specific conditions are met at a future time. Insurance policies are conditional for several reasons:

1. *Contingencies*—Situations that depend upon chance or uncertain conditions, as an accident or random event. Insurance policies are written to deal with the contingency of accidental or uncertain loss. If

the loss does not occur, the insurance company is not obligated to pay benefits.

2. *Condition Precedent*—A requirement under a contract that must be met before a party must perform under a contract. After a loss, the insured must notify the company and provide proof that the loss occurred. If these steps are not taken, the insurer has no obligation to pay a claim.

3. *Condition Subsequent*—A requirement that an insured must cooperate with the insurer after a claim has been paid on a policy. If the insured fails to cooperate, the insurance company may be relieved of its obligation to pay for a loss and may be able to reclaim the benefit paid. For example, the risk manager may collect on a fire policy after a building has burned as a result of the negligence of a third party. After receiving the money, the insured may have to cooperate with the insurer in proving the negligence of the third party and recovering money equal to the amount of the loss.

Negligence and Legal Liability

Liability is defined as the exposure to any legal obligation and the accompanying responsibility to compensate another party for a loss or damage. The possibility of legal liability is a major threat to the long-term financial stability of individuals and organizations.

Liability exposures exist in almost every area of business or social interaction among people. In this section, we cover the general nature of such liability. Later in the chapter, the concepts are applied directly to the need for certain automobile insurance coverage.

Negligence

Negligence may be defined as the failure of a person or organization to exercise a proper degree of care in a given situation. Alternatively, it is the failure to behave as a reasonably prudent individual when faced with certain circumstances. Some of the important characteristics of negligence are:

1. *Prudent Behavior Rule*. The individual or organization must behave prudently. If the behavior is reasonable, negligence does not occur. It does not matter that an accident may have been avoided by different behavior. It only matters that a proper degree of care is exercised.

2. *Commission, Omission, or Both*. Negligence may occur because a person commits a careless or thoughtless act. Or it may occur because a

person fails to perform an act that would be expected of a reasonable person. Or it may occur as a result of a combination of a committed act and an omitted act.

3. *Decision by a Court of Law.* The standard for the existence of negligence is usually not clear when an accident or injury occurs. Or the facts or actions may be disputed between two parties. Essentially, the system in the United States is that a court of law must decide whether negligence did or did not occur.

Legal Liability

Legal liability refers to any obligation of an individual or organization that is enforceable in a court of law. It may arise from statutes passed by Congress or a state legislature, agreements made between two or more parties, or as a result of negligence. With respect to negligence, legal liablility can be created only when a court determines three factual situations:

1. *Negligence must have occurred.* One person or organization must have unreasonably or unlawfully failed to exercise a prudent level of care for a specific situation.

2. *Loss must have occurred.* A person or organization must have suffered a loss. The simple existence of negligence imposes no legal liability if no damage or loss occurred.

3. *Negligence must have been a proximate cause of the loss.* A *proximate cause* is the behavior that, in a natural and continuous sequence, results in some outcome. Legal liability exists only when an unbroken chain of events connects the negligence and the loss.

As an example of legal liability, assume that a service station attendant negligently lights a cigarette while filling a motor vehicle with gasoline. If a fire occurs, is a legal liability created? First, a court must decide that lighting the cigarette near a flammable liquid is negligent. Then, the fire must have damaged something, such as the automobile, or injured somebody, such as the driver. Finally, the fire must have started when the cigarette was lighted. If it started 15 minutes later, a court may decide that the action of the attendant was not the proximate cause of the loss.

Exceptions to Legal Liability

Legal liability is a creation of the law. The legal system in the United States also has created categories of individuals and organizations that cannot be held legally liable under certain conditions or circumstances. The major categories are:

1. *Mentally Incompetent Persons.* Some individuals lack the mental capacity to perform as a reasonable person in different circumstances. If it is determined that a person lacks mental competency, that person cannot be held legally liable.

2. *Children.* State laws vary on the point in time when a child can be expected to behave as a prudent person. In all states, an infant cannot distinguish between right and wrong with respect to prudent behavior. A child, however, at some point becomes legally liable for his or her behavior. This is set by state law or determinable by the court.

3. *Governmental Entities.* In some cases, governmental bodies enjoy immunity from being sued for negligence. As an example, the U.S. Army cannot be sued for negligently causing the death of a soldier in combat. This immunity was once quite extensive and virtually no lawsuits were permitted alleging negligence by a government entity. This situation, however, has been modified in recent years both by statute and by court decisions.

Legal Principles

Insurance policies are issued in a framework of legal guidelines and requirements. In this section, we examine some of these principles that affect contracts in all areas of insurance.

Indemnifying Losses

Indemnity is the compensation or reimbursement for any loss or damage suffered by a person or organization. When a loss occurs, it may be indemnified by insurance in accordance with terms of the policy. Two legal principles apply to indemnifying an insured who has suffered a loss:

1. *Indemnity Principle.* This legal concept states that payments of claims under an insurance policy must be limited to the actual loss suffered by the insured. This limitation avoids situations where individuals might gamble with the purchase of insurance.

2. *Actual Cash Value of Loss. Overinsurance* is a situation where an individual or organization purchases a policy with a higher face value than the possible loss, for example, the purchase of a $1 million policy on a warehouse valued at $700,000. Derived from the indemnity principle

is the legal concept that an insured may collect no more than the actual cash value of a loss. This avoids situations of overinsurance and reduces the possibility of intentional destruction of property in order to collect insurance.

Valuation of Losses

When a loss occurs, the form of insurance policy affects the application of the indemnity principle. Two policy forms are common:

1. *Indemnification Policy*—Reimburses the insured up to the actual cash value of the loss. Any dispute must be resolved by negotiation between the parties. If not, the matter is settled either by arbitration or appeal to a court of law.

2. *Valued or Cash Payment Policy*—Obligates the insurance company to pay a stated sum as the benefit of an insurance contract. It is used in several situations, including:

    a. When it is difficult to assess the actual cash value of a loss, such as objects of art. A painting may be worth millions of dollars to a collector, but how can anyone "prove" value?

    b. When a valued policy is required by law, such as workers compensation where legal guidelines provide a schedule of benefits to an injured worker.

    c. To avoid disputes. An example is ocean marine insurance. If a vessel is lost at sea, no physical evidence exists of its current condition or value.

    d. In life insurance. Here, the concept of value of the loss has limited meaning. What is the value of a life?

    e. In disability insurance. Policies are written so that an individual collects a stated sum of money on a regular basis if he or she is disabled and cannot earn a living.

Multiple Insurance Policies

Individuals and organizations can purchase insurance from many companies and can overlap coverage. Thus it is possible to violate the indemnity principle. An example is medical coverage provided by an employer and also by an individual's automobile insurance. If a person is injured in an automobile accident, both policies might be liable for the payment of medical expenses.

Most indemnity policies carry provisions that do not allow the collection of benefits from more than one policy. In some cases, this is enforceable. In other cases, individuals may collect benefits in excess of actual loss.

With respect to valued and actual cash value policies, it is possible to collect benefits under all policies in effect at the time of loss. Since these are not indemnification policies, there is no requirement to establish the extent of loss and no concern about multiple coverage.

Insurable Interest

An *insurable interest* is the existence of a relationship where a person is affected by a loss. The relationship may be between a person and property or between two people. The loss may be financial or may involve a blood relative or family member. If an insurable interest exists, the situation may be covered by insurance. Without an insurable interest, no insurance coverage is possible.

Individuals and organizations must ensure that their policies cover situations where they have insurable interests. If a loss occurs and it is determined that an insurable interest does not exist, the benefits from the policy may not be collectible. This means that money being paid in the form of premiums is wasted since no insurance coverage exists.

Some of the common examples of insurable interest are:

1. *Ownership.* The owner of property suffers a financial loss if the property is destroyed. This is a common basis for insurable interest.

2. *Leasehold Interest.* An individual or organization that rents or otherwise uses property owned by another person may have an insurable interest if damage to the property adversely affects the life of the person or the operations of the organization.

3. *Creditor Interest.* The organization holding a mortgage or lien on property has an insurable interest in the property.

4. *Bailee Interest.* A *bailee* is a person who receives goods from another person and is responsible for safeguarding the goods prior to returning them. The person may protect the goods until they are moved to another location. Or the bailee may hold the goods on consignment. This means that the goods are sold by the bailee and payment made to the owner. In either case, the bailee does not own the goods. Still, a person in this situation has an insurable interest in the property.

5. *One's Own Life.* Every person has an insurable interest in his or her own life.

6. *Family Members.* Because family relationships are based upon love and affection, the loss of a close relative is a personal loss to an individual. On this basis, an insurable interest exists among family members.

7. *Business Relationships.* People who work together often develop

financial ties that result in losses in the event of death or disability. Partners in a business or employee-employer relationships are examples. Insurable interest exists in these situations.

Timing of the Insurable Interest

The timing of the insurable interest is critical to the collection of insurance benefits. The two rules are:

1. *At the Time of the Loss.* In property insurance, a person can collect benefits only when the insurable interest exists at the time of the loss. Once the interest is completed, as with the sale of property, the insurance policy is no longer in force.

2. *At the Time of Purchase.* In life insurance, the insurable interest must exist only when the policy is purchased. Afterward, benefits can be collected as long as the policy remains in good standing with the insurance company.

Subrogation

Subrogation is the right of an insurance company to be reimbursed for payments when a loss is caused by a third party. For example, assume that an insured automobile is struck by a negligent driver. The insurance company will pay damages and then may sue the negligent driver to recover its money. This right to recover its payments in this situation is a basic legal right of the insurance company. Normally, it is also stated in the insurance policy.

The right of subrogation has several important features:

1. *Common-Law Right.* It is not necessary to state the right in the insurance policy, although it commonly is done. The claim of insurance companies against third parties is a common-law right in the United States.

2. *Not Applicable in Life Insurance.* The right of subrogation applies only in property-casualty insurance, not in life insurance. Thus if an insured individual is killed in an automobile accident, the insurance company must pay the claim without recourse to a negligent driver of the other car.

3. *Generally Not Applicable in Disability or Health Insurance or Workers Compensation.* State laws usually forbid subrogation in the case of disability and health policies. Thus a disabled person may collect her insurance benefits and also collect damages from a negligent party who caused the

injury. Nor is subrogation applicable to workers compensation where lawsuits against the employer are generally prohibited by law.

Expectations Principle

The *expectations principle* holds that the reasonable expectations of insureds will be honored by the courts in interpreting insurance contracts. Thus detailed small print is not allowed to deny the expectations. Basically, this principle applies in three steps:

1. *Determine the reasonable expectations.* If the insured believes he is purchasing disability insurance, the contract should provide benefits if the person is accidentally disabled.

2. *Do not expect technical competence.* An insurance contract should be written so that it can be understood by individuals who do not have a legal, medical, or other technical background. Courts expect insurance policies to be basically understandable to a layperson without a knowledge of insurance law. This does not fully apply in providing large commercial coverages where an organization is expected to be somewhat knowledgeable of the technical aspects of insurance policies.

3. *Interpret ambiguity in favor of the insured.* An insurance contract should not contain ambiguous provisions. If it does, they are usually interpreted by the courts in favor of the insured. With regard to ambiguity, the expectations principle recognizes the fact that insurance agreements are contracts of adhesion and thus are usually better understood by the insurer than by the insured.

Exercises

1. Snowville Industries sends an order to United Garments for $300,000 of textiles in various shapes and sizes. United offers to fill the order but at a price of $320,000. Snowville does not respond but instead orders the goods from another supplier. Two months later, United ships the goods and bills Snowville for $300,000. Snowville refuses to pay and United sues. Is United entitled to collect for breach of contract? Why or why not?
2. Endicott Industries orders $220,000 of goods from Claremont Products. At the time of the order, Claremont indicates that it will also provide $15,000 of other goods at no charge. When the order is filled, Claremont does not provide the extra goods. Endicott sues for $15,000. Is Endicott entitled to collect? Why or why not?
3. A car dealer has a car in the showroom with a marked price of $16,000.

The dealer offers to sell it to an individual for $13,000. The dealer then draws up a purchase order and it is signed by the purchaser. On the bottom of page two, the contract states that the purchaser must pay an additional $1,000 in preparation fees. Is this an aleatory contract? a commutative contract? a contract of adhesion? a conditional contract? Explain.

4. An individual purchases a one-year insurance policy covering his new automobile. After six months, he sells the car but does not cancel the policy. In the seventh month, the car is in an accident. Is the car still covered by the original policy? Why or why not?

5. A company purchases an insurance policy that provides for reimbursement for theft, burglary, or the disappearance of valuable items. The policy requires the company to lock up all valuables in a safe at the end of the day. An employee leaves some jewels on a desk overnight. They are missing the next morning. The company files a claim for $22,000 from the insurance company but refuses to provide proof of the value of the jewelry. Will the company collect? Why or why not?

6. A company purchases an insurance policy on a rare painting by an Old Master. The policy has a face value of $65,000. The painting was recently offered at auction, but the top bid was only $40,000. The owner withdrew the painting and refused to sell it. Two months later, it is stolen. How much will be collected if the policy is an indemnification policy? a valued or cash payment policy?

7. A father has a son who works in the family business. The son has a fiancée who borrows $25,000 from him to help her mother pay off a mortgage. The father has applied for two life insurance policies, one on the son for $300,000 and the other on the son's fiancée for $25,000. The father is the beneficiary of both policies. Does an insurable interest exist on the son? on the fiancée? Why or why not?

8. A company owns a hardware store and leases the neighboring garage. In the garage, it stores inventory. It also allows a local butcher to store some equipment in return for a small payment. The owner of the company wants to purchase property insurance on the hardware store, garage, and inventory and equipment stored in the garage. Does an insurable interest exist on each? Why or why not?

9. Al Holpp is the beneficiary of life insurance on his son Robert. With the same company, he also has automobile coverage on his car. A third policy with the same company protects Al for up to six months against loss of income from disability. All three policies require Al to cooperate with the insurance company after a loss. One day Robert is driving Al's car and Al is a passenger. The car is hit by a speeding driver who is given a ticket by a policeman. Robert is killed in the accident and the car is a total wreck. Al himself is disabled for three months. Al's insurance company agrees to pay the death and disability benefits only

if Al cooperates in a lawsuit against the negligent driver. The company takes the same position with respect to paying for the car. Must Al cooperate?

10. An individual buys automobile insurance for her 16-year-old son. The policy contains a clause stating "Payments will not be made under this policy if at variance with state law." The son drives the car to a neighboring state where the legal driving age is 17. He has an accident in that state. The insurance company cites the clause and refuses to pay the policy. Will a court uphold this position?

5

Insurance Contracts

As noted in the previous chapter, insurance contracts are governed by general contract law. They are also unique in many respects.

In this chapter, we examine the insurance contract as a unique legal entity. We begin with the structure of a typical contract. Then, we identify some of the common features of insurance contracts. Finally, we discuss the enforcement of insurance contracts after a loss has occurred.

Structure of Insurance Contracts

Although insurance contracts are usually fairly complicated legal documents, most contracts consist of seven distinct parts. In this section, we examine the components of an insurance contract.

Declarations

A *declaration* is defined as any statement that provides information about the person or property covered by an insurance contract. The declarations component is the first part of most insurance policies.

Typical information contained in the declarations section includes:

1. *Identity of the Insured*—Possibly the name of a person in life insurance, an identifier of a building, or the model and serial number of an automobile. The purpose is to specify exactly the individual or property being covered by the policy.

2. *Identity of Insurer*—Name, address, and any other information on the company providing coverage under the policy. The purpose is to identify the party that will receive and process claims for losses.

3. *Location Information*—The address of the person insured under the policy or the physical location of the property covered. The purpose is to provide a geographic identifier for the person or property.

4. *Time Period of Coverage*—The specified period of time covered by the policy. A life insurance policy may specify the time in years. Or it may provide coverage for an indefinite period as long as premium payments are made. A property policy is likely to exist for a fixed period of time. It may be renewed by mutual consent. One declaration is to name the period of coverage.

5. *Amount of the Premium*—The payment for insurance coverage. The declarations contain the amount of money that must be paid in order for the policy to be effective.

6. *Amount of Coverage*—A specified amount of coverage in the event of a loss.

The declarations also contain other information that is needed to understand the scope and restrictions of the policy.

Definitions

Most insurance policies contain a separate section defining key terms used in the policy. Examples are:

1. *Additional Insureds.* In the declarations section, an insured is named under the policy. In life insurance, a single person is normally covered. In property contracts, other insureds may be covered under the policy. As an example, an automobile insurance policy covers the owner or driver of a car. It usually also covers other persons such as other immediate family members who drive any vehicle or any driver of the insured vehicle who has permission to use it. These additional insureds are included in the policy by defining them as insured in the definitions section.

2. *Property Identifiers.* The definitions section clarifies terms used in property insurance contracts. In a homeowners policy, the residence premises may be defined as the private residence on the property and other structures attached to the main dwelling. In an automobile policy, a covered auto may be defined to include a trailer.

3. *Parts of Speech.* The definitions section may clarify verbs or other parts of speech contained in the policy. An automobile policy that covers a person occupying a vehicle may define "occupying" as being inside a vehicle, on top of it, getting in it, or getting out of it.

4. *Restrictions of Broad Terms.* Some common English terms may have unclear meanings. For example, *bodily injury* can mean anything from death to a minor cut on a finger. A health insurance policy might define *bodily injury* as bodily harm, sickness, or disease, including required care, loss of services, and death resulting therefrom.

Insuring Agreement

The *insuring agreement* is a summary of the major requirements imposed on the insurance company by the policy. Common elements of an insuring agreement are:

1. *Payment for Losses.* The insurer agrees to pay for losses arising from certain causes. Normally, this is expressed in two basic forms:
   a. *All-Risk Agreement.* With this approach, all losses to the property are covered except for losses that are specifically excluded. In property insurance, for example, an all-risk policy may exclude damage caused by floods. Separate coverage is needed for a house in a flood plain.
   b. *Named-Perils Agreement.* With this approach, the policy covers only losses from causes specifically listed. A flood insurance policy is issued on a named-perils basis since it only covers damage from floods and other water causes.

2. *Restrictions on Coverage.* In some cases, the insuring agreement contains limitations on coverage. For example, a homeowners policy may cover a garage only so long as it is not used for business purposes. A life insurance policy may exclude payment of a death benefit if a person commits suicide within the first two years of the effective date of a policy.

3. *Provision of Services.* The policy may require the insurer to take actions other than pay for losses. As an example, it may require the payment of legal fees associated with a loss. Or it may require the insurer to pay for annual inspections of a premises covered for loss from fire.

Exclusions

An *exclusion* is any loss or cause of loss not covered under an insurance policy. Three major categories of exclusions are commonly identified in insurance contracts:

1. *Excluded Losses.* Insurance policies must carefully delineate the losses they cover, because premiums are based on statistical data for categories of losses. Yet, after an accident or other cause of damage, most people suffer economic damage that was not covered. For example, a health insurance policy may cover all medical bills. After an injury, an insured may lose income because he is not able to work. A health policy that is not designed to reimburse lost income will exclude losses from indirect sources.

A second example covers policies designed for specific purposes. A lawyer may purchase malpractice insurance to protect against losses from professional lawsuits. What happens if a client trips on the front step of her law office and sues for bodily injury? The answer is that such a loss is excluded from the malpractice coverage. It must be covered under the property damage provisions of the building's coverage.

2. *Excluded Perils.* A *peril* was earlier defined as a cause of a loss. An all-risk policy may exclude certain perils. For example, the peril of war or death from an accident for an airline pilot may be exclusions in a life insurance policy. An earthquake may be an exclusion in a property policy.

Perils are commonly excluded because they are impossible to cover or are better covered in separate policies. No insurance company is large enough to cover the death benefits payable in a nuclear war. Flood coverage is not needed by houses located on hilltops. In the first example, the insurance policy excludes a peril that would be catastrophic to the insurance company. In the second example, the policy excludes a peril that does not apply equally to all insureds under a policy.

3. *Excluded Property.* Insurance policies are designed to cover certain properties and not others. However, sometimes properties get mixed. A homeowners policy may specifically cover personal property inside the house. What happens if the owner brings home $300,000 of jewelry that is normally stored in a vault and, while the jewelry is in the house, the house burns down? Is the jewelry covered?

The answer is no because jewelry and other valuable properties are an exclusion to homeowner coverage. To cover money, jewelry, or rare art work, the person must purchase specific coverage.

Conditions

A *condition* is a provision of a policy that changes the scope of coverage. Some typical conditions are:

1. *Insurable Interest.* A $300,000 boat may be owned by three individuals. One owner's insurable interest in the boat is $100,000. One owner may not collect more than $100,000 in the event of loss of the boat. A limit of payment equal to the insurable interest is a normal condition of a property policy.

2. *Duties After a Loss.* The insurance company requires the insured or his or her beneficiary to take certain steps after a loss. A life insurance policy may require the filing of a claim and proof of death. An automobile policy may require the insured to safeguard the vehicle from further loss or to notify the police after an accident.

3. *Loss Settlement.* After a loss, an insured may disagree with the

insurance company on the extent of loss. A policy may contain conditions for settling such a disagreement.

4. *Cooperation With Insurance Company.* After a loss, the insured may be required to work with the insurance company to mitigate the loss. As an example, an insurance company may pay benefits for property damaged by a third party. Then, the company may seek damages from the third party as a result of his or her negligence. The insured must cooperate in pursuing such damages.

Miscellaneous Provisions

Virtually all insurance contracts contain other clauses, paragraphs, or sections that affect the scope of coverage. This list of possible miscellaneous provisions is quite long. Examples are:

1. *Relationship Between Insured and Insurer.* An insured may wish to change the terms of a policy. Or the insurer may seek certain behavior from the insured. Some provisions cover the conduct required of the insured and insurer when dealing with each other.

2. *Cancellation of Policy.* Under some circumstances either the insured or insurer may seek to cancel a policy. The terms for termination may be specified.

3. *Transfer of Interest in a Policy.* An insured may transfer his rights under a policy. The insurance company may seek to approve such transfer. A provision can deal with this matter.

4. *Life Insurance Provisions.* A life insurance policy has a number of items that deal with the rights of the insured, beneficiaries, and owners of policies. These are all miscellaneous provisions in a life policy.

Endorsements and Riders

An *endorsement* is a written provision that expands, reduces, or otherwise modifies the coverage under a basic property insurance policy. A *rider* achieves the same goal in life and health policies. In many cases, the terms are used interchangeably.

Some common endorsements or riders are:

1. *Expand Coverage.* The endorsement can cover perils that are not included in the basic coverage. For example, an earthquake endorsement might be added to a basic property policy.

2. *Delete Coverage.* The endorsement can reduce coverage. As an example, certain items of property can be excluded from a standard property contract.

3. *Add Provision.* An endorsement can be used to add a clause of any kind that is not included in the basic coverage. For instance, an endorsement to a life insurance policy can waive the payment of premiums if an insured becomes totally disabled.

4. *Modify a Provision.* An endorsement takes precedence over the basic terms of a contract. Thus an endorsement can modify any aspect of coverage. This is true only as long as the modification is not prohibited by state law.

Common Features of Insurance Policies

Insurance contracts contain a number of features that are relatively common with different policies. In this section, we examine some of these features.

Deductible

A *deductible* is a requirement under an insurance policy that limits the coverage to losses above a certain minimum level. The insurance company pays only for losses above that level. For example, suppose a policy covers a $4,000 loss with a $1,000 deductible. The insurance company only pays $3,000 (4,000 − 1,000).

Deductibles are included in insurance policies to achieve several goals, including:

1. *Reduced Premiums.* An insurance policy that contains a deductible costs less than a similar policy with no deductible. The larger the deductible, the greater the savings.

2. *Reduced Administrative Costs.* Small dollar claims involve processing costs similar to those of larger claims. Thus the proportion of dollars available to pay claims is higher if smaller claims are eliminated. The deductible eliminates all claims below a certain dollar level. It also eliminates the associated administrative costs.

3. *Reduced Moral Hazard.* The deductible tends to reduce the temptation to intentionally cause a loss and benefit from it. Suppose, for example, an individual intentionally sets fire to an insured car worth $5,000. With a $500 deductible, the insured does not get the full benefit of the fire. It would be better to sell the car.

4. *Reduced Morale or Behavioral Hazard.* People may be more careless when losses are fully insured. If the insured must pay for part of the loss, the financial loss encourages safety practices.

Percentage Participation Clause

A *percentage participation clause* refers to any requirement for the insured to pay a specified percentage of any loss. For example, a health insurance policy may require the individual to pay 20 percent of all claims. This may be stated as all claims above a deductible.

When combined with a deductible, the percentage participation clause achieves goals similar to those of deductibles. Even without the deductible, the clause achieves all goals except the elimination of small claims.

Enforcement of Contracts

An insurance policy is a contract enforceable under the law. In this section, we examine some of the issues that affect the validity of an insurance contract.

Void and Voidable Contracts

In the law, the term *void* refers to an agreement that has no legal force. The term *null and void* is redundant. A void agreement is also a null agreement in that it is invalid and is not binding on the parties.

Under the law, *voidable* refers to an agreement that can be made void, at the option of one of the parties. A voidable contract is currently valid but can be made invalid if two circumstances occur.

1. *Contingency Occurs.* First, an event must occur that allows the contract to be voided. The event can be the discovery of an untruth during the negotiation of the contract. Or it can simply be the inclusion in the agreement of an option that allows one party to void the contract if it wishes to do so.

2. *Positive Action to Void.* The voiding party must advise the other party that the agreement is no longer valid. Such notice is normally given in writing with insurance contracts. Final resolution of whether the contract is actually void is often made in courts of law.

Utmost Good Faith

Utmost good faith is a legal requirement that both parties must make a full and fair disclosure of all facts affecting an insurance contract. Any material information about the risks covered by the policy must be known to both parties. The risk manager must advise the underwriter of all important aspects of the requested coverage. Failure to do so can allow the insurer to void the policy at a later time.

Utmost good faith when negotiating for insurance is different from legal requirements with respect to other contracts. Most contractual negotiations simply require equal knowledge and access to the facts by each party. If a business is being sold, both parties can agree on a price. If it turns out that one party failed to provide all the information or was deceptive, the contract may still stand. This is not true in insurance. Any willful failure to meet the standard of utmost good faith can endanger the coverage.

With respect to supplying information, several concepts are important:

1. *Representation*—A statement of fact made by an applicant in the process of obtaining an insurance policy. It concerns the risk and is made to induce the underwriter to provide insurance coverage. It can be oral or written but must be true to the best knowledge of the applicant. It can be made prior to the application or concurrently with it. It can be in response to questions on an application form or in general conversation with an insurance agent or underwriter.

2. *Material Fact*—An aspect of the risk that is so significant as to affect the terms of a policy. It can even be sufficient to cause an insurer to deny coverage.

3. *Misrepresentation*—A statement that is false with respect to a fact. If it is intentional and deals with a material fact, it can be the basis for the insurer to void the policy at a future time.

4. *Concealment*—The failure to voluntarily disclose material facts that may affect the terms and availability of an insurance policy. The risk manager must do more than simply answer all questions correctly. He or she must also recognize significant facts that can affect coverage and volunteer them. If a warehouse is located next door to a factory that manufactures explosives, this fact must be made known to the insurance company. Failure to do so can be the basis for voiding the policy at a future time.

5. *Warranty*—A statement made to secure insurance coverage that must be absolutely and strictly true. Unlike representations, it is not enough that they be made to the best knowledge of the applicant. A warranty does not even need to be material. It must simply be true. If a risk manager purchases theft insurance and warrants that the company has a safe in every sales office, this must be true. If it turns out that 3 of 27 offices do not have safes, the policy can be voided by the insurer.

6. *Fraud*—An intentional deception to cause a person to give up property or some lawful right. With respect to an insurance policy, it is

a willful false representation, concealment, or deliberate action that is relied upon by the insurer and causes the insurance company economic injury. It is more serious than concealment and may lead to civil or criminal penalties.

Strict Compliance Rule

The *strict compliance rule* states that a contract is enforced in accordance with its terms. If the terms are clear, the meaning may not be distorted by interpretations. Insurance policies are generally covered by this rule.

Parole is oral evidence offered to vary the terms of a written contract. Normally, parole is not permitted to modify an insurance contract. The exceptions are:

1. *Obvious Factual Error.* If both parties make a transparent factual error, oral evidence may be used to modify the contract. For example, an individual owns a building at 26 Main Street. She purchases a fire insurance policy in which a clerical error lists the address as 25 Main Street. The policy probably would be enforced to cover fire damages at 26 Main Street.

2. *Fraudulent Statement.* Individuals may not make fraudulent oral statements that mislead the insurer. If they do, the statement can be used to modify the contract.

3. *Factual Conflict.* If the applicant makes an oral statement that conflicts with the written representations and warranties, it is the obligation of the insurer to investigate the discrepancy. Failure to do so can lead to a subsequent modification of the contract as a result of the oral statement.

Waiver and Estoppel

A *waiver* is the intentional relinquishing or abandonment of a known right. If the insurer issues a policy knowing that its terms and conditions are not being met, the insurer may be waiving its future right to void the policy.

Estoppel is the prevention of a person from making an affirmation or denial, because it is contrary to a previous action that he or she has made. This applies to the enforcement of a policy after an apparent waiver. If the insurer knowingly issues a policy whose terms are not being met, the insurer may be waiving the terms. Estoppel will prevent the insurer from claiming at a later time that the failure to meet the terms voids the policy. If the insurer wishes to void the policy, it must be done when the knowledge becomes known. Otherwise, the insurer will be estopped from denying payment on a claim under the policy.

Exercises

1. An insurance policy contains the following sentence:

   We will pay those sums that the insured becomes legally obligated to pay as damages because of bodily injury or property damage to which this insurance applies.

   In what section of an insurance agreement will this statement be found?
2. An insurance policy contains the following sentence:

   We will pay for loss to covered property from any of the covered causes of loss.

   An agent claims that the policy is an all-risk contract. Is this true? Why or why not?
3. An insurance policy contains the following words:

   Endorsements Attached to this Policy:
   #45545   Broad Form Nuclear Exclusion
   #40677   Extended Reporting Period

   In what section of an insurance agreement will this statement be found?
4. An insurance policy contains the following words:

   "Residence employee" means:
   a. an employee of an insured whose duties are related to the maintenance or use of the residence premises; or
   b. one who performs similar duties elsewhere not related to the business of the insured.

   In what section of an insurance agreement will this statement be found?
5. An insurance policy contains the following words:

   We do not insure for loss caused directly or indirectly by any of the following. Such loss is excluded regardless of any other cause or event contributing concurrently or in any sequence to the loss.

   In what section of an insurance agreement will this statement be found?
6. An insurance policy states that the insured will pay the first $500 of any covered loss. What is this provision called? Where is it likely to be found in the policy?
7. An insurance policy states that the insured will pay 20 percent of any

covered loss up to the limit of the policy. What is this provision called? Where is it likely to be found in the policy?

8. An insurance policy allows the company to void a policy for misrepresentation or concealment. An individual has taken out insurance on a classic car. He forged a bill of sale showing the car cost $35,000, the face value of the policy. It actually cost $20,000. The insurance company learned of the real price in June but took no action. In December the car was involved in an accident with $3,000 of damage. Does the insurance company have to pay the claim?

9. A homeowner purchases burglary insurance on a collection of rare sculptures. Some are kept in his home. He warrants to the insurance company that a working alarm system is installed on the house and connected directly to the local police station.

   He also has some sculptures in his business office three miles away. He tells the insurance company that he believes the office building has 24-hour security. This is not true, as a watchman locks up at 10 p.m. and does not return until 6 a.m. The homeowner also keeps some of the sculptures in a carriage house 200 yards from his home but on the same property. He fails to tell the insurance company that the carriage house cannot be locked.

   Some of the sculptures do not exist at all. They are listed on the sheet because the individual plans to file a false claim at a later date.

   While the homeowner is on vacation, he is cleaned out. A burglar actually takes the entire collection from all three locations. The insurance company learns that the alarm system was not working because of dead batteries. It also learns of the absence of 24-hour security and the lack of a lock on the carriage house. It further learns that some nonexistent sculptures were listed on the policy. Is this loss covered? Why or why not?

10. An individual applies for insurance for her coin collection. She purchases an indemnity policy. She writes its value as $16,000 on the application but tells the agent that it really is worth $40,000. She purchases $30,000 worth of insurance. The collection is stolen. How much can she collect?

11. An insurance company issues a fire policy on a house and garage. At one place in the policy it states that no business activity will be conducted on the premises. When bringing the policy to the applicant, the agent notes that a pizza restaurant is operating on the ground floor. Six months later, a fire starts in the restaurant and damages the building. The insurance company notifies the insured that the policy is voided. Will this stand up in court? Why or why not?

6

Life Insurance

Life insurance is a versatile and important financial product that can meet a number of individual needs. It provides a death benefit to assist survivors in carrying on when a person dies. It can provide retirement benefits when an individual has stopped working.

Life insurance is increasingly being provided to employees as part of the fringe benefit package. This is equally true for employees of businesses, private nonprofit employers, and government organizations. At the same time, life insurance coverage is needed by individuals who do not receive it as a fringe benefit. Whether it is provided by an employer or purchased individually, an understanding of life insurance is an important part of personal financial planning.

In this chapter, we examine the fundamentals of insurance policies that provide either death benefits or funds for retirement. In practice, either policy can achieve the goals of the other. That is, a life insurance policy can provide retirement benefits and a retirement policy can provide death benefits. Thus the two policies are somewhat interchangeable and are discussed together under the general heading of life insurance.

Nature of Life Insurance

Life insurance has a number of features found in all policy forms. In this section, we examine the financial components of life insurance, the parties to the policy, and the ownership rights.

Life Insurance Economics

Life insurance is defined as an insurance arrangement that provides for the payment of a specified amount upon the death of an insured individual. As with other forms of insurance, it is based upon the pooling of risks and the prediction of the probability of death for an individual. The financial components of life insurance are:

1. *Premium.* A premium is paid, either in a single installment at the time of purchase of the policy or in periodic payments. The premium provides one source of money that can be used to later pay a death benefit.

2. *Investment Income.* The premiums are invested by the insurance company to earn a return. This return is also available to pay the death benefit.

3. *Expenses.* A sales commission is normally paid when an insurance policy is written. The writing of the policy and investigating the health of an applicant cost money. Recording the premiums also involves costs. Expenses must be covered by the premiums and investment income.

4. *Death Benefit.* When an individual dies, the face value of the policy must be paid.

5. *Profit.* For a private insurer, a profit is expected when insurance is sold.

The financial relationship is expressed noting that the premiums and investment income must equal the expenses and death benefits and profit. As an example, a company may write policies with premiums of $2 million. Investing the premiums produces an additional $2.4 million of investment income over the life of the contracts. Death benefits of $3.8 million will be paid and expenses to service policies will be $400,000. For this line of business and these policies, the financial relationship is:

$$2,000,000 + 2,400,000 = 400,000 + 3,800,000 + 200,000$$

where the $200,000 is a profit or increase in capital for the company.

Parties to the Policy

A life insurance policy has three parties who have an interest in the contract. These are:

1. *Insured*—The individual whose death will create the death benefit.

2. *Beneficiary*—The individual who will receive the death benefit when it is paid. A *primary beneficiary* is the person entitled to receive the proceeds following the death of the insured. A *contingent beneficiary* is

entitled to benefits only if the primary beneficiary is deceased at the time of death of the insured.

3. *Owner*—The person who may make decisions with respect to the policy. The owner can overlap either of the other two parties. That is, the policy can be owned by the insured, a situation where the policy has a *revocable beneficiary*. Or it can be owned by the beneficiary, a situation that normally involves an *irrevocable beneficiary*. An example is when a company insures a key employee and pays the premiums itself.

Rights of the Owner

The owner of a policy may exercise a number of decision-making rights including:

1. *Naming the Beneficiary*. A person or a charitable or other organization may be named as beneficiary. An *estate,* defined as the assets and liabilities of a dead person, may also be named. The owner of the policy has the right to change the beneficiary by following specific rules, such as advising the insurance company.

2. *Taking Cash From the Policy*. Some life insurance policies have a *cash surrender value,* defined as an amount of money available upon voluntary termination of a policy prior to the death of the insured. An important feature of a cash value is that the insured can borrow against the policy at a relatively low rate of interest without surrendering the policy.

3. *Exercising Policy Options*. Some life insurance policies contain options that provide benefits or rights. These options can be exercised by the owner of a policy.

Forms of Life Insurance

Life insurance is available in many forms. In this section, we examine some of the major categories of life insurance.

Whole Life Insurance

One of the most common forms of life insurance is *whole life,* a policy that provides a death benefit in return for a fixed premium. Three forms of whole life are available:

1. *Straight Life*—Also called *ordinary life* and requires a periodic premium paid for the entire life of the insured or until age 100. If the

premiums are paid without an interruption that cancels the policy, the face value of the policy is paid upon the death of the insured.

2. *Limited Payment Life*—Requires a fixed periodic premium for a specified period of time. Ten-pay life requires premiums for 10 years. Life paid up at 65 requires premiums to be paid until the insured is 65 years of age.

3. *Single Payment Life*—Requires a large single premium to be paid at the start of the policy period. Once paid, no further premiums are required.

Term Insurance

A second form of life insurance is *term insurance* where a death benefit is paid only if the insured dies during a specified period of time. Two basic policy forms are:

1. *Periodic Term*. This policy promises to pay a death benefit if the insured dies during a fixed period of time, such as 1 year, 5 years, or 10 years. Normally, the premium is level during the period. If the insured outlives the period, no cash value or other benefit is paid.

2. *Specified Age Term*. This policy pays a death benefit if the insured dies prior to a named age, such as 65 years. Again, nothing is owed if the individual lives to the designated age.

Modifications to Term Insurance

In addition to the basic forms of term insurance, a number of variations are available:

1. *Decreasing or Increasing Term*. Policies can change the death benefit. A *decreasing term policy* provides lower benefits as each year passes. This would fit a situation where the proceeds are designed to pay off a loan that is declining in value each year. An *increasing term policy* has benefits that rise each year. This would be helpful in an inflationary economy.

2. *Renewable Term*. The insured can continue the coverage after the policy expires. This is commonly done by providing an option exercisable by the owner to extend the period of coverage in return for the payment of additional premiums.

3. *Convertible Term*. The owner can convert the policy to whole life under specified conditions and at a designated cost.

Variable Life Insurance

Variable life is a modification to whole life with characteristics as follows:

1. *Fixed Premiums.* The monthly or periodic premium payment is fixed and does not vary.

2. *Variable Face Value.* The death benefit and cash value of the policy vary in response to the rate of return on a named group of securities. The policy is normally indexed to an equity fund or index of returns on stocks and bonds. If returns are higher than expected, the death benefit and cash value rise.

3. *Minimum Death Benefit.* The death benefit varies only in an upward direction above the initial face value. If the return on the underlying fund is less than expected, the face value of the policy may decline but will not drop below a minimum death benefit.

Universal Life Insurance

Universal life is another modification to whole life with characteristics as follows:

1. *New Premiums.* The owner can increase, decrease, or continue premium payments on a level basis at his or her option.

2. *Guaranteed Interest.* The insurance company guarantees a minimum return on the invested premiums from past periods. This is set quite low, normally around 4 percent.

3. *Excess Interest.* The insurance company invests the premiums to earn a return, normally exceeding the rate of guaranteed interest. The excess earnings are credited to the cash value of the policy.

The important feature of universal life involves the situation where the premiums and interest exceed the mortality charge and expenses. In such a situation, which is expected but not guaranteed, the policy generates a profit that is given to the owner. This may be in the form of lower premiums, higher cash surrender value, or higher death benefit.

Variable Universal Life Insurance

Variable universal life is a combination of universal life and variable life insurance. It allows a high level of flexibility with regard to premium payments, cash values, and the investments that support the policy. The owner can request the cash value to be invested in a variety of investments that offer different risk and return levels.

Variable universal life reflects the fact that life insurance can be both a way of providing a death benefit and a means to building cash value. Policies have become increasingly flexible in recent years to achieve both goals for policyholders.

Endowment Insurance

This form of life insurance promises to pay a benefit whether or not an insured individual dies during the period of the policy. It is really a combination of term insurance and a savings program. The benefits are:

1. *Death Benefit*. If the insured dies during a specified time period, a death benefit is paid. In effect, this is term insurance.

2. *Survival Benefit*. If the insured lives until the end of the period, a lump sum cash payment is made. This is the savings feature.

Annuity Contracts

An *annuity* is a periodic payment of money over a designated period of time. An *annuity contract* is an agreement that provides for a periodic payment to be paid over a period of time and/or for the duration of a life or lives. The person who receives the payments is called the *annuitant*. The period during which payments are made is called the *liquidation period*.

In this section, we examine annuities.

Kinds of Annuities

A number of annuities are available in the area of life insurance:

1. *Temporary Annuity*—Makes payments for a designated liquidation period, such as 10 years.

2. *Single Life Annuity*—Makes payments for an uncertain liquidation period, namely, the duration of a person's life.

3. *Temporary Life Annuity*—Makes payments for a variable liquidation period, either a specified length of time or when a person dies, whichever comes first.

4. *Joint and Survivor Annuity*—Makes payments when two or more individuals are named as annuitants and continues as long as one is still alive.

Annuity insurance policies carry a wide variety of features to meet the needs of insureds. Individuals and employers can select the options that best meet the needs of themselves, their families, or their employees.

Immediate vs. Deferred Annuities

One classification of annuities distinguishes between the following:

1. *Immediate Annuity*—Exists when payments begin at the next payment interval after purchase. For example, if a monthly annuity is purchased today, payments begin in one month.

2. *Deferred Annuity*—Exists when payments begin sometime in the future. An example is a policy that begins payments at the retirement age of 70.

Pure vs. Guaranteed Annuities

A second classification of annuities distinguishes the following:

1. *Pure Annuity*—No refund or cash value if the insured dies before the start of periodic payments. In effect, this is retirement insurance only. Death prior to the designated start of payments eliminates all responsibility for the insurance company.

2. *Guaranteed Annuity*—Pays a specified number of annuity payments whether or not the insured lives for the entire liquidation period. If the insured outlives the guaranteed period, payments continue until the end of the designated period or until death.

3. *Premium Refund Annuity*—Refunds part or all of the premiums paid if the insured dies before the start of the liquidation period.

Fixed vs. Variable Annuities

A third classification of annuities is:

1. *Fixed Return Annuity*—Guarantees a certain payment during the liquidation period.

2. *Variable Return Annuity*—Invests premiums and past income in variable return securities, such as common stock and bonds. The eventual benefits will fluctuate depending upon stock and bond prices, dividends, and interest.

Life Insurance Contracts

The agreement between the owner of a life insurance policy and the insurance company is contractual in nature. A wide variety of features are available to provide individuals with proper life or retirement insurance. In this section, we cover some of the major features of life insurance and retirement contracts.

Required Clauses

A *clause* is a stipulation in a formal legal document. Although life insurance policies vary widely, a number of common clauses are required under most state laws. These are:

1. *Ownership Clause.* The person who may exercise ownership privileges is identified. Options include changing the beneficiary, borrowing against the policy, or cancelling it and collecting its cash value.

2. *Beneficiary Clause.* Person or persons are named who will receive the proceeds at maturity of the policy. It also supplies details on the rights of direct and contingent beneficiaries and how beneficiaries can be designated.

3. *Incontestable Clause.* The contract's validity cannot be challenged after it has been in force for a stated period of time, normally two years, provided the insured lives for the two years. It is designed to avoid disputes in the distant future when the insurance company may learn that the insured misrepresented his or her health or other matters.

4. *Premium Clause.* The effect of failing to pay premiums on a timely basis is covered. A *default* is the failure to make payment when due. This is accompanied by a *grace period*, defined as a span of time when the policy remains in force following a default. One month is common. If the insured dies during this period, the benefits will be paid, less the amount of the overdue premium.

5. *Reinstatement Clause.* A *lapsed policy* is an insurance contract that is no longer valid. This occurs when an overdue premium is not paid during the grace period. After a policy lapses, an individual may wish to purchase insurance again. She would have a higher premium because of a shorter life expectancy. The reinstatement clause provides for returning the contract to a valid state without an increase in the premium. It does require proof of insurability and payment of all overdue premiums with interest. Normally a policy may be reinstated within a five-year period.

6. *Assignment Clause.* An *assignment* is the transfer of contract rights to another party. The owner of a policy can assign all or part of the

policy rights. The assignment clause provides that such assignment is not effective until the company has received notice.

7. *Suicide Clause.* A refund of premiums only is allowed if the insured commits suicide within a certain period of time, normally one year.

8. *Misstatement of Age Clause.* A change in benefits occurs if the age of the insured is incorrect. Although telling an incorrect age is a misrepresentation, the insurance company may not use it to void the policy. The benefits are simply recalculated to the correct age and paid to the beneficiary.

Optional Clauses

The following optional clauses are commonly included in life insurance policies:

1. *Dividend Clause.* Some policies have dividend clauses that provide for the payment of dividends to policyholders if the company makes more money than expected.

2. *Cash Value Clause.* The cash surrender value calculation and any restrictions on it are spelled out.

3. *Loan Clause.* If a policy has a cash value, the owner can borrow against it.

4. *Payment of Policy Benefits Clause.* The different methods of collecting the benefits of the policy are spelled out.

5. *Aviation or War Exclusion Clauses. Adverse selection* is the tendency of individuals to purchase insurance to cover below-average risks, for example, a higher than normal likelihood of dying. Some insurance policies contain clauses that exclude payment of benefits in these situations. Examples are the aviation clause, which excludes payments to pilots or passengers of aircraft. Another is a war clause, excluding payments to individuals killed in war.

Endorsements and Riders

An *endorsement,* also called a *rider,* is a provision added to an insurance policy to change one or more of the basic conditions or terms of the contract.

Normally, the owner must pay additional premium amounts to pay for endorsements or riders that add to the benefits of a policy. Some of the common endorsements are:

1. *Renewability or Conversion Option.* The *renewability option* allows an individual to renew a term insurance policy for an additional period with

the payment of an additional premium. The *conversion option* allows the owner to convert a term policy to another form such as whole life.

2. *Disability Waiver of Premium Option.* If a person becomes disabled and cannot earn a living, the person may not be able to make premium payments. That would cause the policy to lapse. This option allows all premiums to be waived in the event of disability.

3. *Accidental Death Benefit.* An additional death benefit is provided if the death of the insured is caused by an accident. Commonly, the death benefit is doubled.

4. *Guaranteed Insurability Option.* The owner can purchase additional amounts of insurance in the future without providing evidence of insurability.

5. *Spendthrift Clause.* The beneficiary is denied the right to assign or otherwise encumber the benefits prior to collecting them. The clause forbids creditors from attaching or claiming the benefits until they are received by the beneficiary and makes it difficult for a beneficiary to spend the proceeds prior to receiving them. It also provides some protection to surviving spouses or other beneficiaries from the creditors of the deceased.

6. *Common Disaster Clause.* This clause involves the deaths of insured and beneficiary in a common accident. If the beneficiary outlives the insured for even a moment, the death benefit is paid to the estate of the beneficiary rather than to the contingent beneficiary. If that result is not the intent of the insured, a common disaster clause may be added as an endorsement. It provides that proceeds be withheld for a designated time, normally a month, in case the insured and beneficiary die in a common accident. If both die at approximately the same time, the proceeds go to the contingent beneficiary.

Nonforfeiture Options

An important feature of life insurance is that a cash surrender value can build up as a form of savings. When a policy lapses as a result of failure to pay premiums, the cash surrender value remains. A *nonforfeiture option* ensures that the owner will not lose the accumulated cash benefit. In addition, it allows the owner to select the method of disposition of the cash surrender value. Three options are commonly available:

1. *Cash Settlement.* The owner can accept the surrender value in cash.

2. *Paid-Up Insurance.* In effect, this option is a policy that will remain in force until death without further premium payments. It will have a lower death benefit than the original policy.

3. *Term Insurance.* The insurance company uses the surrender value to provide term insurance. The period depends upon the face value of the insurance and the size of the cash surrender value.

Settlement Options

Earlier in this chapter, we noted that a life insurance policy may provide retirement benefits, and vice-versa. This is achieved by changing the *settlement option,* defined as the method of payment of the proceeds of an insurance policy. Some of the most common options are:

1. *Lump Sum*—The payment of cash equal to the cash value or death benefit of a policy.

2. *Interest Only*—Leaves the death benefit under the management of the insurance company and involves periodic payments of interest earnings on the proceeds. Thus the death benefit could later be paid to a second beneficiary. As an example, the mother receives interest while she lives and the principal goes to children upon her death.

3. *Fixed Period Annuity*—A series of fixed payments for a designated period of time.

4. *Fixed Amount Annuity*—A series of fixed payments until the proceeds are exhausted. The amount can be changed by the beneficiary, which has the effect of changing the period.

5. *Life Income Annuity*—A series of fixed payments during the life of the beneficiary. When the beneficiary dies, the payments stop. The size of the annuity payment depends upon the age of the beneficiary, the assumed rate of interest, and other actuarial factors.

6. *Period Certain Life Income Annuity*—Guaranteed payments until the death of the beneficiary but guarantees a minimum number of payments. If the beneficiary dies before the minimum number of payments is reached, they are continued to his or her estate or to another beneficiary.

Exercises

1. Mark Hartwell purchases a policy paying him $100,000 in the event of the death of his wife, Margaret. If he is not alive at her death, the money goes to George Washington University. Margaret purchases a policy on her own life for $50,000, with benefits payable to Smith College. For each policy, name the (a) insured, (b) primary beneficiary, (c) contingent beneficiary, (d) owner, (e) irrevocable beneficiary, (f) revocable beneficiary.

2. An agent sells the following policies this month. What kind of policy is each one?
   a. A 10-year policy, no cash value, face value begins at $25,000 and declines in decrements to $5,000. May be renewed for two 5-year periods at $10,000 face value. May be converted to $20,000 whole life with proof of insurability and at an annual premium of $600.
   b. Annual payments for 20 years; then the policy is fully paid up; interest guaranteed at 6 percent, excess earnings credited as earned; owner can increase or decrease premiums at his or her option.
   c. Pay $10,000 today and receive lifetime coverage. Death benefit of $25,000.
   d. Pay $600 a month for insurance coverage until age 65; if still alive, collect $50,000.
   e. Pay $120 a year to receive $10,000 coverage. Indefinite period. Growing cash value.
   f. Pay $100 a month to receive $40,000 of coverage until age 70. The policy has no cash surrender value.
3. An agent sells the following annuities. Name the category of annuity for each one.
   a. At age 65, he makes monthly payments of $1,200 to either John or Edith Handleson, so long as either shall live.
   b. At age 67, he makes quarterly payments of $4,000 to Mike Lyons or his heirs until he reaches age 80. If he dies before age 67, no payments are made.
   c. At age 62, makes monthly payments of $2,200 to either Ruth or Al Wilson, for 20 years or until both are dead, whichever comes first.
   d. At age 70, makes monthly payments of $800 until death of Sam Lewis.
   e. At age 65, pays $1,300 a month for 25 years to Martin Laurence or his heirs.
   f. At age 70, pays $1,500 a month for 10 years to Hoke Cartewell or his heirs. If death occurs prior to age 70, 50 percent of premiums are refunded.
4. Three years after issuing a life insurance policy, the insurance company learns that an individual misrepresented both his age and the fact that he was in ill health. The insurance company sends him a notice that the policy is void. Three weeks later, he dies. Does the insurance company have to pay the face value of the policy?
5. Sandra Closkey makes an insurance premium payment on the 10th of each month. She fails to make it in July. In October, she sends three payments. Is the policy still in force? If not, what must happen to reinstate the policy?
6. Charles Abdul wants some options with his insurance policy. He wants to have the premium payments made even if he is unemployed or permanently disabled. He wants the right to purchase additional insur-

ance without a health checkup if he needs more in the future. He wants to be sure that the policy will maintain its value in both dollars and pesos, in case his beneficiary chooses to live in Mexico. He wants to be sure that no creditors can file a court claim against his benefits. And he wants to be sure that the proceeds go to a contingent beneficiary if he and the primary beneficiary die at the same time. What options does Charles need?

7. An insurance policy contains the clause "In the event of a failure to make four consecutive payments, the cash surrender value of this policy will be forfeited. It may be reinstated only upon application from the insured and repayment of the overdue premiums plus interest at 7 percent plus a penalty to be determined by the company." What is wrong with this statement?

8. An individual has reached the age of 65 and has retired. She has a cash value in her group life insurance totalling $450,000. She writes to the company as follows: "I want my cash surrender value of my policy. Can I have:

   a. ". . . a series of guaranteed payments until I die?"

   b. ". . . the earnings only on the policy, leaving the principal for my daughter when I die?"

   c. ". . . a growing annuity each year guaranteed to keep up with the rate of inflation, payable until I die and for five additional years payable to my daughter?"

   d. ". . . a series of guaranteed payments for the next 30 years, payable to my daughter if I die before the time period is over?"

   What are the answers to these questions?

7

Life Insurance in Organizations

Life insurance benefits provided to and through organizations can achieve a number of goals. The group policies benefit both the organization and its employees.

In this chapter, we examine some of the features of group life insurance and retirement policies.

Purposes of Group Life

The group life insurance program of a business, nonprofit organization, or government agency can achieve a number of purposes, which are covered in this section.

Employee Retention

A group life insurance program can increase the chances of retaining employees. Group insurance is attractive for several reasons:

1. *It is easy to obtain.* A group policy covers all employees who are eligible and who elect membership. Thus it is easy for an individual to obtain life insurance.

2. *Its rates are economical.* Group insurance is provided under a master policy. The selling and administrative costs are lower than for individual policies. Thus the cost of group insurance is less than the cost of individual policies.

3. *It is subsidized by the employer.* Employers tend to pay a large portion or all of the cost of group life. *Split-dollar insurance* is an agreement whereby the employer and employee share the cost of life insur-

ance. The employer subsidy becomes an added benefit to the employee that would be lost if the employee changed jobs.

Key Person Insurance

A *key person* is defined as an employee who makes a critical contribution to the success of an organization. If such an individual dies unexpectedly, the organization will probably suffer financial loss. *Key person insurance* is life insurance to offset such loss. It is owned by the employer and purchased to cover the key person. In the event of death of the covered individual, the organization is provided funds to make up losses that occur until a new person can be hired and become effective.

Business Continuation

The death of an owner or partner in a closely held business can threaten its continuance by the other owners or partners. The estate of the deceased may require liquidation of the assets. A *cross-purchase plan* is an agreement whereby each owner or partner purchases sufficient life insurance on the other owners or partners to permit a purchase of each other's assets. If a person dies, money is available to buy out the person's interest and continue the business.

Group Life Insurance

Life insurance is extensively used by private and public employers as an employee benefit. Although this is essentially a human resources function in most organizations, it reflects the compensation program of organizations. *Group life insurance* is defined as an insurance plan covering a number of employees under a single policy issued to the employer. In this section, we examine group life insurance.

Group Life Underwriting

Group underwriting is defined as the acceptance of applications by an insurance company without a review of whether each individual is insurable. Instead of processing each detailed application, the insurance company agrees to accept all full-time employees who meet two requirements for eligibility, namely:

1. *Sign up during eligibility period.* An eligibility period is defined as a designated time period during which an individual may enroll in a

group insurance program. Normally, this is a 30-day period at the start of employment or following a probationary period.

2. *Be actively at work.* On the day coverage becomes effective, the employee must be actively working. This is deemed to be evidence of good health and a requirement that reduces the likelihood of adverse selection.

If the employee fails to meet these requirements, he or she may be able to sign up at a later time. This will require the individual to furnish evidence of insurability.

Group vs. Individual Life Insurance

Group life insurance differs from individual life insurance in the administration of the program. Some of the differences are:

1. *Record Keeping.* For large groups, the employer may be the administrator of the program. The insurance company provides a *master policy*, defined as a contract containing the terms and conditions of coverage for all employees. The employer then provides each insured employee with a certificate showing the amount of insurance and beneficiary and a booklet describing the terms of the policy.

2. *Relatively Standardized Benefits.* A *flexible benefit program* is group insurance where the employee can make some decisions on the amount and conditions of life insurance. A *supplemental plan* is part of some master policies that allows the employee to select additional coverage. In spite of these efforts to meet employee needs, group insurance does not offer the variety of coverage and terms that is available with individual life insurance.

3. *Formula Benefits.* Mechanical formulas are typically used to determine coverage. This has two effects. Employees with longer terms of service or higher salaries can receive a higher level of coverage than newer or lower-paid employees. Also, mechanical formulas are used to reduce the chances of adverse selection.

4. *Shared Cost.* The cost of group insurance is normally borne partly by the employer and partly by the employee. The employer generally covers the bulk of the cost.

5. *Lower Cost.* Because of economies from low marketing costs, group underwriting, and standardized administration, the premium on group insurance is less than the premium for comparable individual insurance.

6. *Tax Benefits.* Premiums paid by employers are normally deductible as a business expense. At the same time, employees generally do not

have to pay taxes on the employer's contribution. These tax benefits make group insurance less costly than individual insurance.

Cost of Group Life Insurance

The premiums for group life insurance are affected by several factors, including:

1. *Nature of Plan.* A *contributory plan* requires employees to pay a portion of the cost of life insurance. A *noncontributory plan* is funded entirely by the employer.

2. *Claims Experience.* A group policy may have the cost of premiums determined individually for an organization. Three approaches are used with respect to determining premiums:

  a. *Class Rating.* The premium is determined by grouping an organization with other insureds having similar characteristics. The premium is based on the loss experiences of the class of insureds.

  b. *Experience-Rated Plan.* Historical data are used to determine the premium paid by the employer to the insurance company. This plan can be used only with large organizations who have sufficient employees to develop statistically reliable data; also called a *prospective rated plan.*

  c. *Retrospective Plan.* Under this approach, the insurance company collects an advance premium and adjusts it later, based on the actual loss experience of the insured.

3. *Employee Turnover.* As older employees retire and younger employees join the organization, the average mortality experience is affected. For a growing organization, the effect is likely to reduce the cost of coverage on the average. In contrast, a declining organization may hire few new employees and may have an aging work force, in which case premiums may be higher than for other organizations.

Retirement Insurance

Retirement insurance is also widely used as an employee benefit by public and private organizations. As with life insurance, this is usually a human resources function with some risk management overtones. In this section, we examine retirement insurance.

Private Pension Plans

A *pension* is a regular payment to an individual or family when the individual has fulfilled certain conditions. A *private pension plan* is a program used by an organization to provide for the retirement of its employees. Private pension plans in the United States are administered in accordance with a variety of laws and regulations. Three major federal laws are particularly significant:

1. *Employee Retirement Income Security Act of 1974 (ERISA)*—Prescribes standards for funding, eligibility, vesting, termination, management, and tax treatment of private pension plans.

2. *Tax Equity and Fiscal Responsibility Act of 1982 (TEFRA)*—Attempts to standardize terms and benefits of private plans and ensures that all employees are treated fairly.

3. *Retirement Equity Act of 1984 (1984 Act)*—Further seeks fairness for all employees.

Qualified Pension Plan

A *qualified pension plan* conforms to the requirements of federal laws, such as those above, and is so recognized by the Internal Revenue Service. Qualified plans receive several tax benefits, namely:

1. *Tax-Deductible Employer Contributions.* Under a qualified plan, the employer's contributions may be deducted as a normal business expense. With unqualified plans, this is not the case.

2. *Tax-Deferred Employee Contributions.* With a qualified plan, the contributions made by employees are not taxed until the benefits are actually received. This is usually at a much later time, such as after retirement.

3. *Tax-Deferred Investment Earnings.* After contributions are made, they are invested to yield a return. With a qualified plan, these earnings are not taxed until the benefits are received.

Qualification Requirements

For a plan to be qualified by the Internal Revenue Service, it must meet the following standards:

1. *Designed to Benefit Employees*—Must be designed specifically to benefit employees and their beneficiaries. It must not be designed to primarily benefit officers or owners of an organization. Neither may it discriminate in favor of officers, stockholders, or highly paid employees.

2. *Written and Disseminated*—Must be in writing and be communicated to the employees. This includes the distribution of a written description summarizing major provisions, rights, and obligations.

3. *Permanent*—Must contain provisions so that it cannot easily be terminated by the employer. As one measure of whether it is a permanent plan, it might require the employer to make continuing contributions over a long period of time.

4. *No Diversion of Funds*—Must be set up so that it is impossible for the employer to divert or recapture contributions until all potential liabilities are covered.

5. *ERISA Requirements*—Must meet other requirements as spelled out by ERISA.

Eligibility Criteria

Private pension plans must specify the conditions that qualify an employee for inclusion in the plan. Some of the major considerations are:

1. *Probationary Period.* This is a period of time when a new employee is not included in the plan.

2. *Other Considerations.* An organization may have more than one retirement plan for different geographic locations or subsidiaries. The basis for inclusion in the plan must be specified by category of employee without discriminating in favor of highly paid employees.

Retirement Age

The purpose of a private pension plan is to provide retirement benefits. In fulfilling this goal, three retirement ages must be considered:

1. *Normal Retirement Age*—The specified age for full pension benefits. Most private plans follow the lead of social security and designate age 65 as the normal retirement age.

2. *Mandatory Retirement Age*—The age at which an individual must retire and begin to collect benefits under the plan. Federal law prohibits mandatory retirement prior to age 70.

3. *Early Retirement Age*—The age at which an employee may voluntarily retire and begin to collect retirement benefits. When an employee selects early retirement, benefits will be lower than those provided for employees who continue to the normal or mandatory retirement age.

Vesting

Federal law requires the employer to refund any contributions made by the employee when the employee terminates employment prior to qualifying for retirement. This is not the case for the contributions made by the employer. *Vesting* is the employee's right to collect benefits on the basis of the employer's contributions to a pension plan. Federal law requires qualified plans to provide for full vesting within a reasonable period of time.

Federal law specifies three minimum standards for vesting:

1. *100 Percent Five-Year Rule*—Provides for 100 percent vesting after five years of service. No partial vesting is required. This is sometimes called cliff *vesting*.

2. *Phased-In Seven-Year Vesting*—Requires 20 percent after the third year of service, so that vesting reaches 100 percent after the seventh year.

3. *Top-Heavy Plan Vesting*—Provides a disproportionate share of benefits to owners and other highly paid employees of a firm, with lower benefits paid to lower paid individuals. Special rules exist for vesting under such plans. Either 100 percent vesting must be provided after three years, or 20 percent a year must begin after two years so that 100 percent is achieved after six years of service.

These are minimum standards in the United States. Private pension plans may provide for more rapid vesting.

Defined Benefit Plan

A *defined benefit plan* specifies retirement benefits according to formulas that are known to all participants. The formulas may link benefits to salary, years of service, or other factors. Two of the major approaches are:

1. *Flat Amount Formulas*—Specifies benefits in dollar amounts. An example might be $500 a month for all fully vested employees, or $25 a month for each year of service. An employee with 20 years of service would get 20 times $25, or $500 a month.

2. *Percentage Formulas*—Specifies benefits as a percentage of earnings. An example might be 2 percent of annual earnings for each year of service, with a maximum of 60 percent. Thus an employee who had earnings of $50,000 and 20 years of service would receive .02 times 20 times $50,000, or $20,000 a year. An employee with 30 years of service would receive the maximum benefit of $30,000.

Defined benefit plans that use percentages must specify the earnings and period of time. Some formulas use earnings during the final years of employment. Others use highest earnings over a specified period, such as three years. Still others use the average earnings over the full period of employment.

Defined benefit plans may provide for increases in benefits to cover inflation during the retirement years. A *cost of living adjustment* (COLA) *clause* is a provision that adjusts benefits automatically on the basis of changes in price or wage levels in the economy. In plans without such clauses, the employer may raise retirement benefits periodically to match inflation.

The specified benefits in qualified defined benefit plans are insured by the Pension Benefit Guaranty Corporation (PBGC), an agency of the federal government. All defined benefit plans pay an annual fee for this insurance.

Defined Contribution Plan

A *defined contribution plan* specifies no retirement benefits. Instead, it provides for employer and possibly employee contributions and provides retirement benefits based upon the money available at retirement. Four factors play a key role in the level of benefits:

1. *Size of Contributions.* The amount of money contributed each year is a major factor in the level of benefits. Federal law regulates the maximum contributions that may be made on a tax-deferred basis.

2. *Length of Service.* Long-term employees will have more money in a plan and thus have higher benefits than employees who participate for a shorter period of time.

3. *Investment Earnings.* The contributions are invested to earn a tax-deferred return. If earnings are high, benefits will be larger than if earnings are low.

4. *Retirement Age.* Employees who defer their retirement will receive higher benefits than those who take normal or early retirement.

Defined contribution plans have specific formulas for the amount of contribution by the employer. As an example, a plan may require the employer to contribute 10 percent of earnings to the plan. The plan will provide the employee with periodic statements on the amount of money currently allocated to the employee on the basis of past contributions and earnings.

Financing Defined Benefit Pension Plans

Funding is defined as the accumulation of contributions and earnings to provide for the benefits of a pension plan. Defined contribution plans are, by definition, fully funded. For defined benefit plans, a *funded plan* exists when sufficient earnings are accumulated during an employee's work years to provide the defined benefits after retirement. Virtually all defined benefit plans are fully funded.

Two basic approaches are used to ensure proper financing of defined benefit pension plans:

1. *Trust Plan.* A *trust* is a legal entity established to receive, invest, and safeguard the assets of other persons or entities. It is administered by a *trustee,* such as a lawyer or bank. A trust plan involves creating a trust to accumulate contributions, invest them, and pay benefits to individuals who retire.

2. *Insurer Plan.* An insurance company is the administrator. A variety of designs are available for both defined benefit and defined contribution plans.

Profit Sharing Plans

Another type of pension plan is a *deferred profit sharing plan,* defined as an arrangement where an employer contributes a portion of the company profits to a retirement fund for employees. The major characteristics of profit sharing plans are:

1. *Qualified Plan.* Profit sharing plans may qualify for tax exemption by following similar rules to those applied to pension plans. Thus they can represent a form of tax-deferred retirement benefits.

2. *Variable Contributions.* The employer's contributions to the plan will vary with the profits of the organization. Higher contributions will be made in more profitable years. No contributions will be made during years of losses.

3. *Employee Withdrawals.* Under specified guidelines, employees may withdraw funds from qualified profit sharing plans prior to retirement. If the employee is allowed to withdraw funds at any time, the profit sharing plan will not qualify for tax exemptions.

Exercises

1. Charlie and Frank are partners in a tool die business. Frank is married to Ruth. Bill and Judy are employees. Charlie wants to buy insurance on Frank's life. Business would suffer if Judy dies. He also wants to insure her. Further, Charlie wants insurance sufficient to buy out Ruth if Frank dies. Finally, he wants to offer Bill a fringe benefit by sharing half the

cost of the life insurance he provides for his wife and two small children. Which of these are possible?

2. Elliott and Cheryl joined Batten Industries on the same day. The company offers group life insurance with an eligibility period in January each year. Elliott and Cheryl missed the first January sign-up. In November, Elliott applied and petitioned to join, effective immediately. In January, Cheryl applied and was accepted effective January 17. Unfortunately, she was sick the entire week with influenza and she stayed home. What happened with each application?

3. Fred Peterson is the vice-president of operations at Lifeline Industries. He writes the following: "I object to the company's group life insurance plan. We have to do the record keeping, pay the entire cost of the plan, gain no tax benefits, and pay more than would be the case if individuals bought their own insurance." Is he correct?

4. Joe Winslow proposes a plan to the Bathan Company as follows: "You will get group life insurance, paying 80 percent of the premiums. Employees pay the balance. We will use historical data to determine premiums. We collect a premium in advance and do not modify it if you have a high level of losses." What kind of plan is Joe proposing?

5. Lars Hanson proposes a private pension plan that does not meet the requirements of ERISA, TEFRA, or the 1984 Act. He says the benefits of compliance do not offset the paperwork of compliance. Is he correct?

6. Seflow Corporation establishes a private pension plan. It provides greater benefits to officers of the firm, as befits the importance of the role of the president and vice-presidents, but also takes care of all other employees. It is a contributory plan, with the company paying 60 percent of benefits. The plan is not in writing but most employees understand its features. The plan may not be terminated without giving 60 days notice to employees. Excess funds that accumulate as a result of high interest rates on investments may be recaptured by the firm only at the end of each year. Is this a qualified plan?

7. Mark Sanford's company has a qualified retirement plan with three retirement ages. He makes up a riddle about them for his wife, namely, "65, 70, Boo Hoo. You and me baby, 52 skidoo." What might this mean?

8. John Simpson has worked for his company for six years. He has been a participant in a contributory private pension plan the entire time. When he quits, his employer states that John should stay. Otherwise, he will lose his contributions to the plan. Furthermore, John is not even partially vested, so the employer's contributions will also be lost. Are these statements true?

9. Tom Wallace is 26 years old and Lucinda Jones is age 55. They work for the same company and are married to each other. One day at lunch, Lucinda says she prefers a defined benefit retirement plan with a COLA.

Tom says she is crazy. Rather, a defined contribution plan is better with a 7-Up. Who is right?

10. Tom and Lucinda also disagree on their company's qualified profit sharing plan. Tom says it is identical to the retirement plan. Lucinda says no. Who is right?

11. A company seeks to establish a qualified private pension plan that pays defined benefits. The money will be held in money market accounts administered by the treasurer. Is this permitted if the funds are conservatively managed?

8

Health and Disability Insurance

In addition to life and retirement insurance, corporations, nonprofit organizations, and public agencies provide health and disability insurance as part of their employee fringe benefits. In addition, individuals purchase policies to deal with medical expenses and disability.

In this chapter, we examine the nature of health and disability coverage in the United States. We begin with medical coverages followed by the providers of health care insurance. Then, the major characteristics of disability insurance are examined. Workers compensation programs will be covered in Chapter 17.

Medical Coverage

A *medical expense benefit* is defined as any insurance payment that covers expenses resulting from an accident, nonaccidental injury, or illness. In this section, we cover insurance for medical costs.

Financial Approaches to Health Coverage

Health insurance policies use three different financial approaches to covering medical expenses:

1. *Indemnity Coverage*—Based upon the dollar value of the expenses incurred. The insured is covered for the cost of a loss up to specified limits. For example, a hospitalization policy may cover designated hospital expenses up to a limit of $300 a day, with a deductible of $500 per visit. With indemnity coverage, the insured can select a low-cost provider of a medical service and receive full reimbursement, less the deductible.

2. *Valued Basis Coverage*—Based upon the occurrence of specified

events, such as visits to a doctor or days spent in a hospital. As examples, a policy may pay $50 for each visit to a doctor and $200 a day for hospitalization independently of any actual expenses incurred.

3. *Service Basis Coverage*—Based upon the services provided and is independent of cost. As an example, a policy may cover 80 percent of the cost of removing a gall bladder. This differs from indemnity because it does not cover the full cost at any level, even when the service is rendered by a low-cost provider.

Classifications of Health Insurance

A wide variety of policies and coverages provide for the medical expenses of employees. As a conceptual framework, we identify six broad classifications of coverage:

1. *Hospital Expense*—Pays for the cost of room and board when an insured is confined overnight at a hospital. In addition, the coverage may include certain incidental activities such as X-rays, prescribed drugs, and laboratory tests.

2. *Medical Expense*—Pays for visits to a doctor's office for nonsurgical care, including examinations, referrals to other physicians, and the writing of prescriptions.

3. *Surgical Expense*—Pays for surgical operations, and each coverage is scaled in accordance with the difficulty or severity of the operation. A hernia repair might be covered for $500, an appendectomy at $800.

4. *Major Medical Expense*—Pays for large medical expenses involved with serious illnesses or accidents. These expenses involve a large deductible, such as $1,000 or more to eliminate small claims. They also normally require that the insured share a percentage of expenses.

5. *Comprehensive Major Medical*—Combines the medical expense and major medical coverage into a single policy.

6. *Dental Expense*—Covers routine dental care as well as accidental or emergency damage to an insured's teeth or gums.

Characteristics of Group Insurance

Most employers are primarily interested in major medical and comprehensive insurance coverage. The hospital, surgical, and medical expense coverages present a number of problems, including relatively low benefit limits and gaps in coverage. These problems are eliminated or reduced by group insurance programs on the basis of major medical and comprehensive policies.

The employer should select a policy that provides an efficient relationship of cost to benefits. This involves an evaluation of the details of a group policy proposal. A number of characteristics are important when evaluating the cost of group medical coverage, including:

1. *Breadth of Coverage.* A group plan assumes that employees do not have medical, surgical, or hospital coverage. The goal of the group policy is to assist employees in dealing with medical needs for themselves and their families. The policy should be evaluated on the extent to which it provides broad coverage that minimizes the prospect of financial hardship.

2. *Deductible.* Defined as a portion of a health claim not covered by the policy, the deductible is used to reduce the cost of health coverage by eliminating small claims where the cost of processing can exceed the reimbursement. Deductibles are evaluated against three standards:

   a. *Benefit Period*—A stipulated period of time such as a calendar or policy year. It may also be a stipulated period, such as "18 months from the time of a first claim under a policy." Deductibles may apply during a benefit period and start again once a new period begins. As an example, a policy may require a $100 deductible per policy year. Once this amount is reached, other claims will not involve a deductible during the policy year.

   b. *Family Members.* A deductible can apply to each individual covered or can be a total for all members of a family. Thus it could be expressed as $100 for each person or $400 for a family of four persons.

   c. *Injury or Illness.* A deductible can apply for each accident or illness. Thus a second accident in a benefit period may trigger a second deductible.

3. *Limits.* A *maximum limit* is the total amount that will be paid by an insurer under a health plan. As with deductibles, limits are necessary to keep down the cost of coverage. A limit may be expressed in several ways:

   a. *Per Accident or Illness.* The policy may provide for a limit of $100,000 for each separate injury or illness. This protects the insurer against the catastrophic expenses associated with certain illnesses or serious accidents. For protection above the limit, an employee must purchase additional coverage.

   b. *Per Lifetime of an Employee.* A person who has severe health problems may incur serious hospital and medical bills over a lifetime. One limit of most group policies is the total dollar benefits that will be paid to one individual.

c. *Per Benefit Period.* Some policies restrict the benefits that can be paid in the policy or calendar year or other benefit period. This is another limitation designed to hold down the cost of the policy.

4. *Participation Provision.* The employee is required to pay a fixed percentage of medical bills above the deductible. It is sometimes called a *coinsurance provision.* Its purpose is to encourage employees to keep expenses as low as possible because they must pay a portion of them. An example of such a provision is a policy that requires a $500 deductible and 20 percent participation. For a $5,000 injury, the employee pays the first $500 plus 20 percent of the remaining $4,500, or $1,400 total. The insurance company pays the remaining $3,600.

Evaluating Hospital Benefits

Hospital coverage can be evaluated on the following points:

1. *Room and Board*—Covers room and board at the hospital. Does it also cover:
    a. Private nursing services?
    b. Treatment in the emergency room of the hospital if the employee does not remain overnight?
2. *Ancillary Charges*—Costs of hospital services, such as X-rays or blood tests. Issues are:
    a. *Schedule or Blanket Coverage.* A *schedule basis* is the payment of benefits with a fixed dollar amount for each service. Thus an X-ray may be reimbursed at $50 even though the hospital charges more for this service. A *blanket basis* reimburses ancillary charges in total. The policy may cover $100 a day for all such services.
    b. *Participation Requirement*—May require the employee to pay a percentage of the cost of ancillary charges.
3. *Maternity Benefits*—Coverage provides for the cost of giving birth in a hospital. Some policies cover room and board and care of the newborn infant. Others cover only the *complications of pregnancy*, defined as medical procedures that do not accompany a routine pregnancy. Full maternity coverage is normally sought in group health programs.

Medical and Surgical Benefits

Medical and surgical coverage can be evaluated on the following points:

1. *Surgical Limits.* Surgical procedure is covered in one of two ways.

A *stated limit benefit* provides a fixed dollar maximum for each kind of operation. A *usual and customary limit* provides reimbursement up to a "normal" charge for the operation. A participation provision may be required in either case.

2. *Nonsurgical Limits.* Policies cover doctors' fees, laboratory charges, and nonsurgical procedures on an outpatient basis. The limits should be sufficiently large to encourage outpatient care rather than the more expensive alternative of checking into a hospital.

3. *Exclusions.* Policies may not provide any coverage for a variety of medical expenses, including eye examinations, dental care, prescriptions, and laboratory tests. As a general rule, a policy with fewer exclusions provides more valuable coverage and costs more to the employer.

Providers of Health Care Insurance

Individuals and organizations can purchase medical insurance from a variety of providers. The major ones are covered in this section.

Insurance Companies

Many individual and group health insurance programs are offered by insurance companies. These include life insurance companies, property-casualty companies, single-line health insurance providers, and multiple line insurance companies.

Approximately 1,000 insurance companies offer health insurance policies. These provide coverage for approximately 100 million persons.

Blue Cross Hospital Insurance

Blue Cross is a nationwide plan that provides hospital insurance for some 90 million persons. Seventy nonprofit Blue Cross organizations have major characteristics as follows:

1. *Service Basis Benefits.* Blue Cross pays for services performed in a hospital approved under the plan.

2. *Payment Direct to Hospital.* Blue Cross pays the hospital directly rather than reimbursing a covered person for expenses already paid.

3. *Broad Coverage.* Blue Cross benefits are broad and comprehensive. They cover much of the cost of a hospital room, nursing services, use of operating rooms, and medications. Some plans also cover outpatient

services, diagnostic testing, physical therapy, and other hospital expenses.

4. *Reciprocity*. Although each Blue Cross organization is independent, all subscribers are covered nationwide under a reciprocity agreement.

Blue Shield Medical Insurance

A Blue Shield plan is a nonprofit medical insurance organization. It operates similarly to and coverages are coordinated with Blue Cross. The difference is the items covered. Blue Cross handles hospital expenses; Blue Shield covers surgical or nonhospital medical care.

Independent Providers

Independent organizations are set up to provide medical coverage for designated groups of individuals. They include community plans, health clinics owned by physicians, and other entities. About 10 million persons are covered by independent providers, who may exist on a profit or nonprofit basis.

Health Maintenance Organizations

An *HMO* provides a wide range of health care services. Characteristics are:

1. *Comprehensive Coverage*. An HMO provides hospital, surgical, medical, and other services in a single comprehensive approach to health care.

2. *Operating Entity*. An HMO is an organization with its own physicians, other medical and administrative personnel, and facilities. It also has arrangements with hospitals.

3. *Fixed Periodic Premium*. An HMO does not charge covered individuals for each medical service. Rather, the individual or employer pays a fixed premium on a regular basis, such as once a month. In return for the premium, the individual receives whatever services are needed.

4. *Sole Provider*. The HMO is the only source of covered health care service for individuals who are enrolled. An individual may not receive benefits if he or she uses a physician or hospital that is not part of the HMO.

5. *Profit or Nonprofit*. HMOs exist under both profit and nonprofit arrangements.

Preferred Provider Organizations

A *preferred provider organization* (PPO) is another entity that provides health care services to individuals. Some characteristics are:

1. *Pay for Service.* The PPO charges the individual or employer each time a service is provided. The cost of the service is negotiated in advance with the employer.

2. *Discounted Cost of Services.* The PPO normally charges less for each service than the prevailing fee in the area.

3. *Not a Sole Provider.* The PPO does not restrict the individual's choice of physician or hospital. Since an outside service usually costs more than the PPO charge, an individual has a financial incentive to make use of the PPO.

4. *Profit Basis.* PPOs are generally profit-seeking operations, frequently owned by physicians, hospitals, or insurance companies.

Size of Health Care Market

Health care in the United States is a sizeable financial cost for individuals and employers. Figure 8-1 shows the size of the market in terms of benefits paid in a recent year.

The cost of health care services has grown considerably in recent years. A hospital room alone costs almost $300 a day (national average) in 1990. Medical costs and procedures raise the cost of staying in a hospital by another $300 a day. Since the average hospital stay is seven days, the average hospital visit costs over $4,200.

Disability Coverage

Disability insurance is defined as any program that provides an income to a person who is no longer able to work as a result of an accident, injury, or illness. It is an important benefit to provide to employees. Over one-third of all employees suffer temporary disability at some point during their careers. Approximately 10 percent will be permanently disabled before reaching mandatory retirement.

In this section, we examine the characteristics of disability insurance.

General Definition of Disability

The general term *disability* refers to any situation where a person is no longer able to perform the duties of an occupation as a result of injury or illness. Two dimensions of disability can be identified:

Figure 8-1. Health care benefits paid by various providers in the United States, 1988.

Insurance companies and other private providers	$ 83 Billion
Blue Cross or Blue Shield	48 Billion
HMOs, PPOs, and independent providers	63 Billion
Government programs	140 Billion
Total	$ 334 Billion

1. *Extent*—Refers to the seriousness of the injury or illness. *Total disability* means that a person is unable to perform any of the important duties pertaining to the occupation. *Partial disability* means that a person can perform some but not all of the important duties of the occupation.

2. *Duration*—Refers to the time period of the inability to work. *Permanent disability* is a situation where the inability to perform the occupation will continue until the mandatory retirement age. *Temporary disability* exists when the person will recover from the injury or illness and may resume the occupation.

Legal Definition of Disability

For the purpose of purchasing disability insurance, we can identify three legal definitions of disability:

1. *Primary Occupation*—An inability to engage in a person's previous primary occupation. An example is a surgeon who can no longer operate on patients.

2. *Any Reasonable Occupation*—An inability to engage in a reasonable occupation for which a person can be fitted as a result of prior education, training, or experience. The surgeon may not be able to operate but may be able to treat patients as a general practitioner.

3. *Any Occupation*—An inability to engage in any occupation where a disabled person can earn a living. If the surgeon cannot practice medicine, he or she might be able to work in a nonmedical job.

The definition of disability is the most important aspect of a disability insurance contract. If disability is defined as an employee's own occupation, the policy is the most expensive. If disability is defined as any occupation, it offers little benefit to employees.

Probably, the most cost-effective, yet valuable disability policy combines two definitions and two time periods:

1. *Short-Term, Own Occupation.* When a person is initially disabled, he must deal with the injury or illness. This is a time when disability should be defined narrowly to one's own occupation. This definition should exist for a sufficient period to allow the employee to recover from the injury or retrain for another occupation. Such a period might range from six months to two years.

2. *Long-Term, Any Reasonable Occupation.* Over the long term, many disabled persons can retrain for similar occupations that utilize their skills and talents. A fireman may no longer be able to fight fires but can perform other useful, less stressful work. It is logical to expect injured employees to retrain for other suitable positions.

Causes of Disability

Disability contracts are matched against disability from specific sources. This is an important part of the value of the insurance and substantially affects the premium. Some definitions of the cause of disability are:

1. *Accidental Bodily Injury.* This broad definition involves a person who is accidentally injured, whether by accident or otherwise. A person working with paint solvents may become dizzy over a period of time. If the dizziness is disabling, it is an accidental bodily injury that occurred without an accident. It is covered within this definition.

2. *Bodily Injury by Accidental Means.* With this definition, an accident must occur and be the source of the injury. This is not a complete definition and policies that use it leave gaps in an organization's disability coverage.

3. *Sickness Commencing After Start of Policy.* An illness or disease is contracted after the effective date of a policy. This excludes illnesses that originate prior to the start of coverage.

4. *Sickness With First Symptoms After Start of Policy.* This broader definition covers illness or disease that is discovered after the effective date of the policy. This covers a person who contracted a disease with a long incubation period.

Some sources of injury are excluded in different disability policies. Examples are injuries resulting from war, self-inflicted wounds, or injuries that occur in conjunction with alcohol or narcotics. Although exclusions are usually not major, the employer should evaluate each policy separately to ensure that the causes of disability are not overly restrictive.

Exercises

1. An employee benefits manager is offered the following group health coverages. What type of insurer provides each?
   a. Medical and dental coverage provided by doctors who are employees of the insurer
   b. A full range of services available from physicians who choose to participate in the plan
   c. A limited range of services provided at a health clinic, with back-up surgical and hospital benefits from physicians chosen by the individual
2. A benefits manager has the following three alternatives for paying for health care under a group proposal. Name each one.
   a. Hospital stays are covered at $300 a day, less a $50 deductible, and surgical procedures are covered up to 80 percent of the surgeon's fee.
   b. Hospital stays at actual cost up to $400 a day, with a $75 deductible, and surgical procedures also up to specified limits for each procedure, with a deductible.
   c. Hospital stays at 85 percent of actual cost, less a $25 deductible per day, and surgical procedures according to a chart of procedures, with no deductible.
3. Each of the following represents a class of coverage for group health insurance. Name each one.
   a. Hospital, surgical, and physicians' expenses are covered in a single package.
   b. Covers medical operations, such as removal of cancerous tumor.
   c. Covers room and board in a hospital, maybe including some related procedures performed while in the hospital.
   d. Visits to a physician's office.
   e. Significant medical or surgical procedures, with a large deductible.
4. A hospitalization plan covers X-rays, blood tests, and similar services at a rate of $150 per day while the patient is in the hospital. What kind of charges are these? What kind of coverage is provided? is not provided?
5. A hospitalization plan provides some maternity coverage but not for routine pregnancies. What kind of coverage is probably provided?
6. A surgical expense plan provides reimbursement up to 80 percent of the "normal" cost of an operation in a geographical area. What kind of coverage is this? what is it not?
7. A cab driver is injured in an accident and will be in a body cast for six weeks. Afterward, he will be in bed for 10 weeks. Then, he should gradually be able to return to work. Name the extent and duration of this disability.
8. A computer operator is injured in an accident and can no longer sit at a

computer for long periods of time. She can, however, perform the duties of a receptionist or telephone operator. She has requested permanent, total disability but has been denied. What definition of disability is probably used under her coverage?

9. An insurance company representative seeks to sell a disability policy to a company. He argues that the least-cost definition of disability is any reasonable occupation. Is this true? What definition should the company select?

10. A computer operator has been experiencing dizzy spells over the past two years. Her doctor believes that they are the result of watching television at night and a computer screen during the day. One morning, she is unable to make out the letters on the screen and files for disability. The application is approved. What definition is probably used as the cause of disability in the company's plan?

11. An employee joins the company six months after contracting a disabling virus. No symptoms appear for two years. In another year, he is totally disabled. He applies for permanent disability and it is granted. What definition of the cause of disability is probably used in the company's disability policy?

12. An insurance company sells a group health policy that specifies that all coverages are on an indemnity basis. When claims are filed, the company pays 60 percent of claims with specified limits. The company is being sued for additional monies based on misrepresenting the coverage. Is this indemnity coverage?

13. A corporation purchases a health policy that covers a percentage of doctor's fees up to a usual and customary limit. The company bases its reimbursements on prices set in Houston, Texas, for medical expenses incurred by employees in a San Francisco manufacturing operation. The Texas corporation sues. Is it likely to win?

14. An individual climbs a ladder to work on his house. While standing on the twelfth rung, he has a heart attack and falls to the ground. He suffers only mild injury from the fall, but the heart attack leaves him partially disabled. His group health policy defines a higher level of payment if the disability occurs from bodily injury by accidental means. Does this injury qualify for this definition?

9

Automobile Insurance

In 1988 the United States had 184 million vehicles registered for operation on the nation's roadways. These vehicles were involved in 26 million accidents in which over 50,000 people were killed and hundreds of thousands were injured. Physical damage to vehicles and other property exceeded $30 billion.

As a result of the large number of vehicles, automobile insurance is the largest single component of the property-casualty insurance business. In 1988 it comprised 43 percent of premiums written for the entire industry.

In this chapter, we examine automobile insurance. We begin with the nature of such insurance and the various issues that affect financial responsibility. Next, we examine various approaches to the compensation of accident victims. These include the tort system and no-fault insurance. Then, we cover the problems associated with high-risk drivers. Finally, we review in detail the Personal Auto Policy.

Nature of Automobile Insurance

Legal liability represents a major source of economic exposure for individuals and organizations who operate motor vehicles. Other exposures also exist. A number of steps can be taken to provide protection against the consequences of catastrophic loss resulting from owning or operating a motor vehicle. In this section, we examine the nature of automobile insurance and its role in providing financial protection to individuals and families.

Categories of Automobile Loss

Three major categories of loss can occur as a result of the ownership or operation of a motor vehicle:

1. *Injuries or Death of Insureds.* The driver of the automobile or passengers, such as family members who are insured under the vehicle's auto policy, can be injured or killed in an accident.

2. *Third-Person Injuries or Death.* Individuals outside the vehicle, such as pedestrians or occupants of other cars, or noninsured passengers in the vehicle can be injured or killed.

3. *Property Damage.* The vehicle itself, other vehicles, and property near a street or other thoroughfare can be damaged or destroyed as a result of an accident.

The Need for Automobile Insurance

The large automobile insurance market has developed as a result of a recognition by consumers and politicians that coverage is necessary for most individuals. Basically, we can identify four motives for purchasing automobile insurance:

1. *Large Exposure.* An automobile accident can produce damage and injuries that will cost a great deal of money. A seriously injured person can have medical bills that cannot be paid by most individuals or families. And the loss of income from an injury that disables a working adult can produce legal exposure if negligence is proved and damages are awarded in lawsuits. An automobile accident exposes individuals to financial ruin and organizations to bankruptcy.

2. *Asset Protection.* The vehicles owned by individuals and organizations can represent a large portion of their total assets. Individuals have a financial need to protect automobiles that are expensive compared to their budgets or annual incomes. Organizations need to protect the cars and trucks that are used in the conduct of their activities.

3. *Vicarious Liability.* In this situation, one party is deemed responsible for the negligence of another party. An owner of a vehicle may be judged liable for damages awarded when a friend borrows his car. A company may be judged liable for damages levied against an employee. The exposures from being sued under vicarious liability can be as substantial as those from being negligent directly.

4. *Legal Requirements.* In many states, it is mandatory to carry automobile insurance.

Compensating Accident Victims

The laws governing automobile insurance are administered at the state level. Thus the United States has a variety of systems for compensating the victims of automobile accidents. In this section, we examine the different state approaches.

Financial Responsibility Law

A common feature of all state laws is the concept of financial responsibility on the part of the owner or driver of a car. A *financial responsibility law* requires the owner or driver to demonstrate the ability to pay damages resulting from an automobile accident. Failure to meet a minimum level of financial responsibility may result in a suspension of an individual's right to drive an automobile.

Financial responsibility laws vary from state to state. They all involve a state-imposed requirement for a *minimum liability limit*, defined as an amount of money that an individual must be able to pay to settle a liability judgment imposed by a court. Individuals who cannot prove that they have the resources to cover the minimum liability limit must either purchase insurance or they will be denied the right to drive.

Within the framework of a minimum liability limit, proof of financial responsibility is imposed in different ways. Broadly speaking, the approaches may be categorized as follows:

1. *Current Accident.* In this category, a motor vehicle accident, under the state law, causes a minimum amount of property damage or results in bodily injury. In either event, an individual must show proof that she can pay the minimum liability limit. If not, driving privileges will be revoked.

2. *Current and Future Accident.* A more stringent law requires a driver to show that he can pay the minimum liability limit from both a current accident and a future accident.

3. *Judgment and Future Accident.* Some state financial responsibility laws require proof after a judgment has been obtained in a court. Basically, the liable party must pay actual judgment plus the minimum liability limit for a future accident. If the actual judgment is large, only payment up to the minimum liability limit is required.

4. *Conviction of Driving Violation.* When an individual is convicted of a serious driving violation, proof of financial responsibility is usually required even though no accident occurs. Examples are driving while intoxicated or under the influence of drugs and reckless driving. Failure to stop after an accident also falls in this category.

If the individual is unable to demonstrate financial responsibility under the state law, his or her driver's license and automobile registration are revoked. Normally, the individual will have a certain time period, such as 90 days, to provide such proof.

Most states, even those with mandatory automobile insurance requirements, have financial responsibility laws. The provisions of the law are most easily met by carrying sufficient insurance at the time of the accident or conviction to meet the legal requirements. After an accident or conviction, the insured simply notifies the insurance company and asks it to file the proper form with the state authorities.

Expressing Minimum Liability Limits

Financial responsibility laws specify minimum liability limits in three categories. An example is a limit expressed as 50/100/25. This means:

1. *Bodily Injury per Person per Accident.* The first number is the limit for each individual injured in a single accident. In the above example, the requirement is $50,000.

2. *Total Bodily Injury for All Persons per Accident.* The second number in the above example is the limit for all individuals injured in a single accident. For most states, and also for our example of $100,000, this is double the first number.

3. *Property Damage per Accident.* The third number in the above example is the limit for all property that is damaged or destroyed in a single accident. In our example, the requirement is $25,000.

Compulsory Insurance Law

In addition to financial responsibility laws, many states require owners and operators of motor vehicles to carry liability insurance. A compulsory insurance law makes it more likely that a negligent individual will have the resources to pay the minimum liability limit if a court orders a judgment for bodily injury or property damage. This is true because insurance companies are generally more reliable than individuals as sources of funds.

Compulsory insurance requirements do not assure that an insurance company will be available to pay a judgment up to the minimum liability limit. Some gaps in the system are:

1. *Uninsured Driver.* A driver may fail to purchase insurance. This individual may have an accident while driving without a license and operating an unregistered vehicle.

2. *Lapsed Coverage Driver.* A driver may fail to pay premiums and thus allow his insurance coverage to lapse.

3. *Out-of-State Driver.* An individual may be licensed in a state that does not have a compulsory insurance law.

4. *Unknown or Illegal Driver.* Some accidents are caused by drivers who are not known or who have violated the law. Examples are hit-and-run drivers, operators of stolen vehicles, or operators of fraudulently registered automobiles.

Unsatisfied Judgment Fund

A small number of states have attempted to close the gap in coverage when a negligent driver does not pay for the loss from an accident. An *unsatisfied judgment fund* is a pool of money available to compensate accident victims when a negligent party is unable or unavailable to pay for a loss. Major characteristics of the system are:

1. *Unsatisfied Judgment.* A court must hand down a verdict that a party was negligent and has legal liability for an accident.

2. *Loss of License for Negligent Party.* The individual who caused the loss must reimburse the fund for any monies paid. Until this occurs, the negligent party may not hold a valid driver's license.

A system of unsatisfied judgment funds probably has more drawbacks than benefits. Although it affords some reimbursement for losses suffered when another party is negligent, the process can take a long time. This is particularly so since a court case must be won. And they are difficult to finance properly. Only small amounts of money are collected from the negligent drivers who were uninsured in the first place. Most of the funding comes from insured drivers or their insurance companies. The funding has generally been inadequate in recent years.

Uninsured Motorist's Coverage

A second approach to closing the gap in coverage can be taken by a responsible driver himself. This involves the purchase of *uninsured motorist's coverage,* defined as insurance that compensates for losses caused by negligent parties when the negligent parties are not financially responsible. Characteristics of the coverage are:

1. *Judgment Not Needed.* It is not necessary for the insured to obtain a court judgment against the other party. It is only necessary to establish negligence.

2. *Collection From One's Own Insurance Company.* The coverage is

purchased as part of the insurance on one's own vehicle. Hence, the injured party collects directly from her own insurance company.

3. *Widely Available.* This insurance is widely available in the United States.

4. *Mandatory in Many States.* The insurance is required in a number of states. It is automatically included in liability coverage, unless specifically declined, in other states.

5. *Relatively Inexpensive.* The insurance premium is fairly small compared to the total cost of automobile insurance.

Underinsured Motorist's Coverage

In some cases, a negligent driver will meet the state's minimum liability limit, but a court will return a verdict for a larger amount of money. *Underinsured motorist's coverage* pays any damages awarded above the limit. It operates similarly to uninsured motorist's coverage and is widely available.

Weaknesses of Fault Systems

Financial responsibility laws, compulsory insurance, and the tort approach to assessing fault in an automobile accident have visible weaknesses as systems for covering losses from automobile accidents. These include:

1. *Individuals Causing Their Own Losses.* Although seriously injured as a result of his own negligence, a person may lack the resources to pay his medical bills or replace his damaged property. In serious injuries, a person may be temporarily or permanently disabled and be unable to earn a living. These individuals need insurance protection from accidents separately from any issue of negligence.

2. *Difficulty of Proving Fault.* Automobile accidents occur on busy highways, late at night, in the pouring rain, and under other circumstances where it may be difficult or impossible to determine the party who caused the accident. It is probably safe to say that most persons involved in accidents believe they were caused by the other party.

3. *High Costs.* A fault system is expensive. Legal costs are incurred to prove or to deny fault. Judgments against uninsured or unknown motorists may not be paid. If they are paid, the funds are basically provided by insured motorists who fund unsatisfied judgment funds or who buy uninsured motorist's coverage.

No-Fault Automobile Insurance

In an attempt to overcome the weaknesses of a tort approach to compensating automobile victims, a number of states have adopted no-fault systems. *No-fault* refers broadly to any system where a person's financial losses resulting from an automobile accident are paid by one's own insurance company without regard to any issue of negligence. After an accident, each party is reimbursed for loss by his or her own insurance company.

Many states have adopted different versions of no-fault insurance systems since the first law was passed in 1971. In this section, we discuss the different approaches to no-fault.

Pure No-Fault

A *pure no-fault* system has the following broad characteristics:

1. *Negligence Not an Issue.* An accident victim collects for damages according to the coverage in his insurance policy. Negligence is not a factor.

2. *Unlimited Medical Expense Coverage.* An injured person is fully covered for all hospital, doctor, rehabilitation, and other medical expenses that result from the accident.

3. *Unlimited Loss of Wages Coverage.* An injured person collects monies from the insurance company to compensate her for lost wages while recovering from the injury.

4. *No Pain and Suffering Payments.* The insured may not collect any monies to compensate for the pain and suffering caused by an automobile accident.

5. *No Right to Sue for Negligence.* The insured gives up the right to sue a negligent party who caused the accident. Also, the insurance company has no right of subrogation against a negligent driver. The tort system is effectively abolished under pure no-fault.

Modified No-Fault

A number of states have systems that increase the benefits paid from one's own insurer as a result of an automobile accident. Such systems are called *modified no-fault* and have the following characteristics:

1. *Thresholds.* A *no-fault threshold* is defined as a minimum level below which an individual may not sue another party for negligence in an automobile accident. Two thresholds may be used:

a. *Dollar Threshold*. The law may specify that lawsuits cannot be brought if damages do not achieve a certain dollar figure. As an example, no lawsuits are permitted if medical expenses and property damage are less than $2,000.

b. *Verbal Threshold*. The law may specify the minimum level in terms of words rather than dollars. For example, a lawsuit may not be brought unless a victim suffers death, disfigurement, dismemberment, or permanent loss of a bodily function.

2. *Collection From Own Insurer*. For injuries below the established threshold, the accident victim collects from his own insurance company.

3. *Tort Recovery Above Threshold*. If a person has suffered losses higher than the threshold, he may sue a negligent party for medical expenses and property damages.

4. *Limits on Pain and Suffering Damages*. A modified no-fault system places limits on monies that may be collected to reimburse an accident victim for pain and suffering. In some states, such reimbursements are completely eliminated.

Expanded First-Party Coverage

A number of states have programs to reimburse victims without regard to fault in an automobile accident. Also called *add-on plans*, the major characteristics of expanded first-party coverage are:

1. *Some No-Fault Reimbursement*. Medical expenses and other damages may be reimbursed by one's own insurance company without regard to fault.

2. *Right to Sue Negligent Party*. For losses in excess of the no-fault reimbursement, an accident victim has the right to sue the party causing the accident.

3. *Retention of Insurer Subrogation Rights*. *Subrogation* was earlier defined as an assignment of the rights of one party to another party. A subrogation clause is retained in automobile insurance policies under expanded first-party coverage. After reimbursing losses on a no-fault basis to its own policyholder, the insurance company may sue a negligent third party.

Movement Toward No-Fault

For 20 or more years, the United States has been moving in the direction of no-fault insurance systems in most states. The pressures underlying this movement are as follows:

1. *High Cost of Insurance.* Automobile insurance has become very expensive for the average individual. The reasons for the high cost are in dispute among insurance companies, consumer groups, and others. The most commonly cited reasons are (a) a large number of losses, (b) inefficient systems, and (c) frivolous or fraudulent claims.

2. *Need to Cover Economic Losses.* Automobiles kill or maim individuals and destroy property. Society has to locate funds to pay medical bills, rebuild property, and otherwise cover losses. This is a social need independent of fault. Two problems exist with fault systems that affect the ability of society to cover its economic losses from automobile accidents:

   a. *Timing of Payments.* It takes time to decide who is at fault in an accident. Thus money may not be available on a timely basis after an accident to pay hospital bills and replace property.
   b. *Negligent Party Has No Money.* The person at fault may be an uninsured driver with no resources. Thus no money is obtainable to pay damages.

3. *Inefficient Tort System.* The system of using lawsuits to determine fault and identify funds to pay damages is inefficient in three respects:

   a. *Processing Time.* The process is slow. Monies may not be available for years after an accident occurs.
   b. *Cost.* The system has high administrative costs, including legal fees and courtroom time.
   c. *Erratic Outcomes.* The result of litigation is not reliable as a source of funds to cover losses. With identical circumstances, two juries can reach different conclusions on liability for a loss. One individual can receive a judgment that far exceeds any rational estimate of the real loss; another person can receive no money at all to cover medical expenses.

Reform #1: Personal Protection Policy

The Personal Protection Policy approach is a modification of existing automobile insurance coverage. It is being considered in many states and is likely to replace existing coverage for many individuals in the future. It differs from existing systems in the following ways:

1. *Choice of Involvement With Litigation.* The individual could choose whether to use the courts to resolve liability questions in the event of an accident. With this option, the current system of filing suits would be retained.

2. *Choice of Nonlitigation.* The individual could choose never to sue another driver and never to be sued. Injuries would be covered as first-

party damages by one's own insurance company. At the same time, the law would prohibit other parties from suing the insured. The only exception would be for cases involving drunken driving or similar offenses.

3. *Choice of Coverages.* The individual could choose the level of property damage, medical expenses, and other coverages, including deductibles. This choice already exists to some degree, but more flexibility would be available.

4. *Possibility of Lower Premiums.* Some choices would result in lower premiums. By reducing legal costs or declining unneeded coverage, the premiums would be lower than current programs.

This policy may become a viable option for states without strong no-fault laws. The high cost of auto insurance causes many problems. At the same time, some individuals wish to retain the right to sue negligent parties. The Personal Protection Policy approach is a way to meet the needs of both groups.

Reform #2: Buy-at-the-Pump Proposals

A number of reformers have proposed no-fault systems to replace all current systems. Essentially, they involve adding the cost of insurance to the price of gasoline or diesel fuel. Hence, they can be called *buy-at-the-pump proposals.* The major characteristics of these systems are:

1. *Elimination of Sales Costs.* Insurance companies have selling costs equal to 12–15 percent of premium dollars. If insurance charges are collected as part of gasoline prices, selling costs could be reduced.

2. *Mandatory Automatic Coverage.* Since the insurance premiums are effectively collected at the pump, the system would achieve 100 percent coverage of all drivers with no possibility of uninsured drivers.

3. *Full Medical and Lost Wages Coverage.* The system would cover all medical expenses and provide full reimbursement for lost wages. This is similar to a pure no-fault system.

4. *General Damages for Injury Indemnification.* The system would set a schedule of payments to indemnify injured persons based on the severity of the injury. Individuals who wish a higher level of payment could purchase additional optional insurance.

5. *Lower Claims Processing Costs.* With 100 percent coverage of individuals, full reimbursement of medical expenses and lost wages, and general damages payable by schedule, claims costs would decline dramatically.

6. *No Tort Costs.* With no right to sue for negligence under the pure no-fault philosophy, lawsuits would cease to be a means of covering losses. The costs of lawsuits would be saved.

High-Risk Drivers

Whatever the system, states have the social goal of encouraging highway and road safety. Partly, this is a matter of dealing with drivers who have excessive numbers of accidents. In this section, we discuss high-risk drivers.

Identifying High-Risk Drivers

Although the laws with respect to automobile insurance vary widely from state to state, the most common problem involves *high-risk drivers,* defined as individuals who are above-average risks for insurance companies. There are three categories of such drivers:

1. *Individuals With Poor Driving Records.* Some drivers have a large number of accidents compared to other drivers. They may drive at excessive speeds, drive while drinking alcohol or under the influence of drugs, lack the visual skills or reflex actions that assist in avoiding accidents, or simply fail to take proper precautions when driving a motor vehicle. Whatever the reason, they compile records with an excessive number of accidents for the miles driven.

2. *Membership in a Group With Poor Driving Records.* Some drivers are statistically included in a group that has a large number of individuals with poor driving records. The most common example is unmarried male drivers under 25 years of age. Because of immaturity or other factors, these drivers are involved in accidents out of proportion to their numbers in the driver pool. In a recent year, drivers under the age of 25 accounted for 20 percent of all drivers but were engaged in one-third of all fatal accidents. Although an individual who is under age 25 may be a conservative and safe driver, statistical inclusion in a high-risk group may identify that person as a high-risk driver.

3. *Membership in an Insurance Classification.* Insurance companies classify drivers in many ways as they match losses with premiums. One classification may separate urban, suburban, and rural drivers. Because of a large number of cars on crowded streets, urban drivers may be a high-risk classification compared to rural drivers. Regardless of driving record, by living in a city, an individual can become a high-risk driver.

The Issue of High-Risk Drivers

Most states encourage all drivers to obtain automobile insurance. This facilitates the payment of medical expenses and other losses when accidents occur. At the same time, insurance companies are often unable to provide automobile insurance to high-risk drivers at reasonable cost. Because of excessive losses, the premiums would exceed the individual's ability to pay them.

To deal with this problem, most states have established mechanisms to provide coverage for high-risk drivers. The most common ones are:

1. *Automobile Insurance Plans.* This mechanism shares high-risk drivers among all companies that write automobile insurance in a state. Drivers who are unable to purchase insurance from an insurance company are assigned to a *high-risk pool*. They can apply to the plan and be assigned to a company that must provide coverage. The assignments are based on the percentage of business held by each company in the state. Thus a company with 5 percent of the automobile insurance business will be assigned 5 percent of the drivers in the pool.

Although automobile insurance plans vary by state, they have common characteristics. Most plans allow a surcharge to be paid by high-risk drivers. Most plans also allow the insurance company to cancel coverage under certain conditions, such as nonpayment of premium.

Automobile insurance plans are the most common approach to providing insurance for high-risk drivers, with more than 40 states offering some version of the mechanism.

2. *Reinsurance Pool.* A few states have established a system of reinsuring high-risk drivers in a statewide insurance pool. Every company must accept all applicants but can assign high-risk drivers to the reinsurance facility. Premiums for these drivers are forwarded to the facility, which then pays for losses. The policy is serviced, however, by the company that writes it.

This system has two benefits for the individual as compared to automobile insurance plans. First, it allows the individual to choose an insurance company. Second, it avoids the stigma of purchasing insurance through a plan for high-risk drivers.

3. *Joint Underwriting Association (JUA) or State Fund.* A few states have established a statewide association or insurance fund to insure high-risk drivers. Premiums are accepted and losses are covered. Then, any deficiency is made up by assessing all insurance companies who do business in the state.

Personal Auto Policy

Automobile insurance coverage in the United States has traditionally been provided using a number of different basic policy forms. The Personal Auto Policy is the most widely used for the coverage of individual and family automobiles.

In this section, we examine the features of the Personal Auto Policy.

Structure of Personal Auto Policy

The Personal Auto Policy is organized in a number of parts, as follows:

1. *Declarations and Definitions*—Contains the representations of the insured and definitions of some terms used in the policy.

2. *Part A: Liability Coverage*—Covers the rights of the insured when sued by another party after an accident.

3. *Part B: Medical Payments*—Covers the rights of the insured with respect to medical expenses for covered persons.

4. *Part C: Uninsured Motorist Coverage*—Covers rights of the insured when an accident is caused by a negligent person who has insufficient insurance.

5. *Part D: Damage to a Covered Auto*—Covers rights of the insured when a covered auto is damaged in an accident or by other means.

Exercises

1. An individual lends his car to a friend who has an accident in it. The owner of the car is sued, as well as the friend. The owner alleges that he was not negligent and cannot be sued. Is he correct?
2. A friend tells Josephine Lawson that her state has a financial responsibility law of 25/100/15. The friend lives in a no-fault state that requires every driver, no matter how wealthy, to carry automobile insurance. What does 25/100/15 mean? Is the friend correct?
3. Sally Ellison lives in a state governed by a law of pure no-fault insurance. While driving her car home after a party, she is injured in an accident caused by a drunk driver. After getting out of the hospital, she hires a lawyer to sue for reimbursement of her medical expenses. She also seeks damages for pain and suffering. Is she likely to win if the accident report places the blame on the other driver who lost his license after causing the accident?
4. Christopher Manwick lives in a modified no-fault insurance state. He carries a large amount of automobile insurance. He is injured in an

automobile accident that is the fault of the other party. His insurance company pays his medical expenses but wants to sue the other party. In addition, Chris thinks he should be compensated for pain and suffering. Is he allowed to sue?

5. Peter Spero receives a notice from his insurance company that he is identified as a high-risk driver. So does Bonnie Taylor. Peter is 22 years old and has never had an accident. Neither has Bonnie, who lives in downtown Los Angeles. Is it likely that the insurance company has made mistakes in these cases?

6. A state is evaluating how to deal with high-risk drivers. It is considering (a) an automobile insurance plan, (b) a reinsurance pool, (c) a state fund (JUA). Lena Herman, a state legislator, has criticized all three plans because they do not allow drivers the right to choose their insurance company. She also objects to using state tax money to pay for losses. The state insurance commissioner says she is not correct. Who is right?

7. Jennifer Consolo objects to a proposed personal protection policy offered by her company because she does not want to give up her right to sue if she is injured by negligence in an automobile accident. Is this a valid objection?

8. Some insurance reformers have proposed a new automobile system with no selling expenses, automatic coverage, and a reduction of lawsuits. How might they achieve these goals?

9. An individual is covered under the Personal Auto Policy. He is injured in an accident caused by another party and sues the negligent driver to pay his medical expenses. He collects only $7,000 of the $15,000 medical bills. Is he covered for the remaining $8,000?

10. A negligent driver has no money and carries no insurance. A court rules that he is liable for causing $10,000 of property damage to the covered auto of another driver. He also is judged liable for causing $6,000 of bodily injury to the other driver. The injured driver is covered under his own Personal Auto Policy. Who pays for the damages?

10

Personal Property Insurance

As with the automobile, the residence of an individual poses a number of risks and exposures. If a person owns the home, it is more than his or her castle. It is a highly valuable asset. For many people, it is the most costly purchase they will ever make and the largest single asset they own. Whether owned or rented, personal property inside the dwelling can also pose a risk. If lost, stolen, or destroyed, jewelry, electronic items, and other valuables can be costly to replace.

Outside the home, individuals face exposures that endanger their assets. Some property, such as a boat, small plane, or rental assets, may involve sizeable sums of money.

In this chapter, we examine the nonauto risks that face the property owned or used by individuals. As part of this process, we cover some of the policies that reimburse individuals for personal property losses.

Homeowners Policy

A *package policy* is an insurance contract that combines two or more separate coverages into one policy. A *homeowners policy* is a package policy designed to protect individuals who own or rent residences.

For millions of homeowners and tenants in the United States, a homeowners policy represents a fairly standardized approach that is widely used to protect owners and tenants from residential losses. At the same time, there are multiple forms to achieve multiple purposes. There is no existing single homeowners policy that best meets the needs of all individuals.

In this section, we cover the homeowners policy as a comprehensive property insurance contract for protecting individuals who own or rent a residence.

Property Risks of Residences

Whether owned or rented, an individual's residence poses a number of major property risks, including:

1. *Physical Damage.* The home or leased unit can be damaged by fire, flood, or other causes.

2. *Loss of Use.* A damaged house may not be suitable as a residence until it is repaired. The loss of use involves costs to the individual.

3. *Destruction of Personal Property.* A residence contains furniture and other personal property that might be damaged along with the dwelling.

Section I: Property Coverages

The homeowners policy contains two sections. Section I is structured to cover five property exposures. Not all the forms provide all five coverages, which are:

1. *Coverage A: Dwelling*—Covers risks of damage or destruction of the actual residence, plus any attached structures.

2. *Coverage B: Other Structures*—Covers risks to other structures on the premises that are not attached to the main dwelling.

3. *Coverage C: Personal Property*—Covers damage to personal property owned or used by the policyholder.

4. *Coverage D: Loss of Use*—Covers additional living expenses incurred as a result of the inability to live in a residence while it is being repaired or rebuilt.

5. *Additional Coverages*—Covers miscellaneous expenses not itemized in the other areas.

Section II: Liability Coverage

Section II of the homeowners policy provides liability insurance against claims from third parties arising out of an occurrence covered by the policy. Section II coverages are discussed in Chapter 11.

Endorsements

An *endorsement* or *rider* is a written provision that adds to, deletes, or modifies an insurance policy. Endorsements can be added to any of the homeowners forms to achieve an individual's property insurance goals.

Key Definitions

Homeowners policies contain a number of key terms and definitions, including:

    1. *Insured*—The individual purchasing the policy and relatives and children who are residents of the household.

    2. *Residence Premises*—The dwelling and other structures or grounds or that part of a building where the insured resides.

    3. *Other Structures*—Covers buildings separated from the residence premises by clear space.

    4. *Personal Property*—Covers nonresidential possessions owned or used by the insured anywhere in the world.

    5. *Occurrence*—An accident that results in bodily injury or property damage.

Nature of the Coverages

Homeowners policies provide different coverages under their various forms. All forms, however, have the following approach to specifying the coverages:

    1. *All-Risk Coverage*—Exists when property is insured against any exposure, peril, or risk not specifically excluded in the policy; sometimes called *open-perils coverage*.

    2. *Named-Perils Coverage*—Exists when a peril, exposure, or risk must be named specifically to be covered under the policy.

    3. *Exclusions*—Restrict coverage under named circumstances or for designated perils. The various homeowners policies have many exclusions.

    4. *Limits of Liability*—Restrict coverage to specific dollar amounts of loss for different items. Homeowners policies also have many limits of liability.

Measurement of the Amount of the Loss

When a loss occurs, the insurance policy must specify how it will be measured. That is, the policy must identify a method for determining the dollar amount of the loss. Two approaches may be used:

    1. *Replacement Cost*—The amount of money required to construct a new and similar house on the site of a house that is totally destroyed. It

excludes the cost of carpeting, appliances, awnings, and outdoor equipment.

2. *Actual Cash Value of the Loss*—Defined as the replacement cost minus depreciation on the damaged portion of the house. A new roof may cost $10,000. The old roof with a life span of 20 years may be 12 years old. Thus it has depreciated by 12/20, or 60 percent. If the roof is destroyed in a fire, the policy will pay $4,000 (10,000 minus 60% of 10,000). Measuring depreciation is the major problem with this calculation. The insurance company will have tables of depreciation for different kinds of houses, or professional appraisers may be used to determine depreciation.

Loss Settlement on Dwelling and Other Structures

Most homeowners policies settle losses on the dwelling and other structures at replacement cost, provided the insurance coverage is at least 80 percent of such cost. Most losses are partial in nature for relatively small amounts. To ensure full payment of partial losses, the insured should ensure that the policy limit is always equal to at least 80 percent of replacement cost. In the event of a total loss, however, an 80 percent policy limit means that insurance will not pay for full replacement of the residence.

In the event of a policy limit below 80 percent of replacement cost, the company will pay for losses on a proportional basis. The policy will pay the *greater of*:

1. *Actual Cash Value.* Or,

2. *Have/Should Times the Loss.* This is a formula where the policy limit (the "have") is divided by 80 percent of the replacement cost (the "should") and the result is multiplied by the amount of the loss. *Example:* A $120,000 policy is taken out on a house with a replacement cost of $200,000. Depreciation on the loss totals 30 percent. A fire causes $50,000 of damage. How much will be paid by the insurance company? *Answer:* $37,500. This is the greater of actual cash value and have/should times the loss. These are:

   a. Actual cash value equals $50,000 minus 30 percent of $50,000, or $35,000.
   b. The "have" equals $120,000; the "should" equals 80 percent of $200,000, or $160,000; have/should equals 120,000/160,000, or 75 percent; have/should times the loss equals 75 percent times $50,000, or $37,500.
   c. $37,500 is greater than $35,000.

Underinsurance

Underinsurance is defined as any situation where the policy limit is below 100 percent of replacement cost. Two effects are important when a property is underinsured:

1. *Total Loss.* For a total loss, underinsurance will result in a failure of the policy to provide sufficient money to replace the dwelling with a similar dwelling. In our example above, suppose the house was a total loss. The actual cash value would be 70 percent of $200,000, or $140,000. The have/should value would be 120,000/160,000 times $200,000, or $150,000. Yet, the policy limit of $120,000 would be all that is paid. In this case, the owner would be $80,000 short of being able to replace the house with a similar dwelling.

2. *Partial Loss.* The overwhelming percentage of dwelling losses are partial in nature. We have seen that 80 percent is a key level of coverage, since full replacement cost is paid for losses. Any level above 80 percent will result in full reimbursement for partial losses up to the limit of the policy.

Homeowners Policy Forms

A number of basic forms of homeowners policies are available in the different states. In this section, we examine some of the most common.

HO-1: Basic Form

Homeowners One is commonly called the *basic form*. Its major characteristics are:

1. *Ownership Coverage.* The basic form insures the dwelling and other structures. Hence, it is designed for individuals who own the residence.

2. *Dwelling and Structures, Not Land.* The insurance will pay for damages to the dwelling and other structures but not to the land beneath them.

3. *Other Structures at 10 Percent.* The policy will reimburse damage to other structures up to a limit of 10 percent of the dwelling coverage.

4. *Personal Property Coverage.* Losses to personal property are reimbursed up to 50 percent of the dwelling coverage.

5. *Loss of Use.* Additional living expenses or the loss of rent from a tenant are covered up to 10 percent of the dwelling coverage.

6. *Named-Perils on Dwelling.* This policy offers named-perils coverage only. The perils are:
    a. *Natural Perils*—Fire, lightning, windstorm, hail, explosion, smoke, and volcanic eruption.
    b. *Third-Party Perils*—Riot, civil commotion, vandalism, and theft.
    c. *Other Perils*—Aircraft, vehicles, and glass breakage.

HO-2: Broad Form

Homeowners Two is commonly called the *broad form*. As its name implies, HO-2 expands the coverage under the basic form by adding named perils, as follows:

1. *Additional Natural Perils*—Water damage or losses from the weight of ice, snow, or sleet.

2. *Internal Systems Perils*—Losses as a result of freezing of the plumbing system or damage to heating or air-conditioning systems.

3. *Additional Other Perils*—Losses from falling objects or artificially generated electricity.

HO-3: Special Form

Homeowners Three is the most commonly used form. Some important characteristics are:

1. *Open Perils for Coverages A and B.* HO-3 provides all-risk protection to the dwelling and other structures.

2. *Named Perils for Coverage C.* Personal property is protected from the same perils as are named on the HO-2 broad form.

3. *Open Perils for Glass Breakage.* Glass breakage is covered on an all-risk basis. This differs from HO-2 where glass breakage is covered on a named-perils basis.

4. *Endorsement Can Provide Open Perils for Coverage C.* An endorsement is available that converts personal property coverage from named-perils to all-risk basis.

5. *Long List of Exclusions.* HO-3 uses many exclusions to minimize the chances of adverse selection, homeowner carelessness, and catastrophic loss. Although the policy does cover dwelling, other structures, and glass breakage on an open-perils basis, the exclusions are significant. Endorsements or additional coverage may be needed to achieve proper protection of the residence premises.

HO-4: Contents Broad Form

Homeowners Four is commonly called the *contents broad form*. As its name implies, HO-4 is designed to deal primarily with personal property. Its major characteristics are:

1. *Coverages A and B Not Provided.* Since the policy does not provide insurance against perils that threaten the dwelling and other structures, it is intended for a tenant who rents a house or apartment.

2. *Required Minimums for Coverages C and D.* The insured is required to take out stipulated minimum amounts of coverage on personal property and loss of use. Additional amounts of coverage can be purchased above the minimums.

3. *Named-Perils Basis.* The coverage is provided using the same perils as named on the HO-2 broad form.

HO-5: Special Form

This policy provides open-perils coverage on the dwelling, other structures, and personal property. It is similar to HO-3 with an all-risk endorsement for Coverage C.

HO-6: Condominium Unit Owners Form

A *condominium* is a legal arrangement under which an individual holds title to a residential unit in a building with multiple residential units. This policy is designed for the owner of a unit in a situation where a condominium association has purchased coverages A and B on the building and other structures. The characteristics are:

1. *Coverage A for Improvements Only.* Instead of full dwelling coverage, HO-6 provides insurance for dwelling improvements, such as carpeting, kitchen cabinets, and light fixtures.

2. *Required Minimums for Coverages C and D.* As with HO-4, the insured is required to take out minimum amounts of coverage on personal property and loss of use. Additional amounts of coverage can be purchased above the minimums.

3. *Named-Perils Basis.* The coverage is provided using the same perils as named on the HO-2 broad form.

4. *Loss-Assessment Coverage.* Although the condominium association carries insurance, it may experience a loss that is not fully covered. In this case, it will assess all owners to cover the loss. HO-6 provides insurance in the event of such an assessment.

HO-8: Modified Coverage Form

This is similar to the HO-1 basic form with an important exception. Only the actual cash value of the loss is covered. The policy specifically denies coverage on a replacement cost basis.

The Homeowners Eight form is designed for dwellings whose market value is significantly below the replacement cost. Typically, this happens in two situations:

1. *Older Homes.* A home built many years ago may have intricate hand work or craftsmanship that cannot be duplicated at a reasonable cost or at any cost. A house that can be purchased for $150,000 could not be built today for twice that amount.

2. *Weak Housing Market.* The housing market in the United States is cyclical in nature. Prices rise and new homes are built. At some point, an area may have an excess number of houses available for sale. Then, market prices will decline. A house available on the market for $150,000 may have a replacement cost of $250,000. To reduce the moral hazard where an owner might seek to destroy the house and collect the high replacement cost from insurance, a company may offer a policy that covers only actual cash value.

Analysis of HO-3 Special Form

Homeowners Three is the most widely used of the various homeowners policies. In this section, we analyze this policy in greater detail.

Coverages A and B: Dwelling and Other Structures

Some of the major features of the HO-3 coverages on the dwelling and other structures are:

1. *Dwelling and Structures, Not Land.* HO-3 will pay for losses to the dwelling and structures, attached to it or detached, but not to the land beneath them.

2. *Construction Materials and Supplies.* The policy covers materials used to construct or repair the dwelling or other structures when located on or next to the residence premises.

3. *Strict Limit on Other Structures.* The limit of loss payment on the detached structures is quite severe. It may not exceed 10 percent of the dwelling coverage. In cases where other structures are sizeable, a separate endorsement is needed to ensure adequate coverage.

Coverage C: Personal Property

Some of the major features of the HO-3 coverage of personal property are:

1. *Property Owned or Used by Insured Covered Anywhere in the World.* The personal property of the insured is covered whether or not it is located on the residence premises.

2. *Property of Others While on Residence Premises.* HO-3 covers personal property on the residence premises as long as an insured also occupies the premises.

3. *Property of Guests or Residence Employees at Any Residence Occupied by an Insured.* Personal property is covered if the insured rents a summer cottage while on vacation.

4. *Named-Perils Coverage.* Unlike the open-perils coverage on the dwelling and other structures, personal property is covered on a named-perils basis.

5. *Special Limits of Liability.* The policy contains a listing of specific limits on different categories of property. These are covered below. If the insured has large amounts of jewelry, goldware, or other items included under the limits, additional coverage may be needed to provide proper protection.

Coverage D: Loss of Use

Some of the major features of the loss-of-use coverage are:

1. *Additional Living Expenses.* The policy covers any increase in living expenses needed to maintain the household's normal living standard while damage to the residence premises is being repaired.

2. *Fair Rental Value.* Alternatively, the insured can choose to receive money equal to the fair rental value of the residence premises. This is reduced by any savings in expenses that result from the damage.

3. *Time Period.* Loss-of-use coverage is provided until the damage is repaired or the household permanently relocates, both of which must take place on a timely basis.

4. *Rental to Others.* If a portion of the property was rented to others but can no longer be occupied, the policy covers the fair rental value of that area.

5. *Damage to Neighboring Property.* In some cases, damage to a neighboring premises requires an insured to vacate the residence premises. If such damage is caused by a peril insured against in the policy

and if the insured is ordered to vacate the residence premises by a civil authority, up to two weeks of additional living expenses or fair rental value are covered.

Additional Coverages

The major additional coverages provided by Homeowners Three are:

1. *Debris Removal.* The policy covers removing debris from the damage, including fallen trees. This is limited to a dollar amount or percentage of the policy limit.

2. *Reasonable Repairs.* The policy covers necessary repairs to protect the property from further damage.

3. *Trees, Shrubs, and Plants.* Subject to limits and named perils, coverage is provided for damaged trees, plants, and the lawn.

4. *Fire Department Service Charge.* Subject to a limit and conditions, the policy reimburses a fire department service charge.

5. *Property Removed.* Covered personal property is insured against loss while it is being removed from a threatened or damaged premises and for 30 days thereafter. This is designed to encourage an insured to safeguard property by removing it from an area of danger.

6. *Credit Card, Fund Transfer Card, Forgery, and Counterfeit Money.* The policy reimburses losses from unauthorized use of bank cards, forgery of checks, and the acceptance of counterfeit money. These coverages have limits and conditions.

7. *Loss Assessments.* The policy reimburses assessments to cover losses to common property when such charges are made against an insured as the owner or tenant of the residence premises. Conditions and a limit apply.

Exclusions for All Coverages

The policy has a number of exclusions to apply to the dwelling, other structures, and personal property. These are:

1. *Ordinance or Law.* The policy excludes losses that occur from ordinances or laws that govern construction, repair, or demolition of a building or structure. Local zoning boards and government agencies occasionally require changes involving the construction, repair, or demolition of a building. If these were covered, a local board could upgrade an entire community at the expense of the insurance company.

2. *Earth Movement.* The policy excludes losses directly or indirectly

caused by the movement of earth, except for direct loss from fire, explosion, theft, or glass breakage caused by the movement.

3. *Water Damage.* The policy excludes water damage from flood, waves, overflow of sewers or drains, and water below the surface of the ground, except for direct loss by fire, explosion, or theft caused by the water.

4. *Power or Utility Interruption.* The policy excludes losses from the interruption of power or another utility service when such interruption takes place away from the residence premises. This can cause food to rot in refrigerators and heating systems to fail. If not excluded, an insured would not have to take steps to monitor a residence to ensure that damage is not done as a result of a power failure.

5. *Neglect After a Loss.* The policy excludes further damage caused by the failure of the insured to use all reasonable means to preserve property at and after the time of a loss.

6. *Catastrophe Exclusions.* The policy excludes damage from war, rebellion, discharge of a nuclear weapon, and other nuclear hazards.

7. *Intentional Loss.* If an insured intends to cause a loss, it is not covered. Thus vandalism by a child angry at an insured parent is an excluded loss.

8. *Administrative Decisions.* The policy excludes losses that result from acts or decisions of any person, group, organization, or government body. Thus the failure of a zoning board to make a favorable decision is not an insured loss.

9. *Faulty Construction or Maintenance.* The policy excludes any loss from faulty construction, materials, or maintenance of property, whether on or off the residence premises.

Coverages A and B Exclusions

In addition to the general exclusions, the dwelling and other structures have a number of exclusions to the open-perils coverage, including:

1. *Collapse as a Named Risk.* The collapse of a building is identified as a named risk in the policy. Collapse is covered only for:
   a. Any peril named in Coverage C
   b. Hidden decay, hidden insect damage, or vermin damage
   c. Weight of contents, equipment, animals, or people
   d. Weight of rain that collects on a roof
   e. Use of defective materials or methods in construction or renovation, only if the collapse occurs during construction or renovation

  f. Awnings, fences, and other listed nondwelling property if the
   loss is a direct result of the collapse

The policy specifically states that collapse does not include settling,
cracking, shrinking, bulging, or expansion.

  2. *Other Structures Used for Business.* Any shed, garage, or other
structure used in whole or part for business purposes is excluded.

  3. *Other Structures Rented to Nonresident.* Any other structure that is
rented to someone who is not a resident of the dwelling is not covered.
An exception is made for the rental of a structure for use as a private
garage.

  4. *Under-Construction Exclusions.* The all-risk coverage is modified
somewhat during the period of construction of the dwelling. For damage
caused by plumbing, heating, and other systems and appliances, coverage is provided only if the owner has taken certain reasonable precautions.

  5. *Vacancy Exclusions.* Coverage may be reduced considerably if a
residence is not occupied. This includes coverage for damage from
internal systems, vandalism, and glass breakage.

  6. *Freezing, Ice, and Water Damage to Other Structures.* The policy
excludes freezing, thawing, and weight of water or ice damage to fences,
pavement, patios, swimming pools, foundations, and piers located on
the residence premises.

  7. *Seepage or Leakage.* The policy excludes constant or repeated
leakage of water or steam from a household system or appliance.

  8. *Wear and Tear.* The policy excludes normal deterioration of property caused by wear and tear, smog, rust, release of pollutants, settling,
cracking, rodents, insects, domestic animals, and other factors.

Personal Property Named Perils

HO-3 Coverage C is provided for direct physical loss only on the perils
named in the policy. These are:

  1. *Fire or Lightning.*

  2. *Windstorm or Hail.* Damage is covered only if the wind or hail
causes an opening in the building. Thus a window may not be left open.
Watercraft and its related equipment are not covered from this peril
unless they are located inside a fully enclosed building. Then, they are
covered up to the special limit of liability discussed below.

  3. *Explosion, Riot, or Civil Commotion.*

  4. *Aircraft and Vehicles.*

5. *Sudden and Accidental Damage From Smoke.* This excludes damage caused by agricultural smudging or industrial operations.

6. *Vandalism or Malicious Mischief.*

7. *Theft, Attempted Theft, and Likely Theft.* This has a number of exclusions:

   a. The theft cannot be committed by an insured.
   b. It cannot take place in a dwelling that is under construction or unoccupied.
   c. It cannot involve theft in an area of the residence premises rented to a tenant who is not an insured.
   d. It cannot involve property stored at any other residence owned by, rented to, or occupied by an insured, except while an insured is temporarily living there.
   e. For a student who is an insured and who resides away from home, personal property is covered if the student has been at the other residence at any time during the 45 days immediately before the loss.
   f. Watercraft and accessories are excluded.
   g. Trailers and campers are excluded.

8. *Falling Objects.* Loss to property stored in a building is covered if the falling object damages the roof or outside wall of the building. It excludes damage to the falling object itself.

9. *Weight of Ice, Snow, or Sleet.* Only property contained in a building is covered.

10. *Accidental Discharges, Overflows, Bulging, and Freezing.* The policy covers damage caused by accidents involving plumbing, heating, air conditioning, sprinklers, electric power, and appliances. Restrictions and exclusions apply.

11. *Damage by Glass.* This is not covered if the dwelling has been vacant more than 30 days. It does cover a dwelling being constructed.

12. *Volcanic Eruption.*

Special Limits of Liability

The HO-3 Coverage C has an overall dollar limit equal to 50 percent of the dwelling coverage. In addition, specified types of property have maximums payable on a single loss. The limit is given as the total dollar amount for all items in the category. The limits are:

1. *Liquid Assets.* $200; covers money, bank notes, bullion, gold, silver, platinum, coins, and medals.

2. *Paper Assets.* $1,000; covers securities, accounts, deeds, evidences

of debt, letters of credit, notes, manuscripts, passports, tickets, and stamps.

3. *Watercraft.* $1,000; includes trailers, furnishings, equipment, and outboard motors for watercraft.

4. *Trailers.* $1,000.

5. *Grave Markers.* $1,000.

6. *Theft of Precious Valuables.* $1,000; covers theft of jewelry, watches, furs, precious stones, and semiprecious stones.

7. *Theft of Firearms.* $2,000.

8. *Theft of Serving Pieces.* $2,500; covers silverware, goldware, other utensils and serving pieces, and trophies.

9. *Business Property.* Two limits apply. The limit is $2,500 for any business property if the loss occurs on the residence premises. It drops to $250 for losses that occur elsewhere.

Personal Property Exclusions

Homeowners Three has a number of exclusions under Coverage C, namely:

1. *Named Articles.* Personal property that is separately described and specifically insured under Coverage C or any other insurance policy is excluded.

2. *Animals, Birds, and Fish.*

3. *Motor Vehicles.* The policy excludes motorized land vehicles and their accessories. This does not include unregistered vehicles used to service an insured's residence or designed for assisting the handicapped.

4. *Aircraft and Parts.*

5. *Property of Tenants.* The policy excludes personal property of roomers, boarders, and tenants not related to the insured. It also excludes all property in an apartment held for rental to others.

6. *Rental Personal Property.* The policy excludes property owned by an insured and held for rental to others off the residence premises.

7. *Business Data Items.* The policy covers the papers and electronic items used in business only up to their blank or unexposed value, subject to the $2,500 or $250 special limitations on business property. It excludes any loss as a result of lost business data stored on paper or electronically.

8. *Credit Card and Bank Transfer Card.* The policy excludes any losses beyond the coverage specifically named under the Additional Coverages section of the policy.

Conditions

The HO-3 policy is subject to conditions listed in a separate area of the contract. These include:

1. *Insurable Interest Limit.* If a residence is owned by more than one party, the policy coverage is limited to the insurable interest of the insured. Thus an insured who owns half a stereo that was stolen can collect only half its value.

2. *Duties After Loss.* The insured must take specific steps after a loss. These include notifying the appropriate parties, protecting property from further damage, filing claims showing proof of loss, and cooperating with the insurance company in investigating the claim.

3. *Loss Settlement.* The policy contains a number of paragraphs explaining the methods for settling covered property losses. It includes calculations on the amount of loss, appraisal and other procedures in the event of a dispute on the amount of loss, and the methods of repairing, replacing, or making a payment for property.

4. *Mortgage Clause.* This clause spells out the rights of individuals holding mortgages on property.

5. *Recovered Property After Payment Is Made.* When lost or stolen property is recovered after the insurance payment has been made, the insured may keep the payment or retain the property and return the payment.

Homeowners Policy Endorsements

The coverages under the various homeowners policies can be increased by purchasing endorsements designed to meet the needs of different individuals. Some of the more popular endorsements are covered in this section.

Inflation Guard Endorsement

Inflation is defined as a rise in general price levels in an economic system. In the United States, housing prices historically tend to rise along with inflationary trends. Replacement costs for dwellings also rise.

Rising replacement costs cause a problem for holders of homeowners policies. To avoid being underinsured, a policyholder must increase the face value of coverage in inflationary periods. An *inflation guard endorsement* automatically increases the dwelling and other coverages periodically. The premium also rises automatically in line with the additional coverage.

Two systems are commonly used with inflation guard endorsements:

1. *Fixed Percentage.* Under this provision, the face value of insurance rises by a fixed percent each period. An example might be 1 percent a quarter or 6 percent a year.

2. *Cost Index.* A *construction cost index* is an economic measure of the cost of building a new home in an area. The index is set to 100 at some point. A year later, it may have risen to 105. This means that construction costs have risen by 5 percent. An inflation guard endorsement can automatically increase coverage on the basis of an index of the cost of constructing a house.

Earthquake Endorsement

All homeowners forms exclude coverage for damage caused by the movement of earth. An *earthquake endorsement* is a policy provision that provides coverage against losses from earthquakes, landslides, and volcanic eruptions. The earthquake endorsement is designed to cover major rather than minor losses. It achieves this goal through deductibles, namely:

1. *Minimum Dollar Deductible.* A minimum deductible is included and is expressed in dollars. As an example, a deductible may be $250 or $500.

2. *Percent Deductible.* A 2 percent deductible is included. With some policies, the deductible may be as high as 5 percent.

3. *Separate Deductibles.* A separate deductible is specified for the dwelling and other structures.

Scheduled Personal Property Endorsement

The homeowners policies may provide inadequate coverage for an individual with respect to personal property. A *scheduled personal property endorsement* provides additional coverage on personal property items that are listed individually. It improves the coverage in two respects:

1. *Increases the Amount of Coverage.* The homeowners policy provides for special limits on items such as jewelry and furs. The endorsement can increase the coverage to replacement cost.

2. *Open-Perils Coverage.* The homeowners policy uses a named-perils

coverage for personal property. The endorsement changes the coverage to an open-perils basis.

Personal Property Replacement Cost Endorsement

A *personal property replacement cost endorsement* changes Coverage C from an actual cash value to a replacement cost basis. The endorsement pays the smallest dollar amount of:

1. *Replacement Cost.* This is the cost of the item at the time of the loss. The policy may specify that the item actually has to be replaced to receive this amount.
2. *Full Cost of Repair.* If a damaged item of personal property can be repaired, the endorsement will cover the full cost of repair.

Both of these payments are subject to the limit of insurance provided under Coverage C and any special limit on items such as jewelry and watercraft.

Other Personal Property Insurance

Automobile and homeowners insurance are two examples of property insurance for individuals. In this section, we cover other forms of personal property insurance.

Flood Insurance

A *flood* is defined as a general and temporary condition of partial or complete inundation of normally dry land. It may arise from tidal waters, an overflow of a river or stream, or a rapid accumulation and runoff of surface waters caused by rain or snow.

Flood insurance is administered in the United States under the guidelines of the federal government. Private insurance companies write the policies sold by brokers and licensed agents. The insuring agreement is called the *Federal Flood Insurance Policy* and contains the following features:

1. *Flood as General Condition.* The policy only covers water damage that is caused by a general flooding of an area. It does not cover water damage resulting from a source that damages only the insured's property.
2. *Three Coverages.* The policy provides insurance on the dwelling,

its contents, and debris removal. The insured may select either dwelling or contents coverage separately.

3. *Dwelling Coverage.* The dwelling is covered as are fully enclosed structures on the property. A number of exclusions are included in the policy.

4. *Contents Coverage.* The personal property owned or in the care of the insured is covered but only while inside a fully enclosed building on the premises. With exclusions and restrictions, flood insurance provides contents coverage, not personal property coverage.

5. *Debris Removal.* The policy covers removal of two kinds of debris:
    a. *Of the Insured Property*—Portions of the dwelling or contents are scattered on or off the property.
    b. *On the Insured Property*—Debris is deposited on the insured property from elsewhere.

6. *Deductible.* The policy contains a deductible on both dwelling and contents coverage.

Personal Property Floaters

A *floater* is an insurance policy that provides protection to movable property. A *personal property floater* provides specific protection for individual items. These include jewelry, furs, silverware, cameras, musical instruments, golf equipment, stamp and coin collections, wedding presents, fine arts, and antiques. Some of the more common provisions of personal property floaters are:

1. *Scheduled Item.* A floater generally covers property that is identified by name. "Blue topaz ring" and "27-foot Cobra powerboat" are examples. A personal jewelry floater will list every item covered.

2. *Newly Acquired Items Covered.* Many floater policies provide for automatic coverage of newly acquired property in the same category as that covered by the floater. As an example, a personal jewelry floater covers new acquisitions for up to 30 days after purchase subject to a limit of 25 percent of the floater coverage.

3. *Valued Items.* A floater generally identifies the value of each item. In many cases, the insurance company requires an appraisal. If not, value may be verified by the bill of sale or store receipt.

4. *All-Risk Coverage.* A floater usually is written on an all-risk basis.

5. *Worldwide Coverage.* Personal property is generally covered wherever it is located anywhere in the world.

6. *General Exclusions.* Most floaters contain the following broad exclusions:

  a. *Wear and Tear.* A personal property floater is not intended to cover items that deteriorate with use. Thus wear and tear, gradual deterioration, and damage from insects and vermin are excluded.
  b. *Inherent Vice.* This refers to a tendency of property to destroy itself. An example is a rare photograph that fades over time.
  c. *Nuclear Radiation or Contamination.*
  d. *War.*

7. *Specific Exclusions.* In addition to the broad exclusions for most floaters, individual policies have exclusions that match the specific property. Theft from an unattended automobile is an exclusion to the stamp and coin collection floater. Many kinds of property, such as money and securities, are excluded from the wedding present floater. A musical instrument used in paid performances is an exclusion under the musical instruments floater.

Title Insurance

A *title* is the legal document that proves ownership of real estate. It must meet specific legal requirements and be filed with an appropriate governmental agency. A *title defect* is a claim against the property that can invalidate the owner's right to it. Such a defect is a risk of ownership. A similar situation can exist with rented property, although the cost of a cancelled lease is usually relatively minor.

A *title insurance policy* is a contract agreeing to indemnify the insured for any loss arising out of undiscovered defects in the title to real property. Some important characteristics of title insurance are:

1. *Single-Premium Policy.* The premium is paid when the insurance policy is issued and no further premiums need be paid by the policyholder.

2. *Dollar Indemnification.* The policy pays for any losses and legal expenses involved with a defective title. It does not guarantee payments to secure a valid title.

3. *Undiscovered Defects Only.* The insurance covers title defects that are not known to the insured at the time of issuance of the title. Any defects listed in the title that cause subsequent loss are not covered.

4. *Indemnifies Past, Not Future, Occurrences.* Most insurance provides protection for events that will happen in the future. This is not the case for title insurance. It covers undiscovered defects prior to the issuance of the title.

Provisions of Personal Property Insurance

When evaluating personal property insurance, care should be taken to recognize certain characteristics that affect the validity of the different contracts. These are covered in this section.

Concealment or Misrepresentation

An insurance policy is a contract of utmost good faith. The intentional concealment of material facts or misrepresentation of circumstances is a serious matter that can make a policy voidable. This applies to property insurance policies. The greatest care should be taken to accurately describe personal property in the insurance application. Coverage may be denied if assets are overvalued or described in misleading language or the representations in the policy are otherwise inaccurate.

Assignment of Policies

Property insurance is a personal contract whereby an insurance company agrees to indemnify an insured against loss. Although it identifies an insured automobile, residence, or other property, the coverage is provided to one or more individuals. As a result, the coverage follows the insured(s), not the property. Except in rare circumstances, coverage does not transfer from the insured to another individual when property is sold, transferred, or when an insurable interest ceases to exist.

An *assignable policy* may be transferred to a new owner with the permission of the insurance company. In making the assignment, the company will assess the possible assignment as follows:

1. *Status of the Property.* The first question asked by the underwriter is whether the property coverage has changed in some fundamental way. Moving jewelry from a safe deposit box to a dresser drawer may affect the degree of risk of theft.

2. *Qualifications of the New Owner.* The new owner or person responsible for the property may be a factor in the decision. A company may not assign a policy to a person who seems to pose a higher risk. If an individual has had five burglaries in the past two years, the company may not transfer a coin collection policy.

In some cases, the insurance company may recognize that the risk level is changing when the policy is being assigned. The company may assign the policy with a higher or lower premium. If the change in risk is not acceptable, the company will refuse to assign the policy.

Duties After Loss

Property insurance contracts require the insured to take certain steps following a loss. A failure to take such steps can endanger collection under the policy. The steps include:

1. *Notification.* The insured must advise the insurance company on a timely basis. This usually includes full details of the loss. It may have to be in writing. In addition, other notifications may be required. An example is the policy requirement to file a police report in the event of a theft of insured property.

2. *Safeguarding Damaged Property.* The insured must take all steps to minimize further loss. An automobile involved in an accident may not be left unattended where it can suffer from vandalism. Property removed from a burning building may not be left where it can be damaged by the weather or stolen.

3. *Cooperation.* The insured is obligated to work closely with the insurance company in the aftermath of a loss. This ranges from providing documentation of the loss to assisting in subrogation when appropriate. A failure to cooperate can cause the insurance company to deny a claim.

Loss Settlement

When property is damaged or destroyed, it is possible that the company and insured will disagree on the monetary value of the loss. The contract will provide procedures for settling the loss, including:

1. *Value.* The loss will be covered at replacement cost, actual cash value, or some other basis, depending upon the terms of the policy.

2. *Appraisal.* This formal evaluation of the value of an item of property may be required to assess the extent of the loss in the event of disagreement on value.

3. *Disagreements.* In the event of disputes or disagreements between the insurance company and insured, a lawsuit becomes a last resort to settling the claim. Usually the policy will require the insured to comply with all policy provisions before a lawsuit can be filed. It may also require the lawsuit to be filed on a timely basis, such as within a year after loss.

Exercises

1. Harry Barlow is seeking a homeowners policy that covers all risks, with no exclusions, for his owned home and personal property. How well

do HO-1, HO-2, HO-3, HO-4, HO-6, and HO-8 achieve this goal? What should Harry do to achieve this goal?

2. A house has a replacement cost of $300,000 and is insured for $200,000. It incurs $25,000 of damage in a windstorm. The actual cash value is estimated at 80 percent of replacement cost. Depreciation is 30 percent of replacement cost. How much will be paid on this loss if the 80 percent formula is included under the homeowners policy?

3. The residence premises are covered under HO-1 for 90 percent of the replacement cost. During a freak arctic storm, 22 inches of snow are dumped on the roof of a garage not attached to the main dwelling on the residence premises. After 24 hours, the roof collapses. Is the loss covered?

4. Larry Saul rents an apartment for $900 a month. He seeks to insure his furniture and other personal property under Homeowners Two broad form. Is this a good idea? Why or why not?

5. The Carlton homestead has a large southern exposure with four glass sliding doors, two French doors, and four plate glass windows, all facing a scenic bay. The residence premises is covered by an HO-2 policy. Is this a good idea? Why or why not?

6. The Barnegat Insurance Company and Avon Insurance Company offer homeowners policies that are essentially similar in terms of dollar coverage on the main dwelling, other structures, and personal property. Barnegat's policy is written on the HO-3 special form and Avon's is written on the HO-5 special form. Is one policy preferable to the other?

7. The Lighthouse Condominium Association has full dwelling and other structures coverage on the 10-story building. In addition, Cynthia Collins has an HO-4 policy to cover her personal property. After a kitchen fire causes damage, Cynthia files for $1,000 to replace a ceiling fan and light fixture, $2,500 to repair a dining room table, and $600 to cover a charge from the condominium association to repair water damage in the hallway. Are these losses covered?

8. The Donaldson Estate is 125 years old, with 4,000 square feet of interior space. Although it could not be built today for under $500,000, it was sold recently for $160,000. Can this main dwelling be covered with homeowners insurance?

9. Kim Chun has an insurance policy issued under the Federal Flood Insurance Program. A heavy rain causes an overflow of a small stream and floods four homes, including Kim's. His garden tractor under a tarpaulin in the backyard is damaged as is a computer on the floor in his basement. Mud and tree branches cover most of the front yard. A storage shed in his backyard is destroyed when it is carried by the waters onto a neighbor's property. Are these losses covered in full?

10. A jewelry floater covers five named articles owned by Sally Booth, up to a limit of $10,000. Two of the articles, plus an onyx ring and diamond

tiara not listed, are stolen from her home. The onyx ring was purchased last year at a cost of $1,000. The tiara was purchased 10 days ago at a cost of $15,000. Are these items covered?

11. Steve Corcoran bought a home five years ago. It is covered with HO-3 and title insurance policies. The township council met last month and declared Steve's property to be in a flood exclusion zone. Steve is ordered to tear down or move the dwelling. Is this loss or expense covered under either of Steve's policies?

12. The Allisons sell their home to the Whittiers, who have no homeowners insurance. After a fire causes $12,000 of damage to the main dwelling, the Whittiers ask the Allisons if their HO-2 policy on the house has been cancelled. It has not. The Allisons mail the policy to the Whittiers with the notarized affidavit "We transfer all rights under this policy to Robert and Edith Whittier." In return, the Whittiers give $1,000 to the Allisons. What coverage have the Whittiers bought?

11

Personal Liability Insurance

Liability is defined as the exposure to any legal obligation or responsibility to compensate another party for a loss or damages. The possibility of legal liability represents one of the greatest threats to the long-term success of individuals and organizations in the United States.

In this chapter, we discuss approaches to dealing with the liability exposures facing an individual.

Civil Lawsuits

In the United States, disputes may be resolved between parties in two legal frameworks. *Tort law* covers dealings where no previous understanding has been reached between the parties. *Contract law* covers dealings where parties have agreed in advance to work together. In this section we compare the two areas of the law.

Charges Under the Law

A person may be brought to court under two categories of legal proceedings in the United States:

1. *Criminal Law*—Covers wrongs against society. The charges are brought by a governmental body for actions that are defined as crimes. A guilty party may be fined or be confined in a prison or other penal facility.

2. *Civil Law*—Covers wrongs against other persons or organizations. The charges are usually brought by the injured party. The penalty is normally the payment of money for damages or the requirement to take or not take some action.

Civil Lawsuits

Civil lawsuits may involve two major categories of wrongs:

1. *Breach of Contract*—Occurs when a person fails to live up to the terms of a legally enforceable contract.

2. *Tort*—Defined as a wrongful act or omission that violates another person's rights or causes that person damage. It is a legal injury that does not involve a contractual agreement. Recovery for damages is permitted in a court of law.

Nature of Contract Law

The first area of dispute resolution under civil law involves contract law. This applies when the dispute is based upon advance agreement and consent between parties. If an agreement meets the requirements of a valid contract, unexpected consequences may be interpreted in the context of contract law. Four concepts are important:

1. *Consent.* If a person agrees to something, future events will be interpreted in this light.

2. *Waiver.* If a person willingly gives up a right, he will not be able to insist upon it at a later time.

3. *Price.* If a person has a limited budget, she may wish to make a trade-off between cost and safety. An example is an airbag that provides a cushion in an automobile during an accident. For a lower price, the person can buy a car without the safety device. This decision results in a lower level of safety than a more costly product.

4. *Enforcement.* A contract contains terms and provisions made between willing parties. Under contract law, the courts will enforce the terms of the contract.

Kinds of Torts

The second area of dispute resolution involves tort law. Here, no prior agreement as to rights or responsibilities exists between two parties. Two kinds of torts may be identified:

1. *Intentional Tort*—Occurs when an individual or organization consciously and deliberately violates the rights of another, thus causing harm.

2. *Negligence Tort*—Occurs when an individual accidentally or unintentionally causes harm to another person.

Torts vs. Contracts

Throughout much of the history of the United States, legal disputes involved far more contractual issues than tort issues. Beginning in the 1950s, a major expansion of tort rights was undertaken by the courts, legislatures, and Congress. Expanded interpretations of negligent behavior dramatically increased the number of liability lawsuits facing individuals and organizations. As a result, liability exposure is more concerned today with negligence than it is with contractual obligations or rights.

Negligence

Earlier, we defined *negligence* as the failure to exercise the degree of care required by law. In this section, we discuss additional elements of and considerations with respect to negligence.

Proof of Negligence

In the United States, negligence can exist when a person fails to behave as a reasonably prudent individual and such failure causes harm. More specifically, negligence occurs when four elements are present and proved in a court of law:

1. *Duty to Act.* An individual must have a legal duty to take an action or not take an action that would be expected of a prudent person. For example, a person has a duty not to cause an open fire in an area when gasoline is being handled or stored.

2. *Failure to Act.* The individual must fail to behave as a reasonably prudent person. Lighting a match to smoke a cigarette in a gasoline storage area may be such a failure.

3. *Injury or Damage Must Occur.* An injury must occur to a person or damage must occur to property. If the person smokes the cigarette and no fire occurs, the act of lighting a match is not negligent behavior.

4. *Proximate Cause.* A cause-effect relationship must exist between the alleged negligent act and the injury. If the person finishes smoking the cigarette and a fire later occurs as a result of some other behavior by another person, the lighting of the match is not negligence.

Burden of Proof on Negligence

A court of law makes the final determination on whether negligence occurred. As a general rule, the burden of proof rests with the injured party. The court must believe that a person failed to act prudently, damage or injury occurred, and the imprudent act was the proximate cause of the injury.

In some cases, the burden of proof shifts to the defendant. These are:

1. *Absolute Liability*—Occurs when an injured party will be awarded damages regardless of whether anyone was at fault. It is also called *strict liability*. Two examples are common:
   a. *Hazardous Activities.* If an activity is inherently dangerous, strict liability may be construed to exist. Examples are activities dealing with explosives, certain chemicals, and keeping wild animals.
   b. *Workers Compensation.* By statute, employers have absolute liability for injuries that occur to employees while on the job.

2. *Negligence Per Se*—Occurs when negligence is assumed if certain conditions are met. For example, a speed limit on a highway should not be exceeded by a motorist. Or a person should not drive an automobile if he has a blood alcohol level higher than permitted by law. In either case, an injury caused by the individual produces negligence per se.

3. *Res Ipsa Loquitur*—Occurs when certain accidents or injuries are assumed to result from negligence in the absence of another explanation. The term comes from the Latin meaning "the thing speaks for itself." Three conditions are required:
   a. *Abnormal Event.* The action that caused the injury or damage must not normally occur in the absence of negligence.
   b. *Defendant Control of Instrumentality Causing the Injury.* The defendant must have exclusive control of the instrumentality that caused the accident or damage.
   c. *No Contributory Negligence by Injured Party.* The party suffering the loss must have not contributed to his own injury.

As an example of res ipsa loquitur, assume that a person is following directions to light a gas grill at a picnic. The grill explodes, causing injury. If it can be determined that the injured party followed directions, the manufacturer of the grill may be found negligent without further evidence.

Major Areas of Negligence Torts

Negligence torts make up the overwhelming majority of liability lawsuits. The lawsuits allege negligence in two primary areas:

1. *Accidents.* An accident is an unexpected occurrence that produces physical harm to a person or property. If a person leaves an open can of

chemicals in his driveway and a neighbor's child is injured, negligence could be claimed.

2. *Personal Injury.* In some cases, physical harm occurs without an accident. An example is prolonged exposure to the cold or an illness resulting from the breaking down of an automobile in a storm. If a mechanic failed to repair the car properly, negligence could be claimed.

Acts of Negligence

Three categories of actions can qualify as negligence under the law. These are:

1. *Positive Voluntary Act*—Occurs when a person takes an action that is not prudent. As an example, the lighting of a cigarette in an area when gasoline is being pumped into automobiles can be a positive voluntary negligent act.

2. *Failure to Act*—Occurs when a person does not take a prudent step to avoid harm. A failure to warn a person who is starting to light a cigarette in a dangerous area can be interpreted as an act of negligence.

3. *Vicarious or Imputed Act*—Occurs when an act of negligence is attributed to a person on the basis of the behavior of someone else. Employers may be sued for the acts of their employees. Principals may be sued for the acts of their agents. A bartender who serves alcohol to an obviously drunk patron may be sued if the patron is later involved in an automobile accident.

Defenses to Negligence Claims

When charged with negligent behavior, a person can defend against the charges by showing that one of the four elements of proof is missing. In addition, certain specific defenses exist even when all four elements are present. These are:

1. *Assumption of Risk.* A defendant may argue that an individual has assumed the risk of harm and must therefore accept the consequences if they involve loss. An example is snow skiing. When a person has been warned that skiing has inherent dangers, state laws may make it difficult to prove negligence in a skiing accident.

2. *Contributory Negligence.* In this situation, the injured party is negligent and contributes to the loss. State laws vary, but individuals may avoid damages by demonstrating that an injured party was partly responsible for the loss.

3. *Comparative Negligence.* In this situation, negligence is apportioned to two or more parties. Most states follow comparative negligence laws with three major systems:

    a. *Common-Law Rule.* If a person is partly negligent for her own injury, no damages may be collected. If an injured party is 10 percent responsible for a loss, the injured party collects no money from the person who is 90 percent responsible.

    b. *Pure Rule.* Each party pays in proportion to his negligence. If an injured party is 10 percent responsible for a $100,000 loss, he collects $90,000 in damages from the other party.

    c. *Wisconsin Rule.* The party who is most responsible for a loss pays the total amount of the loss. If the injured party is 10 percent responsible for a $100,000 loss, the more negligent party pays the entire $100,000.

4. *Last Clear Chance.* In this situation, a party had one final opportunity to avoid an accident caused by negligence but failed to do so. It applies two ways. An injured party can use it to avoid a failure to collect because of contributory negligence. Or a defendant can show that an injured party could have avoided the accident at the last moment.

5. *Immunity by Statute.* A state law prohibits a negligence lawsuit. Some immunities exist under statutes that protect government agencies or charitable organizations from lawsuits. Workers compensation laws also restrict negligence claims.

Liability Exposures

Individuals and organizations are subject to a wide range of liability exposures. In this section, we examine the major sources and costs of legal liability.

Real Property Negligence Liability

A person who owns a residence premises or other real property has the obligation to behave prudently with respect to it. Thus a person's home poses an exposure. A property owner has the obligation to maintain reasonably safe premises for visitors. The owner of potentially dangerous personal property on the residence premises should safeguard it from accidental misuse.

For the residence premises, as well as for all real property, the degree of care that is required is legally determined partly on the basis of the status of the visitor. Four classes of individuals may enter real property:

1. *Trespasser*—A person who enters the property without permission, either express or implied, from the owner, tenant, or other person who has the authority to give permission. The only duty owed to a trespasser is to avoid any actions that cause injury or damage.

2. *Licensee*—A person who enters the property with permission but not the invitation of the owner or other authorized person. Two factors describe a licensee:

   a. *No Benefit to Owner.* The owner knows of or tolerates the presence of the licensee without benefitting from his presence. Examples are door-to-door salespersons and a neighbor seeking to borrow a lawn mower.

   b. *No Expectation of Safe Premises.* The licensee has no reason to believe that the premises have been prepared for and made safe for a visitor. As an example, a homeowner may be using welding equipment when the doorbell rings. The door will be opened without a proper securing of the dangerous equipment.

A licensee is entitled to somewhat more care than a trespasser. The person responsible for the real property has the obligation to warn the licensee of danger that would not be reasonably expected. Examples are warning of a family dog that bites strangers or advising the visitor not to light a match near the welding equipment.

3. *Invitee*—A person who enters the property with the permission and for the benefit of a person who has the authority to extend an invitation. This category includes mail persons, garbage collectors, and other individuals who perform services for the owner. In addition, most states include social guests as invitees. The law requires a higher standard of safety for an invitee as compared to a licensee. The responsible person has the obligation to make the premises safe for the invitee. If a danger cannot be corrected, the owner must warn the invitee of the danger.

4. *Child*—Covered by the highest standard of safety. The law essentially requires a property owner to safeguard children from themselves. It does not matter whether the child is a trespasser, licensee, or invitee. As an example, an *attractive nuisance* may be defined as any dangerous aspect of the property that can lure and injure a child. The responsible person must take steps to separate a child and the attractive nuisance. This includes installing a locked fence around a swimming pool or avoiding leaving a lawn mower running in the driveway.

Other Personal Negligence Liability

In addition to real property exposures, an individual has liability exposures as a result of the activities of daily living. Some examples are:

1. *Automobile Liability.* The driver of an automobile is responsible for its safe operation. A person who owns an automobile can be held responsible for allowing another unsafe person to operate it.

2. *Lessee's Liability.* A person who rents real property has liability exposure to the owner for any damage that occurs on the property. A person who rents a car or boat from another person can be held liable for damages, even though the owner may carry insurance on the property.

3. *Animal Liability.* The owner of a pet is generally responsible for damage or injury that the pet may cause. The more dangerous the pet, the higher the standard of care. Once again, the standard is reasonable behavior by a prudent individual. If a dog has never been vicious, it need not be caged. Once a dog has bitten someone, more care is needed (this is sometimes called the "one free bite doctrine"). A pet lion, however, should always be caged.

4. *Professional Liability.* A *profession* may be defined as a means of earning a living where individuals (a) possess formal training or education, (b) deal with a defined body of skills and knowledge, and (c) are expected to perform their work to high standards. By this definition, lawyers and medical doctors have been members of a profession for a long time. More recently, the courts have begun to view teachers, engineers, real estate brokers, insurance agents, and others as professionals. Since a professional is expected to perform a service to a high standard, the failure to perform can be viewed as negligence.

Potential Costs of Legal Exposures

A lawsuit alleging negligence can be a costly process whether or not negligence is finally proved. The costs arise in the following areas:

1. *Bodily Injury.* A person who has been injured by negligence may receive damages to compensate for physical injury. Monies may be awarded to pay for medical bills, loss of income, and the cost of therapy or other rehabilitation.

2. *Property Damage.* Damage to real and personal property or the loss of use of such property produces monetary damages that can be awarded in a lawsuit.

3. *Pain and Suffering.* An injured individual who endures pain may be compensated by damages.

4. *Punitive Damages.* If a court determines that an individual acted in a grossly negligent manner and deserves to be punished, punitive damages can be awarded.

5. *Personal Injury Damages.* Some injuries are not physical but can result in the awarding of damages. Examples occur when an individual alleges slander, libel, or the invasion of privacy.

6. *Legal Expenses.* Last, but certainly not least, the task of defending lawsuits is a major cost of liability exposures in the United States. In many cases, the legal costs are significantly higher than the eventual damages awarded.

Comprehensive Personal Liability Protection

Comprehensive personal liability (CPL) *insurance* is an insurance coverage designed to protect individuals from nonbusiness and nonautomotive exposures. It is available as follows:

1. *CPL Policy*—A separate policy that may be purchased by an individual.

2. *Section II of Homeowners Policy*—Covers CPL protection.

3. *By Endorsement*—May be added by endorsement to other insurance policies, such as automobile insurance.

In most cases, CPL coverage is provided to individuals in the United States as part of the homeowners policy. We cover it in this section in this context.

Section II: Liability Coverage

Section II of the homeowners policy provides liability insurance against claims from third parties arising out of an occurrence covered by the policy. It provides the following coverages:

1. *Coverage E: Personal Liability*—Claims for damages for bodily injury or property damage. It contains two provisions:
   a. *Damages*—Pays damages up to the limit of liability.
   b. *Legal Fees*—Pays legal fees even though the lawsuit is groundless. The legal fees are paid in addition to the limit of the policy.

2. *Coverage F: Medical Payments to Others*—Provides medical payments for third parties injured by an occurrence covered by the policy. It contains several provisions, including:
   a. *Person at Insured Location.* A person injured at the insured location is covered, whether the injury was caused by the insured or not.

b. *Person Elsewhere.* Any injury caused by the insured to a third party is covered, no matter where it occurs.

c. *Animal Coverage.* Bodily injuries to third parties caused by an animal owned by or in the care of an insured are covered.

3. *Additional Coverages*—Provides other payments in addition to the limit of liability on the policy. Some examples are:

a. *Claims Expenses*—Pays for expenses involved in processing claims, including some loss of earnings paid to an insured who loses work time while helping defend the lawsuit.

b. *Damage to Property of Others*—Replaces property owned by third parties and damaged by an occurrence covered by the policy. The dollar amount of coverage is relatively small.

c. *Loss Assessment*—Pays for assessments from groups such as condominium associations when the assessment results from a covered occurrence.

Section II: Liability Exclusions

The liability coverage of Section II has a long list of exclusions, including:

1. *Business Pursuits.* Most liability resulting from business activities is not covered. The exception is an occasional business activity that is incident to a nonbusiness pursuit. Examples are occasional garage sales or one-time Tupperware parties.

2. *Motor Vehicles.* Liability insurance is not provided for vehicles that are covered under automobile policies.

3. *Watercraft and Aircraft.* A number of watercraft and aircraft exclusions are included.

4. *Double Indemnity Benefits.* If a third party is eligible to receive the same benfits from workers compensation or other sources.

5. *Nuclear Activity or War.* These catastrophe exclusions apply to Section II.

6. *Business Pursuits.* Liability and medical payments coverage are provided for claims arising from business or professional activities. It covers employed persons only, such as teachers, lawyers, or salespersons. It does not cover individuals who own or are otherwise principals in a business. A separate business policy is needed for these situations.

7. *Personal Injury*—Defined as emotional damage done to an individual. This endorsement provides insurance to cover costs of lawsuits when third parties sue the insured for personal, as opposed to bodily, injuries. It covers claims for libel, defamation of character, invasion of privacy, and wrongful eviction.

Other Liability Insurance

The automobile and comprehensive personal liability policies cover specific exposures commonly faced by individuals. Other insurance can be purchased to provide additional protection for individual needs. In this section, we cover these policies.

Umbrella Liability Policy

An *umbrella liability policy* is insurance coverage designed to provide protection against catastrophic losses. It has the following characteristics:

1. *High Limits.* The policy provides a minimum of $1 million of protection against damages and other costs of liability lawsuits.

2. *Excess Coverage.* An umbrella policy is designed to provide coverage for losses above those covered under other policies. The policy generally requires underlying primary coverage. As an example, a policy might require $50,000/100,000/25,000 of automobile liability coverage and $300,000 of comprehensive personal liability insurance. For a medical doctor or other professional, the company may also require professional liability insurance. These requirements can be waived for wealthy individuals who can demonstrate financial responsibility in the absence of insurance.

3. *Broader Coverage.* The umbrella liability policy is designed to provide broader coverage than the underlying automobile or personal liability policy. It is usually written with fewer exclusions than the underlying policies. Because it provides broader coverage, it is often called a *blanket policy*.

4. *Deductible Required.* Some exposures are covered under the umbrella policy but excluded under the other coverages required of the insured. In these cases, a deductible normally applies.

Professional Liability Policy

We earlier defined a *profession* as a career field where individuals have special expertise as a result of education, training, or licensing requirements. Individuals who are identified as professionals are expected to use due care and display a high level of skill in the performance of their duties. When things go wrong, professionals are often sued.

A *professional liability policy* provides legal fees and damages when individuals are accused of malpractice or other failure to provide proper professional services. Such a policy may also be called a *malpractice policy* or *errors-and-omissions policy*. Some of the comon characteristics of most professional liability policies are:

1. *Personal Injuries Only.* A professional liability policy is usually concerned only with injuries to persons but not to their property. Damage to property may be covered under a CPL or other policy.

2. *Practice of the Profession.* The malpractice coverage is normally reserved for actions resulting from the work undertaken by the professional. It may exclude business injuries that specifically result from malpractice. As an example, if a person trips in an accountant's office, no coverage would be provided under the professional liability policy.

3. *Excludes Warranties of Outcomes.* Professional liability policies cover errors, mistakes, or other negligence of the professional. They do not cover guaranties, assurances, or warranties of outcomes. Thus an accountant's error that led to tax penalties may be covered. If the accountant assures the client that a certain filing procedure will eliminate the tax and the accountant is wrong, the assurance or warranty will not be covered. Similarly, a doctor may not warrant a successful operation nor may a lawyer guarantee the outcome of a trial.

4. *Insurer Needs Permission to Settle.* With professional liability insurance, the insurer must normally obtain the permission of the insured prior to settling a claim. Although such settlement is common in liability situations, a professional who admits malpractice or negligence might damage his or her reputation and future activities. Thus this kind of policy generally allows the insured to insist that the insurer defend the allegations brought in the lawsuit.

Miscellaneous Liability Coverages

A variety of other personal liability insurance policies are available to meet the specific needs of individuals. These cover business, leisure, and charitable activities of individuals and their families.

Exercises

1. A storekeeper leaves rat poison outside his store on a neighbor's property near a trash pile. The neighbor's dog eats some of the poison and dies. The neighbor swears out a complaint with the local police department alleging gross negligence against the storekeeper. Is the complaint valid?
2. A college student goes on a ski trip to the Rocky Mountains. When purchasing a lift ticket, she signs a waiver of all rights, acknowledging

that skiing is a dangerous sport and she knowingly is accepting all risks. Near the top of the mountain, a sign reads CLOSED TRAIL. DANGEROUS AREA. DO NOT ENTER. The sign is lying in the snow. She enters the area and is seriously injured. She files a lawsuit against the ski area alleging negligence. Is her lawsuit valid?

3. Two lovers have a quarrel. The man goes to a bar and begins talking to a stranger. The woman enters the bar carrying a gun and shoots the stranger in the arm. The stranger sues for reimbursement of her medical expenses, alleging negligence. The woman denies negligence, stating that the action was not accidental or unintentional. Will the stranger win the lawsuit?

4. Alfred Miller is attacked by two large dogs while walking down the street in front of the home of Willis Johnson. Willis sees the attack from his porch but goes inside without helping. Alfred is hospitalized for two days. When he gets out, he sues Willis for negligence. Is he likely to win?

5. One day Marcus Febreux smokes near a chemical vat below a sign that reads SMOKING ABSOLUTELY AND TOTALLY PROHIBITED AT ALL TIMES WITHIN 50 FEET OF THIS SIGN. The next day, a fire begins at that spot and causes major damage. Marcus is sued for negligence. It is proved in court that Marcus was standing only eight feet from the sign when he smoked. The jury finds negligence to exist, but recommends that Marcus be held liable for only 10 percent of the damage. Will this verdict be upheld on appeal?

6. While walking down the street in a small town in Indiana, Carlos Rodriguez is attacked by a Bengal tiger. He is severely injured. He sues the owner. In court, the owner demonstrates that he (a) was in Brazil at the time of the attack, (b) had left the tiger in the care of a veterinarian and had paid for the care, and (c) had warned the veterinarian that the tiger was dangerous and had to be watched. The owner states in court, "If I had been there, I would never have allowed the tiger to attack this nice man." Can the owner be held negligent?

7. Bill Hanson is driving his Jaguar XKE vintage automobile down the highway at 100 miles per hour. The speed limit is 55 miles per hour. He kills a dog who runs in front of his car. Bill is sued for negligence. He denies the charge. He says, "My duty was to drive safely. My car can easily handle the speed. No other cars were on the highway. The day had perfect weather. I was prudent. The dog should not have been allowed to run loose on a highway. That is the cause of the injury. I am sorry. I like dogs." Is it possible to hold Bill liable for negligence? Was Bill negligent?

8. A business executive is quoted in a national news magazine claiming that a competitor was dishonest. The competitor files a personal injury lawsuit. Is this covered under the executive's homeowners HO-3 policy?

9. The Campanellas throw a party for 28 friends and neighbors. Alcohol is served all night by a hired bartender. When Ralph Lowell becomes drunk, the bartender refuses to serve him any more drinks. The Campanellas' 14-year-old son, Robbie, finds some whiskey in the kitchen and makes Lowell four more drinks. On the way home, Lowell steps off a curb and is almost killed by a taxi. His hospital bills exceed $65,000. He sues the Campanellas, the bartender, and Robbie for negligence. The Campanellas respond to the suit stating that they never served the alcohol and should be severed from the suit. Are they right? The bartender says he behaved prudently when he saw Ralph Lowell's condition. Is he likely to be judged negligent? Robbie says Lowell told him that he was walking home so another drink did not matter. Is Robbie likely to be held negligent?

10. Jacob Coster lives in a state with the Wisconsin rule. He is found guilty of negligence in a case involving an injury to Claudia Stevens. Claudia herself is judged to be 40 percent responsible for the injury as a result of her own negligence. Damages are $20,000. How much must Jacob pay in damages?

11. Lucy Perkins lives in an apartment that has had four burglaries in a period of six months. She is terrified at night. She buys two wild animal traps and sets them in her kitchen and living room. An apparent burglar enters the kitchen window and steps on the trap. Lucy screams, attracting Bob Winslow, her neighbor. He enters the apartment with a baseball bat and steps in the other trap. Both the burglar and Bob sue Lucy for negligence. Is either likely to win?

12. Martha Coyne and Allison Welch are co-owners of a small business. Martha has homeowners insurance with $300,000 of liability coverage. Allison has no insurance but has over $200,000 in marketable securities. They each apply for an umbrella liability insurance policy of $2 million. Under what conditions might each be issued a policy?

13. Dr. Wheaton opens her own practice three years after graduating from medical school. She purchases medical malpractice insurance. While sitting in her office, Michael Wallace is bitten by a dog held on a leash by another patient. He sues both the other patient and Dr. Wheaton for negligence. Is Dr. Wheaton covered under her malpractice policy?

14. Michael Wallace is treated for his dog bite by Dr. Wheaton. She assures him that the wound is clean and he will have no lingering injury. Within a week, his leg is so swollen that it has to be amputated. Two days after the operation, he learns that the dog had rabies. Michael undergoes a painful series of shots. He files a second suit alleging malpractice because (a) Dr. Wheaton told him he would have no lingering injury, yet he lost his leg, and (b) she did not warn him of the possibility of rabies. Is Dr. Wheaton covered under the medical malpractice coverage?

15. Bruce Gordon leaves a package on the floor of a grocery store. A customer trips over it and falls down. A lawsuit is filed. Is it covered under Gordon's homeowners HO-3 policy?

16. An account executive who works for Tiger Advertising and a lawyer in private practice both believe they have liability coverage from their homeowners HO-3 policies. Is this correct?

17. Maria Velez has purchased an umbrella liability policy that provides $3 million of coverage. It requires a personal auto policy with limits of $100,000/200,000/50,000 and a comprehensive personal liability policy with a $500,000 limit. She is being sued under a negligence claim related to a transaction involving the common stock of a closely held firm. The court renders a judgment against her of $1.2 million. Her legal fees are $400,000. Is she covered under the umbrella liability policy? If so, what is the likely coverage?

12

Risk Management

Risk management is a systematic approach to dealing with insurable and noninsurable risks facing an organization. An alternate definition describes risk management as a decision-making process that identifies exposures and creates programs to deal with them.

A *risk manager* is a person who develops and implements the comprehensive strategy for dealing with the various risks and exposures facing an organization. As the environment of business and economic activity has become increasingly complex, new approaches have become essential to have a cost-effective plan for protecting the organization. Insurance plays a role, and an important role at that, but other programs are needed. The risk manager is a professional who is responsible for insurance and noninsurance programs of managing risk.

In this chapter, we introduce the concept of risk management. We identify the risks and exposures facing risk managers. We examine the characteristics of risk management. Finally, we cover some of the tools available to the risk manager.

Risks and Exposures

Organizations face risks that are similar to those faced by individuals. In addition, organizations face exposures that normally do not affect individuals. In this section, we deal with making sense out of risks and exposures.

Two Dimensions of Pure Risk

From the point of view of the risk manager, two dimensions of pure risk must be considered for every exposure facing the organization. These are:

1. *Severity*—The degree of damage to the organization that can

result from an exposure. Risks of high severity can destroy the organization. Low severity risks are of less concern.

2. *Frequency*—The number of times an exposure is likely to become a loss. High frequency risks present regular problems for an organization. Low frequency risks are characterized by long periods of time between losses.

Severity of Exposure

Risk management must evaluate risks in terms of their severity and impact on the organization. Three categories are identified:

1. *Unbearable Risks*—All exposures that would produce losses sufficient to cause bankruptcy or otherwise threaten the survival of the organization.

2. *Important Risks*—All exposures where the organization would suffer serious financial penalty from a loss. An important loss is also likely to hamper future operations.

3. *Unimportant Risks*—All exposures where the organization can cover financial losses without suffering undue financial difficulty. An unimportant loss can be covered as an operating expense without major impact on profitability or other financial results.

Severity and Frequency of Risks

For each of the pure risks facing an organization, the risk manager must design a strategy. For this purpose, it is useful to match general strategies against the severity and frequency of risk, as follows:

1. *High Frequency, High Severity*—A kind of risk that is almost impossible to transfer or share. Insurance companies will not accept the risk or will charge prohibitive premiums for coverage. Fortunately, such risks are generally not common. In some areas of the world, political or religious issues or illegal activities produce such risks. Examples are Beirut, Lebanon, during the 1980s or areas where illegal drug traffic dominates a nation's economy and politics. In these situations, bombings, kidnappings, and other high frequency, high severity losses are common.

2. *High Frequency, Low Severity*—Important risks that affect the economic well-being of the organization. They must be covered by a combination of retention, sharing, and transferring. An example is accidents in the workplace that require treatment but do not involve disability or prolonged absence from the job.

3. *Low Frequency, Low Severity*—Relatively unimportant risks that involve minor economic consequences. It is usually not worth the administrative expenses of purchasing insurance to cover such risks. They are usually retained. An example is the economic loss when a delivery truck breaks down on the highway.

4. *Low Frequency, High Severity*—Important or unbearable risks. They should be covered by a combination of sharing and transferring. An example is fire that might destroy a warehouse.

Characteristics of Risk Management

Dealing with the exposures facing the firm is the subject of risk management. In this section, we examine the major characteristics of the field of risk management.

Goals of Risk Management

The risk manager works to achieve four primary objectives for the organization:

1. *Long-Term Survival.* Corporations and other organizations seek to survive over a long period of time. Programs are needed to ensure that companies can survive the loss of individual employees or external disasters. Risk management is concerned with programs that ensure such survival.

2. *Long-Term Stability.* Disasters and unexpected losses can affect the health and stability of an organization. Instead of being concerned with the company mission, managers need excessive time to overcome the negative effects of the loss. Risk management seeks to minimize the economic effects of disasters, thus assisting in long-term stability of operations.

3. *Cost Control.* Insurance and similar programs of loss control and financing cost money. By properly selecting strategies for each kind of exposure, the risk manager can reduce costs while providing an appropriate level of protection against disasters.

4. *Social and Ethical Responsibility.* Organizations have obligations to behave properly with respect to their communities and employees. This involves being fiscally responsible when losses occur. The risk manager has the goal of ensuring adequate funds so an organization can meet its social and ethical responsibilities.

Risk Management Process

The risk manager is responsible for the systematic task of dealing with pure risk. This involves a multiple-step process:

1. *Set objectives.* The risk manager begins the task by setting objectives for an organization's risk management activities. This is a shared responsibility that also involves the chief executive officer and other members of management.

2. *Identify risks.* The objective is to gain a thorough understanding of the activities of the organization and the exposures affecting them. It generally involves matching each activity against a checklist of pure risks that can affect people, property, and liability.

3. *Evaluate risks.* Exposures are divided into the areas of unbearable, important, and unimportant.

4. *Design a comprehensive program.* Each exposure is matched against a method of dealing with it. The choices basically are to avoid, reduce, retain, share, or transfer each risk. The goal is to achieve a single program that protects the organization at a reasonable cost.

5. *Implement the program.* Once the risk management program has been approved by management, the risk manager takes the steps necessary to cover each exposure. This involves dealing with unit managers, brokers, insurance companies, and others.

6. *Monitor results.* Once a program is operating, the risk manager periodically reviews the results and makes modifications as necessary. Figure 12-1 shows a flowchart of this process beginning with the recognition of risk facing the organization and concluding with the total cost of risk management.

Broad Risk Management Guidelines

In the process of designing a risk management program, the risk manager follows several broad guidelines, including:

1. *Size of Risk.* Some risks are retained and some are transferred or shared. The commonsense rule is that an organization should not risk more than it can afford to lose.

2. *Control After a Loss.* Some losses would severely affect the ability of the organization to survive if the negative impact of the loss were not immediately eliminated. An example is the destruction of a warehouse. If the supply of products were stopped for an extended period of time, customers might find other suppliers. In this situation, it is not enough

Figure 12-1.   Flowchart of the risk management process.

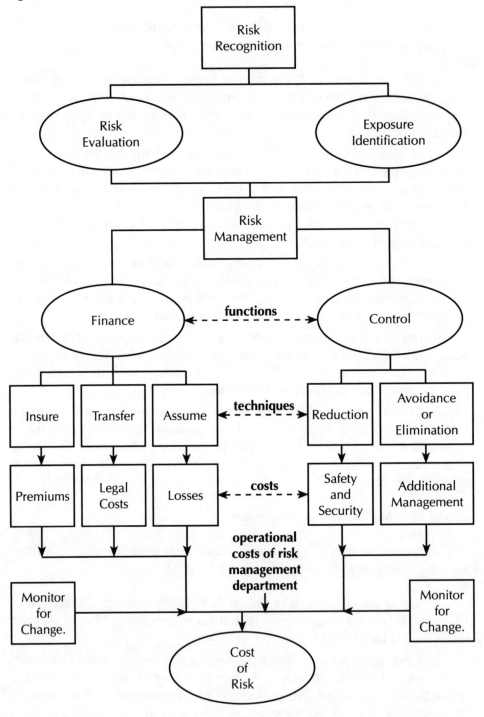

to have insurance to rebuild the warehouse. The risk management program must allow sufficient control after the loss so that a temporary warehouse can be secured and begin operations.

3. *Cost-Benefit Analysis*. Each exposure must be covered on an economical basis. If the cost of insurance is too high, the risk must be retained. If the potential loss is catastrophic in impact, it must be transferred. Overall, the organization should not risk a lot to save a little.

4. *Probability of Loss*. The risk manager must assess the odds of each exposure and determine the probability of loss. Coverage of risks should match the mathematical likelihood of loss and forecasted severity.

5. *Possibility of Transfer*. Some exposures simply cannot be transferred, and this fact must be recognized in risk management programs. In some cases, as with war risks, insurance is not available. In other cases, as with certain foreign currencies, insurance would involve excessive costs.

6. *Amount of Insurance*. Many of the exposures facing an organization will be covered by insurance. The risk manager must design a program to purchase the right amount of coverage. Insufficient insurance can threaten survival; too much insurance wastes the organization's resources.

7. *Ranking of Insurance*. The risk manager must identify insurance expenditures in the categories of (a) essential, (b) important, and (c) optional. Then, the decisions on purchasing insurance must match each category with cost. Essential and important insurance is often purchased, even though cost may be high. Optional insurance is only purchased if the decision is cost-effective.

Tools of Risk Management

In pursuing a program of risk management, an organization has a number of tools to identify, evaluate, and cover exposures. These tools are covered in this section.

Loss Control

Loss control refers to efforts to reduce either the likelihood or severity of a loss by taking steps to reduce the exposure. Two types of loss control efforts are identified:

1. *Avoidance*. In some cases, it is possible to avoid the exposure entirely. An example is a high diving board at a municipal pool. The city can purchase liability insurance to protect against lawsuits if someone is

injured while diving. Or it can remove the diving board entirely. This avoids the exposure.

2. *Reduction*. In some cases, it is possible to reduce the chance of loss. An example is an X-ray machine in a dentist's office. To minimize the chance that a dental technician will receive excess radiation, the switch to operate the machine can be placed in a separate room with lead shielding.

Risk Financing

Risk financing refers to any arrangements that pay for losses that actually occur. The tools of risk financing include:

1. *Retention*. The source of funds to cover retained losses is the organization itself. Retention is unplanned when the organization is unaware of the exposure. It is planned when the organization considers other risk management tools and consciously decides to retain the risk.

2. *Insurance*. For sharing or transferring risk, insurance is the most common device.

3. *Noninsurance Contracts*. The organization can use contractual arrangements to transfer risk. Three examples are:
   a. *Guaranty*—A written promise that one party will be responsible for any negative consequences of a relationship involving the performance of a product or providing of a service.
   b. *Hold-Harmless Agreement*—One party accepting legal liability for damages. A common example involves construction. An injured party on a construction site may sue the owner or the contractor. Under a hold-harmless agreement, the contractor agrees to pay for damages awarded if he or she is negligent.
   c. *Warranty*—A written guaranty on the quality of a product or performance of a service. If the product or service is defective, the manufacturer or provider will be responsible for damages.

Sources of Information

A major task of a risk manager is to identify exposures. Some sources of assistance information are:

1. *Firsthand Observation*. The risk manager can visit property or individuals and observe possible exposures. This can involve a formal visit to a property with an engineer and loss control specialist to check on the quality of construction, fire safety design, and other features. It

can involve asking individuals to undertake a physical examination before being hired.

2. *Interrogation*. Specific questions are asked of individuals familiar with possible exposures. Interrogation can involve the contractor who originally constructed a building or the family doctor who has the medical records of an individual.

3. *Experts*. A number of individuals spend their lives becoming familiar with all aspects of various exposures. These include agents who place insurance, brokers who specialize in certain risks, consultants who advise companies, and professionals such as doctors or lawyers. These experts can be asked to render opinions on the degree of risk and severity of possible loss.

4. *Checklists*. For many years, insurance companies, brokers, and consultants have been developing comprehensive checklists dealing with every conceivable insurable exposure. Such checklists are an excellent source of information on possible risks.

5. *Historical Data*. Insurance companies and other organizations retain statistical information on prior losses. These can be excellent sources of information. As an example, the Insurance Services Office (ISO) is a nonprofit organization that collects data from many companies. It provides historical data to its members that can be used to assess the probability of loss from various exposures.

6. *Professional Associations*. Risk managers often meet in professional organizations devoted to reducing losses from various sources. One prominent professional group is the Risk and Insurance Management Society (RIMS), an organization of risk managers that undertakes education and research activities for its members.

Exercises

For the first seven exercises in this section, identify each item in terms of being an unbearable, important, or unimportant risk. Match each item with its severity and frequency.

1. The possibility of explosion or major fire at the company's single manufacturing facility.
2. The possibility of vehicle accidents that may hinder delivery of completed products.
3. The possibility of a strike at any of the company's 150 suppliers, which would cut off raw materials and components needed for production.
4. The possibility of death or injury of skilled workers among the work force of 2,000 employees.

5. The possibility of the loss of the company president, who is highly respected by major customers.
6. The possibility of customer checks being lost in the mail.
7. The possibility of employees catching colds, the flu, or other illnesses that keep them off the assembly line.
8. Trans-Pacific Shipping carries caustic and poisonous chemicals in ocean-going vessels. It is considering a new program to upgrade all its ships in terms of safety of cargo carriage. Which of the goals of risk management can be achieved by this upgrade?
9. Marcus Corporation has $5 million of insurance on a warehouse worth $22 million. The warehouse is a critical link in the company's business. If it were inactive for more than 60 days, the company would have to declare bankruptcy. In addition to insurance, the company keeps $3 million on hand for emergencies. Match this situation against the guidelines for risk management.
10. First National Bank has instituted a program to train tellers to avoid losses involving either customers or robbers. In addition, the armored car company has agreed to assume all risk of loss while bank assets are being transferred by armored vehicle. As a result, the bank's insurance company has lowered the cost of theft and fraud coverage. Which tools of risk management provide protection to the bank against economic losses from theft and fraud? Which do not?
11. The risk manager of Industrial Products Corporation regularly attends meetings of the Midwest Risk Managers Association to exchange ideas. Although he has never seen a manufacturing operation of Industrial Products, he does review loss records for the company. He also compares them with the experience of other organizations, as published by industry newsletters. When he has questions, he calls the plant manager or others in the company to get answers. Which techniques of information gathering are being used by this risk manager? Which have not been described above?

13

Risk Management Programs

A *risk management program* is a systematic effort to manage the loss exposures facing an organization. It deals with potential losses by identifying and measuring pure risks facing the firm. Then, it involves the development of a comprehensive approach to reducing the impact of personnel, property, and liability losses.

In this chapter, we examine the major elements of programs of risk management in an organization. We begin with the goals of risk management. We examine techniques to identify risk. We discuss risk retention and transfer and loss control programs. The chapter concludes with the administration of a program of risk management.

Goals of Risk Management

Organizations should have a sense of urgency about effecting a sound program of risk management. This vehicle allows the organization to fulfill the following:

1. *Social Responsibilities.* Organizations have obligations to protect the environment and reduce the number of disasters to property and personnel. Risk management can help avoid accidents, injuries, and incidents of pollution.

2. *Employer Responsibilities.* Organizations have obligations to provide a safe workplace and assist in meeting the health, retirement, and other needs of employees. Risk managers devise programs of employee benefits to fulfill these goals.

3. *Financial Responsibilities.* Organizations have obligations to earn a return for shareholders, pay back creditors, and achieve financial stability. Nonprofit organizations have the obligation to use funds properly and protect assets entrusted to them. Risk management provides programs to protect the fiscal integrity of organizations.

A program of risk management basically involves four areas: (1) risk identification, (2) risk retention, (3) risk transfer, and (4) loss control. These four areas are covered in the following sections.

Risk Identification

Pure risks, exposures, hazards, and perils must be identified before they can be evaluated. In this section, we examine risk identification.

Pure Risk Areas

Risks and exposures exist in all areas of the organization. They may be categorized as follows:

1. *Unforeseen Risks*—Future losses that cannot be seen in advance. Even if they could, nothing can be done to protect against them. An example is an explosion at a nuclear power plant followed by a radiation release that affects operations.

2. *Controllable Exposures*—Conditions external to the organization that can be affected by efforts to remove hazards and decrease exposures. An example is the handling of hazardous chemicals. Safer systems can often be designed to reduce the likelihood of future losses.

3. *Uncontrollable Exposures*—External conditions that can be identified but not affected by the organization. An example is the operation of motor vehicles by a firm. Hazards exist on streets and highways that are outside the control of the organization.

4. *Organizational Practices*—Risks that result from the activities or operations of the enterprise. An example is allowing sales personnel to make excessive claims about products, thus exposing the organization to lawsuits.

Techniques of Risk Identification

Three of the four categories of pure risk can be examined using three major techniques of risk identification:

1. *Loss Exposure Survey*—A form or checklist that categorizes risks and quantifies possible losses. The forms can be developed in the areas of personnel, property, and casualty exposures.

2. *Organizational Practices Survey*—A form or checklist that examines the policies and procedures of the organization with a view to identifying practices that cause unnecessary financial, legal, or physical exposures.

3. *Financial Reports*—Balance sheets, income statements, cash flow statements, and other financial data that are generated in the ordinary course of operations.

Characteristics of Loss Exposure Surveys

A loss exposure survey can be developed for the various controllable and uncontrollable risks and organizational practices. Some of the characteristics of a loss exposure survey are:

1. *Factors.* The form will identify physical or operational factors where losses can occur. These factors can include personnel working in hazardous areas, property, or selling practices.

2. *Exposures.* The form may identify the perils, hazards, or other possible causes of loss.

3. *Cost or Value.* The form may identify the actual cash value or replacement cost of tangible property, amount of money at risk in a liability area, or estimates of injury or damage to employees or customers.

4. *Miscellaneous Considerations.* The form may identify other items that provide information on the degree or risk and ways to reduce hazards or exposures.

Figure 13-1 shows a sample loss exposure survey form.

Risks Reflected on Financial Statements

A number of risks can be identified from financial data, including:

1. *Cash and Securities.* The firm's money and other highly liquid assets must be secured from loss by fire, theft, and other causes. The risk manager can note the procedures used to safeguard these assets.

2. *Inventories.* The nature of inventories reflects different risks, depending upon the operations of the organization. Raw materials can include chemicals or toxic substances that must be stored and handled carefully. Jewelry firms have inventories that face the possibility of theft or disappearance. Inflammable or perishable items may require special handling or pose certain risks.

3. *Fixed Assets.* Buildings, machinery, and equipment may be carried on the books at one value but be worth significantly more or less in the market. The loss of certain assets may cripple operations for a long period of time. Leased assets may expose the organization to liability suits from the negligence of third parties.

Figure 13-1. Property loss exposure survey.

	Physical Location	Construction Materials	Replacement Cost	Actual Cash Value
BUILDING				
Main structure				
Second structure				
Warehouse				
Garage				
Storage shed				
EQUIPMENT				
Machinery				
Furnace				
Air conditioner				
Computer				
Fixtures				
INVENTORIES				
Raw materials				
Work in process				
Finished goods				
VEHICLES				
Automobiles				
Small trucks				
Large trucks				

4. *Revenues.* The sources of cash inflows may reflect exposures from product liability suits or distributor negligence. Sales may be excessively dependent upon a single manufacturing plant or small number of customers.

5. *Expenses.* If a large portion of expenses are fixed, the company has exposure from any source of business interruption. Or if employee health or retirement benefits are locked in by agreement, periods of economic downturn may not be accompanied by an ability to reduce certain costs.

6. *Profits.* In many cases, a relatively small interruption of business or loss to tangible assets can eliminate profits entirely. Some organizations are highly vulnerable to minor losses and may even be threatened in terms of their survival.

Risk Retention

Risk retention refers to any conscious effort by an organization to bear the loss from any known sources. It can occur in a number of formal or informal ways. In this section, we examine the conscious decisions not to transfer or share certain risks.

Self-Insurance

Self-insurance refers to a deliberate plan to meet certain and unplanned losses without insurance or other transfer mechanisms. The term is a misnomer, since it deals with retention, not insurance. Several forms of self-insurance are identified:

1. *Assumption*. Risk is accepted without any organization plan. It is appropriate for minor risks or situations where administrative costs of insurance would outweigh the possible exposure.

2. *Full Self-Insurance*—Significant risks are accepted as a conscious decision of management. It is appropriate only when the organization has sufficient resources to cover the specified categories of risk.

3. *Partial Self-Insurance*. Two kinds may be identified:
   a. *Deductibles*. The organization covers losses up to a certain point. Insurance covers exposures above the designated level.
   b. *Retrospective Rating*. The cost of an insurance policy is determined after expiration of the policy, on the basis of the loss experience during the policy period. In effect, this is also a form of partial self-insurance since the organization and its insurer share losses up to a certain point. The higher the level of losses, the greater the premium.

Favorable Conditions for Self-Insurance

Several conditions encourage the use of one or more of the self-insurance forms, including:

1. *Financial Strength*. The level of self-insurance should be relatively small compared to the size of the organization. This can be measured either in terms of assets or cash flow.

2. *Statistically Predictable Losses*. The risk of loss should involve multiple locations, facilities, or people, so that average losses are predictable within relatively narrow limits. A corporation with a single large manufacturing plant should not self-insure against fire. A fast-food chain with 700 retail outlets spread over 50 states may self-insure against fire losses.

3. *Sophisticated Risk Management Structure*. Many administrative tasks are required for processing losses. These include the maintenance of records, analysis of losses, and efforts to encourage safety and security. Some of these tasks are performed by insurance companies and brokers.

With self-insurance, the company should have the capability to perform them internally.

4. *Lower Administrative Costs.* A self-insurance program should have a lower level of processing costs than an insurance company, because insurance companies must pay sales commissions, brokerage, and taxes not required in self-insurance programs. At the same time, the insurance companies and brokers may have economies of scale or experience that lowers processing costs. These may offset savings from self-insurance programs.

5. *Lower Processing Costs of Claims.* A self-insurance program does not require the detailed justification of losses that are required with insurance claims. Hence, processing costs after losses are lower.

Self-Insurance and U.S. Market Cycles

The insurance market in the United States has been notoriously cyclical with respect to the cost of property and liability insurance coverage. At one particular time, insurance premiums would far exceed the actuarial basis of losses covered. A few years later, premium levels would drop to where they could not possibly provide profits to an insurance company. This cyclical pattern may or may not continue.

The risk manager must be aware of the cyclical cost of insurance when making the decision to self-insure or retain risk. If the insurance markets are offering premiums that do not cover the full cost of likely losses, it is more economical to purchase insurance than to retain risk. In a high-premium market, the reverse is true. Comparison of self-insurance and available commercial insurance is a function of risk management.

Cost of Nondeductible Policies

The size of the deductible on a policy represents a form of self-insurance. In most situations, the premium is quoted in a way that encourages the taking of some deductible, because it is economically beneficial to an insurance company to avoid the costs of processing small claims.

The mathematics of a deductible involves a comparison of the size of the deductible, the reduction of the premiums if the deductible is selected, and the likelihood of a claim. As an example, an organization has a quote for a $6 million policy. The likelihood of loss in any year is 1 percent and the likely size of the possible loss is $300,000. The company will reduce the premium by $1,000 if it accepts a $50,000 deductible. Is this cost-effective for the company?

The answer is yes. The premium declines by a certain (100 percent) chance of $1,000 in return for accepting a 1 percent chance of a $50,000 loss. Mathematically, the chance of a $50,000 loss is valued at $500 (50,000 × 1 percent), whereas the savings is $1,000 (1,000 × 100 percent). The deductible is thus cost-effective if the company can afford to take a chance of a $50,000 loss.

Categories of Captive Insurers

A *captive insurer* is an insurance company owned by another organization primarily to provide insurance coverage for the owning entity. In effect, it involves the creation of a wholly owned subsidiary in order to provide self-insurance for a parent. Bermuda is the most popular country in which to establish a captive insurer, but captive insurers are also organized in the Bahamas, Panama, and other countries, including the United States.

Several categories of captive insurance companies are identified:

1. *Pure Captive*—A company that provides insurance to a parent company and its affiliates or subsidiaries.

2. *Broad Captive*—A company created to provide insurance for a parent but that will also offer coverage to other companies.

3. *Association Captive*—A company that provides coverage to a group of companies, frequently in the same line of business.

Rationale for Captives

Captive insurance companies represent a form of self-insurance as well as regular insurance. This is true because risks above a certain dollar amount can be reinsured with other companies. Motives for establishing them include:

1. *Partial Self-Insurance.* A captive is a form of self-insurance, since the organization is retaining a portion of the risk in a subsidiary insurer. At the same time, risks above a certain dollar amount can be reinsured with other companies.

2. *Lower Cost.* Captives are able to take advantage of tax benefits and lower administrative costs and may thus allow the organization to provide coverage at lower rates than available from other sources.

3. *Tailored Coverage.* Captives can specialize in providing the kind of coverage most needed by a parent. Thus the captive may provide product liability, ocean or inland marine, or workers compensation coverage designed to meet the exact needs of the parent.

4. *Foreign Operations Coverage.* Captives can be used to solve individual parent problems in providing proper coverage on exposures in countries with currency restrictions or other regulations involving insurance coverage. Captives can be set up to insure local operations or purchase insurance through state-run companies. Gaps in the coverage or other problems can be resolved to best meet the needs of the parent.

Risk Transfer

One of the most important tasks of a program in risk management is to transfer or share a portion of the exposures facing the firm. This involves the use of insurance. In this section, we discuss the risk transfer responsibilities of the risk manager.

Selection of a Broker

A *broker* is an intermediary who assists in the process of transferring risk through the insurance mechanism. The following factors affect the selection of a broker:

1. *Broker or Agent?* Although the terms are often used interchangeably, a broker should work primarily for the insured, whereas an agent represents the insurer. A first question is whether the risk manager desires a relatively loyal broker or whether the company wishes to deal with a party that basically represents the insurer.

2. *Qualifications.* A broker may be assisting in the placement of complex risks, such as are involved with toxic chemical plants or the manufacture of high-tech equipment. The broker may have engineers, chemists, actuaries, and systems analysts who can assess the details of exposures and design proper coverage.

3. *Service.* A broker can advise on exposures facing a firm, the relative merits of different insurers, the role of self-insurance, and other matters involving risk transfer mechanisms. Similarly, the broker can assist in the settlement of claims.

Selection of Insurance Companies

An important duty of the risk manager is to select the insurance companies that provide coverage for the organization. This involves the following considerations:

1. *Insurance Capacity*—The ability of the carrier to provide the kinds

and amounts of coverage desired by the organization. A small insurer may lack the financial strength to accept large exposures, even when allowing for the fact that reinsurance can be purchased to cover exposures.

2. *Financial Strength*—The ability of the insurer to continue to provide coverage in a period of high losses. Basically, it is a combination of possessing a strong balance sheet and taking other steps to avoid financial strains. The risk manager should have a certain level of financial skills so as to assess the strength of various carriers.

3. *Attitude Toward Specific Exposures*—The philosophy of the insurer with respect to the kind of coverage desired by the organization. As an example, a company may not be comfortable with large pollution exposures. This company will be reluctant to provide adequate coverage to organizations with major chemical or toxic risks.

4. *Underwriting Knowledge*—The level of expertise of the individuals who will evaluate the exposures to be covered. An insurer with experienced engineers and many years of handling chemical companies is more likely to write the appropriate coverage for a refinery.

5. *Ongoing Service*—Refers to the quality of cooperation provided during normal periods of operation. The insurer can make recommendations on minimizing losses and assist in designing proper coverage for unusual exposures.

6. *Postloss Service*—Refers to the quality of assistance after a loss has occurred. The insurer can assess the level of damage, make recommendations to minimize further losses, and pay claims promptly.

Characteristics of Effective Risk Transfer

When evaluating programs involving insurance coverage, a number of guidelines can be helpful, including:

1. *Internal Accountability.* A person within the organization—can be the risk manager or a superior—should be responsible for the provision of adequate insurance coverage. Adequate coverage should not be the responsibility of a broker, agent, consultant, or other individual outside the organization.

2. *Insurance Adequacy.* The organization should have a program that provides the proper level of coverage. Underinsurance exposes the firm to unnecessary risks. Overinsurance is a waste of money. To avoid underinsurance, the firm must routinely assess the value of its assets and the likelihood of exposures. To avoid overinsurance, the firm must delete coverage when it no longer faces a specific exposure.

3. *Comparison of Alternatives.* Insurance is available in a variety of contracts at different prices and from many sources. The risk manager should encourage different sources to propose coverage. Then, perhaps with the aid of a broker, the firm should compare alternatives on the basis of price, coverage, and likely service.

4. *Loss Control.* It is not enough just to purchase insurance. All risk identification and transfer programs should be accompanied by aggressive steps to reduce losses and diminish exposures. An active program of loss control should be part of the risk transfer program.

5. *Disaster Coverage.* No program of risk transfer is complete if it does not consider the effect of a major disaster, such as can occur in liability lawsuits. In addition to basic property and liability coverage, organizations should carry umbrella policies to protect against a loss that would endanger their survival.

6. *Record Keeping.* Once the risk transfer mechanism has been established, the organization should maintain adequate records to document losses. This includes records on the value of property, inventories, and other data. In the absence of such records, it may not be possible to prove that losses actually were incurred.

Loss Control

Loss control refers to any activities that reduce, prevent, or minimize the economic or social losses from accidents. In this section, we cover loss control in the program of risk management.

Twin Goals of Loss Control Programs

The organization's loss control efforts involve two goals:

1. *Reduce Severity of Accidents. Severity* was defined earlier as the degree of damage that can result from an exposure. Programs can reduce the impact of casualty loss. For example, fire walls built in manufacturing plants can restrict the spreading of fires. Airbags installed in automobiles reduce the extent of injuries.

2. *Reduce Frequency of Accidents. Frequency* was defined earlier as the number of times an exposure becomes a loss. Programs can reduce frequency. For example, careful selection of drivers can reduce vehicle accidents. Employee training, safety guards on equipment, and other programs can reduce the number of manufacturing accidents.

Twin Approaches to Loss Control

The organization's loss control efforts involve two approaches:

1. *Physical Engineering*—Efforts to reduce the physical dangers of the workplace or environment of the employee or customer. Examples include eliminating slippery surfaces, improving lighting, reducing noxious vapors, and installing protective devices on machinery.

2. *Human Engineering*—Efforts to reduce accidents that result from careless or unthinking actions of employees or customers. Examples include providing warning labels on products, enforcing safety rules, and avoiding situations of fatigue or inattention.

Techniques of Loss Control

A number of practices or actions can reduce the severity or frequency of accidents. These include:

1. *Reduction of Occurrences.* Accidents are more likely to happen in certain situations, but the likelihood of these situations can be reduced. An example is to decrease the number of people who work in an area of high hazards.

2. *Prevention of Exposure.* Accidents cannot happen if individuals do not enter the hazardous area. An example is to forbid individuals to walk on foot in an area with many moving vehicles.

3. *Time Separation.* Accidents are reduced if people are separated from periods of highest hazard. Employees can clean a plant at night rather than in the daytime when all machines are operating.

4. *Space Separation.* Distance is placed between people or property and hazards. Inventories can be stored in secured areas away from exposure to elements or pilferage.

5. *Implementation of Barriers.* A physical barrier is placed between people or property and hazards. Examples include safety eyeglasses for workers and railings around walkways near construction sites.

6. *Mitigation of Damages.* Systems can reduce the loss if an accident occurs. An example is a sprinkler system in a building or seatbelts in a vehicle.

7. *Restoration or Rehabilitation.* Long-term effects after a loss can be reduced. Examples are rapid replacement of property to resume operations or retraining disabled workers to perform new jobs.

Risk Retention vs. Risk Transfer

One of the major responsibilities of the risk manager is to evaluate various decisions. An example is whether to retain or transfer risk. In this section, we examine the structure of this decision.

Self-Insurance Costs

One approach to risk retention is to self-insure certain exposures. As a minimum, four costs comprise this alternative:

1. *Employee Benefit Costs*—A program that covers health care, disability, and other benefits. The costs, either losses or premiums, borne by the company are included in this section.

2. *Estimated Losses*—Covers the risk manager's best estimate of property and liability losses during the next period of time. The forecast reflects historical data and can be organized into major categories, such as property, auto, transportation, and general liability.

3. *Administrative Expenses*—Covers the personnel and operating costs associated with employee benefits and risk management activities.

4. *Umbrella Policy Premiums*—Some coverages in excess of those that can be handled by the organization, required by most programs of self-insurance. This cost covers premiums for such exposures.

Insurance Costs

Insurance is a second approach to covering exposure. It is comprised of the following costs:

1. *Employee Benefit Costs*—Premiums for health, disability, and other insurance.

2. *Insurance Premiums*—Premiums for property, liability, and other coverages.

3. *Deductibles*—The forecasted deductibles that will apply to losses. If, for example, the risk manager preducts losses of $1 million with 10 percent deductibles, $100,000 is the deductible cost. The remaining $900,000 would be covered by insurance.

4. *Administrative Expenses*—Covers the personnel and operating costs of the employee benefits and risk management areas.

Coverage Gaps

A *coverage gap* is any exposure that is not covered by insurance or another risk financing method. Some examples are:

1. *No Coverage.* In some cases, the gap is created by a conscious choice not to insure against an exposure. An organization may decide to take its chances with an earthquake or may decline to purchase business interruption insurance. These decisions create gaps in coverage.

2. *Inadequate Coverage.* A gap can exist between the maximum exposure from a loss and the coverage in place. For example, a building is worth $2 million and it is insured for $1.8 million. The coverage gap is $200,000 (2 million − 1.8 million).

3. *Retention Gap.* An organization can accept certain gaps in coverage as a sound business decision. As an example, a company has $2 million in coverage on its vehicles. It can also purchase an umbrella policy in the event that losses exceed $3 million. The difference between the $2 million in coverage and $3 million deductible under the umbrella policy is a $1 million gap.

In reviewing coverage alternatives, the risk manager should evaluate the extent of coverage gaps. Large exposures that remain after the risk transfer or retention mechanism is selected can pose an unacceptable danger to the firm. The decision to allow large coverage gaps is not the responsibility of the risk manager. It should be made at the chief executive officer or board level of the organization.

Cost to Organization for Each Risk Area

The evaluation of exposures should involve a calculation of the cost to the organization of each major insurable area. As an example, assume a company can purchase automobile insurance for its fleet of vehicles for $155,000 in annual premiums. At this level, the company estimates that it would be responsible for $25,000 of losses based on the deductibles required. Purchasing the insurance avoids full payment for a predicted $200,000 in losses next year.

The cost to organization comparison is straightforward, as shown in Figure 13-2. Without insurance, the organization is liable for the entire $200,000 of estimated losses in the next year. In addition, full exposure involves the possibility of a single large, unexpected loss. With insurance, the coverage must pay a premium of $155,000 plus cover the expected deductibles of $25,000. Because insurance costs less and also eliminates the single catastrophic loss, it is likely that it would be accepted by the company.

Final Evaluation of Risk Management Program

Complex exposures require large amounts of time to understand their impact on the corporation. Sensitive exposures can harm the organiza-

Figure 13-2. Cost to organization example.

Commercial Auto Coverage

Data:

Projected losses	200,000
Deductibles	25,000
Annual premiums	155,000

Cost to Organization:

Without insurance coverage	200,000
With insurance coverage	
Annual premiums	155,000
Plus deductibles	25,000
Total Cost	180,000

tion. Both categories should be handled in a cost-effective program that includes full participation by top management. At the end of all the technical knowledge and qualitative and quantitative methodology, the organization must conduct its risk management efforts in a framework of cost efficiency. This can be reduced to a risk management philosophy that guides all decisions. As an example:

> This organization will self-insure against minor risks. Large exposures will be assessed for sensitivity and complexity. Risks that can have a significant effect on profits, sales, or the image of the corporation will be covered systematically.

Administration of Risk Management

The risk management function requires a number of administrative activities. In this section, we examine this area of a program of risk management.

Areas of Administrative Responsibility

The risk management function involves a number of areas, including:

1. *Employee Benefits.* Risk managers are commonly assigned responsibilities in the area of employee benefits. This is probably a result of the insurance aspect of group life and health benefits.

2. *Claims Administration.* When losses occur, reports must be filed,

values must be estimated, and communications must begin with insurance companies and brokers. Compliance with insurance policies and company procedures is the responsibility of the risk management area.

3. *Safety and Health.* Risk managers are often asked to design and implement programs that contribute to the health and safety of employees, customers, and visitors.

4. *Crisis Planning.* When a major loss occurs, it has implications for many areas of an organization. Fires, loss of inventories, and damage to facilities or people cause problems for areas outside the immediate zone of the loss. One duty of many risk managers is to plan for coordinated actions to minimize direct and indirect consequences of a loss.

5. *Crisis Management.* Once a major loss occurs, the risk manager participates in efforts to meet the organization's responsibilities to its employees, community, and others. This involves an active management of the negative effects of losses.

Claims Administration

This administrative area involves a number of activities, including:

1. *Loss Notification.* The parties to be notified of a loss vary with the nature of the damage. A fire loss may have to be reported to the local fire department, even though it was extinguished by employess of the organization. Automobile accidents or property thefts may be reported to the local police. All insured losses must be reported to the insuring companies or brokers.

2. *Loss Minimization.* Immediately after a loss, the risk manager is responsible for confining further effects of the accident. Undamaged property must be secured so it is not lost or stolen. Injuries must be treated with prompt medical attention.

3. *Loss Valuation.* Losses must be converted to economic values in order to process claims or begin repair or recovery. The risk manager works with claims adjusters and others to estimate or calculate the extent of losses and request payments to and from appropriate sources.

4. *Loss Disposition.* The risk manager prepares recommendations for top management on the disposition of losses. Should the company accept the loss estimate of the insurance company? Should a building be repaired or replaced? Should a lawsuit be fought or settled?

Record Keeping and Report Preparation

The risk manager must keep records and prepare reports, including:

1. *Insurance Reports.* The organization may have a number of insurance policies to cover property, personnel, and liability exposures. These will have different coverages, time periods, and prices. The risk manager will tabulate information on the various coverages and prepare reports for other managers.

2. *Directives.* The risk manager may issue guidelines or recommendations to other areas of the organization. These can deal with safety procedures in work areas, steps to protect property, and information on employee benefits.

3. *External Reports.* The risk manager may issue reports or respond to surveys from government agencies, trade associations, or other external organizations.

4. *Compliance Reports.* Organizations may be required to inform government agencies, insurance companies, and others of their efforts in dealing with personnel and property. The organization may be required to arrange routine inspections for fire or other hazards and report the results of those visits.

5. *Loss Reports.* Management needs to understand the nature and extent of losses incurred, the extent to which they are reimbursed by insurance, causes of the losses, and efforts to reduce future injuries and damage. Preparation of such reports lies within the administrative duties of the risk manager.

6. *Appraisals.* Keeping track of the actual cash value and replacement cost of property is a key component in proving the extent of loss. This is particularly a problem if the accounting department or other areas of the firm do not maintain detailed records. Risk managers should routinely appraise the value of assets and keep separate records of the values obtained.

Exercises

1. A company president argues that the reason for a solid risk management program is to ensure a profitable company. A consumer activist believes that the goal is to protect consumers and the environment. A union leader claims that the goal is to protect the workers. Who is right?
2. A school bus company is concerned about the following exposures. Match each one with a pure risk area.
    a. The quality of brakes on the vehicles. Should the company upgrade them?
    b. Drunken drivers on the road in the late afternoon. What can the company do to avoid them?

    c. Drivers are difficult to find. Three applicants have bad driving records. Should they be hired anyway?

    d. A court decision against the company that expands liability awards.

3. A risk manager believes that there is no difference between a loss exposure survey and an organizational practices survey. Is she right?

4. A risk manager is concerned about whether the company or its subsidiaries lease any assets that might expose the company to liability lawsuits. What is a quick way to identify such an exposure?

5. What kind of self-insurance is represented by assumption, deductibles, and retrospective rating?

6. A small company is evaluating self-insurance as a means of lowering its administrative and processing costs involved with losses. It has a part-time risk manager who supervises both losses and benefits for the company's 75 employees. Is this a good idea for the company?

7. An organization faces one chance in 1,000 of an earthquake of 6.5 or above at its manufacturing facility in the next year. It would cause over $5 million in damage if it occurred. An earthquake policy is available with a $100,000 deductible. If the deductible is raised to $300,000, the annual premium will drop by $1,000. Should the company accept the deductible?

8. Identify each of the following captives by its category:

    a. Caravan Insurance Company provides coverage only to Sterling Corporation and its worldwide subsidiaries.

    b. Sterling Insurance Company provides insurance for colleges and universities that are members of the American Council on Education.

    c. Volta Insurance Company is a Bermuda company that has 85 percent of its premium volume from a Chicago corporation and the remainder from 16 smaller companies.

9. Taragon Industries is considering setting up a captive in Bermuda to provide only ocean marine coverage. It thinks this can solve some of its problems achieving the right kind of coverage for its overseas operations. Are these valid motives to form a captive? What other reasons might exist to form a captive?

10. A risk manager claims that the only factor that should be involved in selecting an insurance company is the cost of premiums. Is this correct?

11. A risk manager claims that brokers should be selected on the basis of the same factors as those used for selecting insurance companies. Is this correct?

12. A company president believes that the responsibility for adequate insurance coverage belongs to the broker who advises her. Is she correct?

13. A risk manager sees his job primarily in terms of loss control and disaster coverage but not recordkeeping. Is this a good viewpoint for a risk manager?

14. A risk manager has hired an engineer to design systems to avoid the

release of toxic fumes in a factory. He also is developing new safety rules for workers. What are the technical terms for such activities?

15. Modern Terminals Limited is a Hong Kong container terminal. Pedestrians are forbidden to walk in its operations yard where large motorized cranes move containers. What techniques of loss control are being used?

16. A company uses forklifts to move inventory from a warehouse to the factory in the evening when few workers are in the factory. The vehicles follow a path that does not bring them near the evening workers. What techniques of loss control are being used?

17. A chemical storage tank is surrounded by a four-foot-high concrete barrier. Above it is a fire control system that can be activated to put out a fire. What techniques of loss control are being used?

18. A retail jewelry store keeps the bulk of its inventory in a vault that is not located where customers can see it or where employees are working. What techniques of loss control are being used?

19. A company has a SWAT team that is immediately dispatched to an accident in the factory. It consists of a doctor, fireman, and engineer, along with their equipment. Their mission is to deal with the accident and return the situation to normal. The doctor has the additional mission of tracking injured individuals and taking necessary steps to return them to the work force. What techniques of loss control are being used?

20. A risk manager is responsible for employee safety, health care, and benefits and claims administration. She feels that some important responsibility has been omitted. Is she right?

21. A risk manager has been called to the site of a major fire in a warehouse. What steps should he take?

22. Identify each of the following records or reports required to be prepared by risk managers.
    a. The president wants to know the major accidents that have occurred each month.
    b. A safety procedure required by the federal government needs to be disseminated to first-level supervisors.
    c. The insurance company wants a quarterly report on the status of warranties required under insurance policies.
    d. The vice-president of personnel wants a monthly listing of coverages in place and expiration dates.
    e. The vice-president of finance wants to know the value of furniture and fixtures in the company's sales offices.
    f. A trade association wants to know the breakdown in coverage between self-insurance and risk transferred to a captive or other insurance company.

23. A risk manager has stated publicly: "The only costs of self-insurance are losses and administrative expenses." Is this correct?

24. A risk manager stated that insurance involves only one cost that is not also a cost of self-insurance. Is this correct?
25. What is the difference between a coverage gap and a retention gap?
26. A company can pay annual premiums of $400,000, with deductibles of $50,000, for coverage of losses projected between $450,000 and $600,000. Is this a good situation to purchase coverage?

14

Risk Financing Options

Risk financing is the process of managing funds used to pay the costs of property, liability, and personnel losses. It is an integral part of the overall financial management of an organization.

In this chapter, we discuss the role of the risk manager in the process of risk financing. We begin with an examination of the nature of retention. Then, we examine the characteristics of different approaches to funding losses. Finally, we discuss unfunded programs that can be employed by an organization.

Retention and Self-Insurance

Previously, we defined *risk retention* as any conscious effort by an organization to bear the loss from any known sources. As noted, it can occur in formal or informal ways. In this section, we examine the approaches to retaining risk.

Self-Insurance

Self-insurance is an elusive and even contradictory term for several reasons, including:

1. *Lack of Precision*. The term can be used to refer to everything from a risk that is not recognized (and therefore is retained) to a formal program of retention. The lack of agreement on a meaning can cause misunderstandings.

2. *Not a Transfer*. Insurance refers to the transfer of a risk. How can an individual or organization shift a risk to itself? The risk is retained, not transferred.

3. *Misleading Term*. Since the term *insurance* involves a transfer of risk, it leads to a feeling of financial security in the event of a loss. Self-insurance is misleading for individuals who hear the word *insurance*.

In spite of the problems, the term is often used. Care should be taken to define the meaning whenever it is used. As an example, a *self-insured retention* refers to a conscious risk management decision to retain the first portion of a risk.

Retention

Retention is a better term to use when an individual or organization decides not to transfer a risk. This may occur for a number of reasons, including:

1. *Administrative Costs.* It may not be economical to purchase insurance and then process many small claims.

2. *Premium Costs.* In some cases, the market for the desired coverage may require the payment of excessive premiums.

3. *Insurance Not Available.* In many cases, insurers will not offer the kind of coverage needed. Or the company may lack a statistical history to allow an insurer to assess and underwrite a risk.

4. *Improved Loss Control.* A company that retains risk might be more conscious of exposures and take stronger steps to reduce losses.

5. *Easier Claims Administration.* A company may wish to settle claims quickly and smoothly with its employees and customers. An insurance company's efforts to verify losses may make claims settlement more difficult.

Favorable Conditions for Retention

A company should consider a formal program of self-insured retention only if certain conditions exist, including:

1. *Financial Strength.* The company must be sufficiently strong with the balance sheet and income statement to absorb the risks that it retains. If a large loss can cause bankruptcy, the risk should not be retained.

2. *Administrative Capabilities.* The company must have a staff that is able to manage a retention program, including verifying and settling claims.

3. *Management Support and Understanding.* Top management must understand the program and concur with it. It does not work if management is pleased with lower costs but cannot understand why a large loss occurred.

4. *Flexibility.* The company must be flexible to respond to changing circumstances that affect its risks and coverage of them. It particularly

must be aware of current developments and statutory requirements that affect the viability of any retention programs.

Current Expensing of Losses

The simplest method of retaining losses is to treat them as current expenses of the organization and pay them as they occur. Some key features of this approach are:

1. *They are least expensive to administer.* Since it involves little paper-work in advance, current expensing carries few administrative expenses prior to the occurrence of a loss. A greater portion of risk management funds can be used to pay losses.

2. *They should cover minor losses only.* Current expensing provides little assurance that funds will be available to cover a large loss. Thus it is an appropriate retention technique only for risks and exposures that have a limited financial impact on the organization.

3. *There is a delayed income tax effect.* Many losses occur in one accounting period but are not reported, settled, and paid until a later period. With current expensing, the losses from one period may be recognized by the firm in a later period. The result is higher net income (and income taxes) in the earlier period and a lower income (and taxes) when the loss is recognized.

4. *There is a delayed capital assets effect.* The income tax delay is even greater if a loss involves a major asset that must be depreciated over time. The expense of the loss must be recognized in the depreciation of the asset rather than in the payment for a replacement.

Loss Reserves

A *reserve* is a liability account established to recognize current losses that will have to be paid in the future. Normally, we discuss reserves in connection with insurance companies. No reason exists, however, to bar the risk manager from establishing a reserve in the company itself to cover unpaid losses. Two categories of loss reserves may be identified:

1. *Unfunded Loss Reserve*—Not matched with any specific pool of assets that can be directly used to pay losses. The liability is decreased when losses are paid from the general cash account of the organization. As with current expensing, no guaranty exists that funds will be available to pay claims when needed.

2. *Funded Loss Reserve*—Matched by specific liquid assets that are set aside and invested until needed to pay losses. They may be placed in a

specific account of the company or may be held by an insurance company or other external party. Funded reserves offer greater assurance than unfunded reserves that money will be available to pay claims.

With respect to the funding of losses, funded and unfunded programs are discussed.

Insurance Pools

An *insurance pool* refers to an underwriting activity whereby a group of participants agree to share the risks of writing policies. Generally, each member agrees to accept a fixed percentage share of all profits and losses. The term is synonymous with *insurance association* and *insurance syndicate*. When such an agreement is formed to reinsure other risks, it is called a *reinsurance pool*.

Risk Retention Group

A *risk retention group* is an organized effort by a number of organizations, often in the same industry, to retain a portion of their losses through a formal agreement. By joining together, the companies can enlarge their capacity to retain risk and gain a better use of the law of large numbers.

Guaranteed Cost Insurance

One common means of funded risk financing makes use of the purchase of *guaranteed cost insurance*, defined as a fixed premium paid in advance to cover a loss, with no provision to adjust the size of the premium as a result of the level of losses. In this section, we examine this means of risk financing.

Characteristics of Guaranteed Cost Plans

Under a guaranteed cost program, an insured pays a full premium during the policy year. The insurer provides pure insurance under the terms of the policy. A diagram of the arrangement is shown in Figure 14-1.

Advantages of Guaranteed Cost Insurance

A number of benefits accrue to the insured under a program of guaranteed cost insurance, including:

1. *Known Premiums.* The cost of insurance can be budgeted and is

Figure 14-1.   Guaranteed cost insurance.

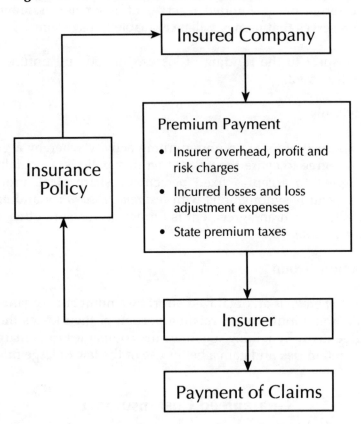

known in advance. The expenses will not fluctuate in response to the level of losses.

2. *Ease of Administration.* The insurance company performs most of the administrative duties under a guaranteed cost plan, including determination of the level of likely losses and settlement of claims.

3. *Known Coverage.* The organization does not have to worry about the payment of losses covered under the program.

4. *Tax-Deductible Premium.* The cost of the insurance in the form of a premium is immediately tax-deductible as a business expense.

Disadvantages of Guaranteed Cost Insurance

A number of disadvantages to the insured may be identified under a program of guaranteed cost insurance, including:

1. *Immediate Cash Outflow.* The premium is paid during the period

of coverage, even though the losses may not be paid until future periods. A cash flow penalty is involved.

2. *No Investment Income.* The funds paid in the premium can be invested by the insurer to earn investment income. The insured does not earn investment income while waiting to pay losses.

3. *Subject to Market Fluctuations.* The amount of the premium and available coverage are both subject to pressures in the commercial insurance marketplace. In some markets, coverage may be unavailable or prohibitively costly.

4. *Favorable Loss Experience Not Immediately Rewarded.* If an organization employs loss control techniques that reduce the frequency or severity of losses, such savings are not passed on to the insured in the current period.

Retention Under Guaranteed Cost Program

A company can retain exposures even though it purchases guaranteed cost insurance if the policy contains a deductible or participation clause. As an example, a policy may contain a $50,000 deductible and 20 percent participation above the deductible up to the limit of the policy. For a $300,000 loss, the organization would have retained $100,000 ($50,000 plus 20 percent of the remaining $250,000) of the loss.

Incurred Loss Retro Insurance

A second means of funded risk financing make use of the purchase of an *incurred loss retrospectively rated plan,* defined as a funded insurance plan where the final level of the premium varies with losses. In this sense, it contains both a transfer and retention component.

Characteristics of Incurred Loss Retro Plans

1. *Standard Premium.* This charge covers the actuarial likelihood of losses and adjusting expenses as well as acquisition and administrative expenses of the insurer. It normally also includes a profit. It is usually paid as an initial or *deposit premium.* The portion reflecting expenses and profit is often identified separately as a *basic premium.*

2. *Investment Income to Insurer.* The insurance company holds the premium cash and thus receives the income from investing it.

3. *Maximum Premium.* This is a multiple of the standard premium and represents an additional charge that can be made if losses exceed expectations. For example, the maximum premium may be 200 percent

of the standard premium. If a large loss occurs, the insured has effectively retained a portion of it equal to a doubling of the standard premium.

4. *Minimum Premium.* A minimum premium is often also specified. If losses do not equal the actuarial forecast, a portion of the premium may be refunded to the insured.

An incurred loss retrospectively rated plan is diagrammed in Figure 14-2.

Advantages of Incurred Loss Retro Plan

A number of benefits accrue to the insured under an incurred loss retro plan, including:

1. *Tax-Deductible Premium When Paid.* The paid premium is deductible as an ordinary business expense.

Figure 14-2.   Incurred loss retrospectively rated plan.

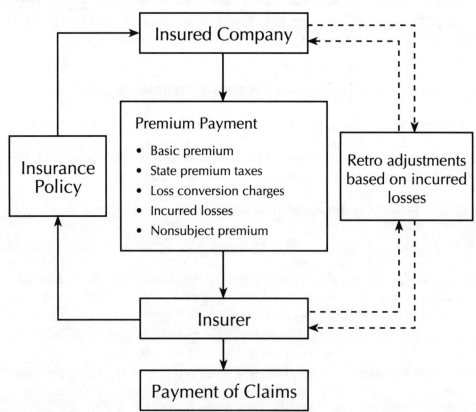

2. *Savings If Loss Experience Is Favorable.* The benefits from a favorable safety record are passed back to the insured in the form of a refund of a portion of the premium.

Disadvantages of Incurred Loss Retro Plan

A number of disadvantages to the insured may be identified under a program of incurred loss retro insurance, including:

1. *Higher Cost If Loss Experience Is Unfavorable.* In a year when high losses are incurred, the insured must pay an additional premium.

2. *Fluctuations in Loss Costs.* The cost of insurance will fluctuate from year to year with variations in annual losses.

3. *Loss of Investment Income.* The insurer invests the premium and receives the investment income. Thus it is lost to the insured.

The Captive

Another means of funding losses involves the use of a captive, earlier defined as an insurance company owned by another organization primarily to provide insurance coverage for the owning entity. Although it is defined as an insurance company, a captive reflects a form of retention, because the parent's fortunes are affected by losses in the affiliated insurance company. A large loss paid by the captive affects the financial performance of the parent.

Is a Captive an Insurance Company?

A captive may be set up so that it fails to meet the definition of insurance. Instead, it may provide certain noninsurance services to its parent. It may allow the parent to transfer premiums and deduct them for tax purposes. It may provide a vehicle for processing claims or obtaining reinsurance without accepting risk itself. If no risk were accepted, it would actually be a financial services company rather than a true insurance company.

Two tests are commonly applied to determine whether a captive is an insurance company in a risk management sense:

1. *Risk Shifting*—Refers to the transfer of the financial consequences of risk and uncertainty from one party to another. If a captive does not bear risk separately from the parent company, it is not a true insurance entity.

2. *Risk Distribution*—Refers to a situation where the financial consequences of loss are shared by one or more parties with the capacity to handle the loss. Stated differently, an insurance company should not routinely be in a position where a single loss causes it to have an overall loss in an accounting period. If a single claim is likely to exceed the premium and investment income of a captive, the risk may not be sufficiently distributed so as to qualify the captive as a true insurance company.

Qualifying a Captive as an Insurance Company

In some cases, tax or other considerations may require a parent to demonstrate that a captive is actually an insurance company. This means it must meet tests for risk shifting and risk distribution. Some steps to ensure that these tests are passed are:

1. *Acceptance of Losses.* The captive can accept risk from the parent under conditions that can cause a profit or loss in the captive, depending upon the level of losses.

2. *Acceptance of Third-Party Business.* A captive can offer insurance services to parties other than its parent. This assists in building up premium volume so the goal of risk distribution is achieved.

3. *Adequate Capital Base.* A captive can be established with adequate surplus to provide stability during a period of high losses. With sufficient capital, it is easier to demonstrate a separate insurance entity.

4. *Premiums Negotiated at Arm's Length.* The premiums to cover risks should be negotiated so that they are adequate to cover likely losses and administrative expenses. No special arrangements should be included that would not be present in a negotiation with a third-party insurer.

5. *Regulation by Insurance Laws.* If a captive is located in a domicile where insurance laws are strict, special financing arrangements between a parent and subsidiary may not be permitted. This supports the position of an insurance rather than financial services operation.

Advantages to Captive Arrangement

A number of benefits accrue to the insured under a captive program, including:

1. *Retention of Risk.* The captive can retain any desired portion of exposures. Those exposures not retained can be covered through reinsurance.

2. *Investment Income.* The captive is able to invest the cash from premiums and earn investment income for the "family" of companies.

3. *Control Over Coverage.* A captive affords less dependence upon commercial insurance markets and offers more control over coverages in a program of risk management.

Disadvantages to Captives

A number of disadvantages are associated with captive arrangements, including:

1. *Capital Commitment.* The insured must put up money to provide the contributed capital base of the captive.

2. *Operating Costs.* A captive involves administrative expenses, including actuarial and legal fees, management and audit costs, and taxes.

3. *Security Costs.* A *letter of credit* is a promise by a bank to provide money to a customer in the future. Insurers or reinsurers who deal with the captive may require a bank letter of credit guaranteeing payment obligations in the event of financial difficulty by the captive.

A Fronting Program

A *fronting program* may be defined as a situation where a company buys coverage from an admitted insurer who immediately reinsures the exposure with a captive of the parent that is not licensed to do business in the jurisdiction. Such a program is needed to avoid the costs of licensing a captive in every state where a parent has business.

The characteristics of a fronting program are:

1. *Premium Paid Through Fronting Carrier.* An admitted insurer accepts the insurance premium and passes most of it on to the captive in return for reinsurance on the exposure.

2. *Security Required.* The fronting carrier will require a letter of credit to ensure that the captive will meet its obligations.

A diagram of a fronting program using a captive is given in Figure 14-3.

Paid Loss Retro Plan

A variation on the incurred loss plan is called the *paid loss retrospectively rated plan.* Paid loss plans vary considerably, but the major difference is that the program is an unfunded form of risk financing.

Figure 14-3.   Captive fronting program.

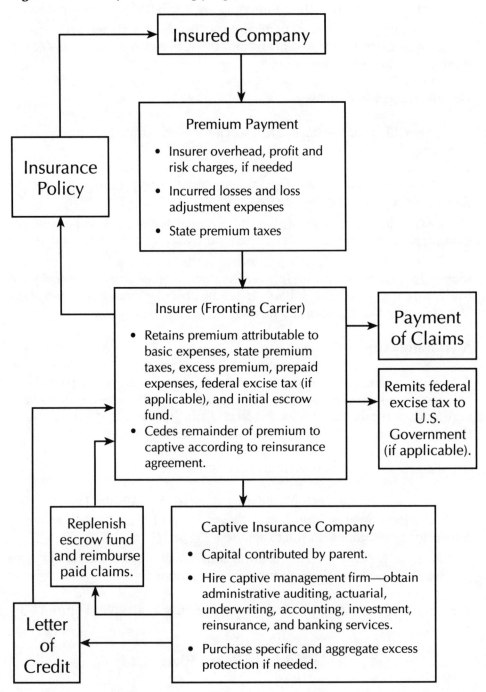

A typical structure is:

1. *Basic premium is paid initially.* Instead of paying the standard premium initially, the insured pays only the basic premium. This gives the insurer coverage of acquisition and administrative expenses and perhaps a profit.

2. *Additional premiums as losses are paid.* When the insurer pays losses in the future, the insured reimburses the insurer up to the maximum premium stipulated in the policy.

3. *Security may be required.* Under a paid loss plan, the insurance company may require security, such as a letter of credit, to be provided up to the level of the standard premium.

4. *Balloon payment occurs at the end.* At some future date, the program must be converted to an incurred loss retro plan. This allows the insurance company to take over responsibility for any delayed or unexpected claims in the future.

Figure 14-4 shows a diagram of a paid loss retro plan.

Advantages to Paid Loss Retro Plan

A paid loss retrospectively rated plan offers several advantages to the insured, including:

1. *Unfunded Losses.* Only the expense portion of the premium is paid to the insurer. The balance can be invested and held until claims are paid.

2. *No Need to Establish Level of Reserves.* The problem of estimating reserves is eliminated since losses are paid without regard to established reserves.

Disadvantages to Paid Loss Retro Plan

A number of disadvantages accrue to the insured under a paid loss retro plan, including:

1. *Fluctuating Costs.* The cost of losses will vary from period to period, as claims are paid.

2. *Balloon Payment at End.* For a line of business with considerable exposure, the balloon payment at the end may be quite large.

Figure 14-4.   Paid loss retrospectively rated plan.

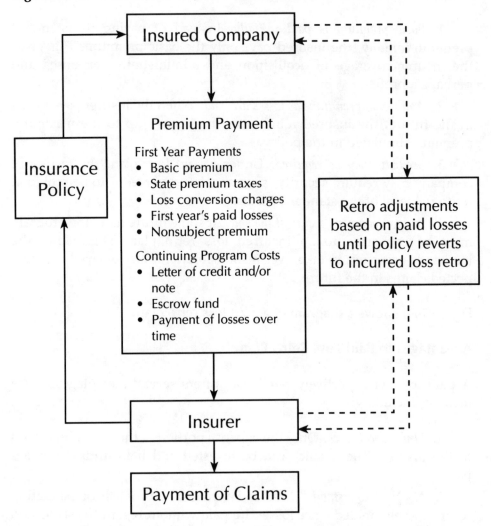

Self-Insurance Programs

A formal program of self-insurance may be desirable for companies in certain areas such as workers compensation and automobile liability, where many relatively small claims are processed. In this section, we examine a qualifying self-insurance program using workers compensation as an example.

Self-Insured Programs

If a state law permits a company to self-insure its workers compensation or automobile obligations, the risk manager can become intimately involved with the process. Figure 14-5 diagrams a self-insurance program. Important items to note in the figure are:

1. *Qualifying as Self-Insurer.* The first step for the company is to qualify under state law. The employer must demonstrate financial capacity to comply with all likely obligations and future claims.

2. *Purchase Excess Insurance.* This insurance is above the level of retention. The state law requires such insurance to guard against a failure to pay if some catastrophe in the workplace exceeds the resources of the employer.

3. *Provide Security.* The state seeks a guaranty that the employer will meet its obligations. Normally, this requires the posting of a surety bond from an insurance company or letter of credit from a bank.

4. *Claims Administration.* The employer must be able to administer claims, either through the establishment of an in-house department or through contracting with an external claims administrator. If an outsider is used, the employer must set up an escrow fund to be drawn down as claims are paid.

Advantages to Self-Insurance

A self-insured program of workers compensation offers the following benefits to an employer:

1. *Maximizes Cash Flow.* The employer retains funds until they are needed to cover losses and expenses.

2. *Lower Costs.* The employer does not have to pay premium taxes, coordinating costs between insured and insurer, and insurer profit. Nor does the employer pay for services that are included but not needed in the insurance program.

3. *Fewer Losses.* Because the employer is working specifically on employee injuries, the entire organization is likely to be more sensitive to safety practices and loss control. Fewer losses should be incurred.

Disadvantages to Self-Insurance

A self-insured program of workers compensation involves the following disadvantages to an employer:

1. *Extra Costs.* The cost of excess insurance, surety bonds, and letters of credit must be paid by the employer.

2. *Multistate Compliance.* If an employer operates in different states, it must qualify in each state where self-insurance is permitted.

Figure 14-5.   Self-insurance program for workers compensation.

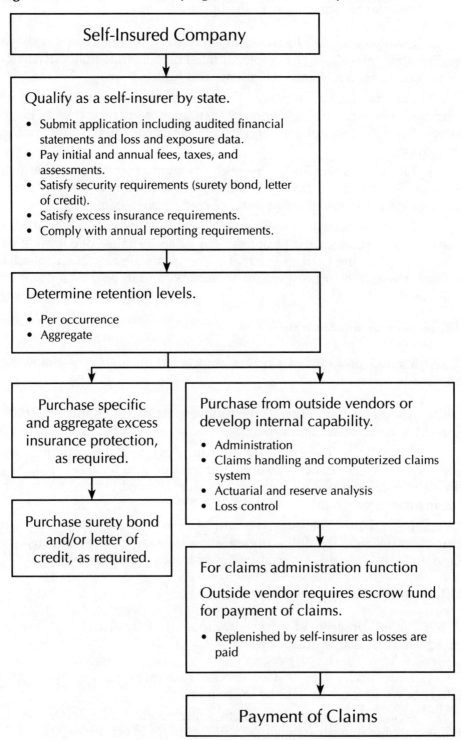

3. *Earnings Affected by Fluctuations.* Losses fluctuate from year to year. The changing costs involved with them will produce variations in the company's reported profits.

4. *Earlier Payment of Taxes.* Only paid losses and expenses are deductible for tax purposes with a program of self-insurance. Although losses have been incurred, the tax benefit is delayed until cash payments are actually made. With insurance, premiums are deductible as expenses when incurred. With self-insurance, the tax benefits may be delayed until the actual loss payments are made.

Exercises

1. Under its commercial automobile policy, a company has average annual losses of $6.5 million. It can achieve significant savings in the cost of insurance if it purchases an incurred loss retro plan in place of its current guaranteed cost plan. Should the company make a change?
2. A company has never had a loss under a commercial general liability policy covering its toxic chemical plant. It can achieve significant savings in the cost of insurance if it purchases a paid loss retro plan in place of its current guaranteed cost plan. The retro plan would have a maximum premium of $2.5 million, whereas the guaranteed cost plan has an annual premium of $800,000. Should the company make the change?
3. A company has never had a loss under a commercial general liability policy covering its construction company. It can achieve significant savings in the cost of insurance if it self-insures instead of continuing to purchase a guaranteed cost plan. Excess insurance is available up to a limit of $3 million. Should the company make a change?
4. A company has the following history of incurred and paid losses:

	Incurred Losses	Paid Losses
Five years ago	270,000	240,000
Four years ago	410,000	280,000
Three years ago	160,000	325,000
Two years ago	650,000	275,000
Last year	305,000	480,000

The company can purchase any of three kinds of insurance policies for the current year, as follows:

a. *Guaranteed Cost Plan.* For a premium of $300,000 and state premium taxes of $15,000, the company will receive a policy with a $50,000 deductible. The company's own administrative expenses are estimated at $25,000 with this program.
b. *Incurred Loss Retro Plan.* For a standard premium of $250,000 and state premium taxes of $12,500, the company will receive a policy

with a maximum premium of $500,000 and a minimum premium of $225,000. The company's own administrative expenses are estimated at $35,000 with this program.

c. *Paid Loss Retro Plan*. For a basic premium of $60,000 and state premium taxes of $3,000, the company will receive a policy with a maximum premium of $600,000 and a minimum premium of $60,000. The company's own administrative expenses are estimated at $50,000 with this program.

If the company chooses a qualified self-insurance plan, it could purchase excess loss insurance above $600,000 for a premium of $60,000, with $3,000 in premium taxes. It estimates its administrative expenses at $100,000 with this program.

What should this company do?

15

Commercial Property Insurance

The exposures facing a business firm are considerably more complex than those facing individuals. In addition to the risks of multiple-purpose vehicles and buildings, the firm faces complex processes when producing goods or services. It also must deal with exposures to many people, including customers, employees, and third parties.

The task of providing risk management coverage to a firm applies in large degree to other organizations, including hospitals, municipalities, colleges, and nonprofit institutions. The exact needs vary, depending upon the nature of activity. As examples, a commercial bank is less likely than a chemical company to face major pollution exposures. A college is less likely than a hospital to be sued for malpractice. However, organizations face property and liability exposures on all sides.

Insurance remains a major tool for protecting an organization against property and liability exposures. Understanding the available insurance coverage is a first step for a risk manager who may be seeking alternative approaches to covering risks. Thus we cover commercial insurance in some detail. Insurance to indemnify an organization for the destruction of property is covered in this chapter. Liability insurance is covered in Chapter 16.

Property Coverage

An organization must understand the nature of risks to its buildings, vehicles, equipment, and other assets. In this section, we examine property exposures and insurance to cover them.

ISO Commercial Portfolio Program

Property insurance in the United States emerged from individual lines of insurance coverage. Thus an organization might purchase fire insurance from one company, earthquake insurance from another, and so on. The different policies employed a range of style, format, language, and coverage. The result was often a variety of coverages that overlapped in some areas and left voids in others.

In 1986 the Insurance Services Office (ISO) introduced a *Commercial Portfolio Program,* defined as a package of insurance forms to standardize business insurance. In addition to eliminating overlap and gaps in coverage, the forms simplify the language of the various coverages.

The following discussion of commercial property insurance takes place in the context of the Commercial Portfolio Program forms.

Building and Personal Property

The building and personal property coverage form is the basic business coverage, similar to the homeowners policy for individuals. The major provisions of this policy are:

1. *Completed Buildings*—Covers property damage to completed buildings listed in the declarations.

2. *Personal Property*—Covers personal property either owned by or in the custody of the insured.

3. *Possible Blanket Coverage*—Refers to a single insurance amount to cover multiple units of property. It differs from *specific coverage,* where a stated policy limit applies to an individual property. This can benefit a firm by simplifying calculations of a loss when it occurs.

4. *Per Occurrence*—Means that each separate loss is covered up to the limit of the policy. The ISO form also has a deductible on a per occurrence basis. For example, a company has $100,000 coverage with a $3,000 deductible. A building listed in the declarations suffers fire damage on two occasions, six months apart. The first has $80,000 damage, the second, $90,000 damage after being repaired. Even though the policy has a $100,000 limit, the first occurrence is covered for $77,000 ($80,000 loss − $3,000 deductible), and the second for $87,000 (90,000 − 3,000).

5. *Coinsurance Clause*—Requires the business to maintain insurance equal to some percentage of the replacement cost or actual cash value of the property. Normally, this will be at least 80 percent. Failure to maintain the percentage will lower the benefit if a loss occurs. The value is computed at the time of the loss, not when the policy is purchased. Thus the responsibility to maintain the percentage belongs to the risk manager.

6. *Duties in the Event of a Loss*—Are similar to those in the homeowners policy. They include notification to the insurance company or police and the safeguarding of property following a loss.

Cause of Loss Forms

The ISO Commercial Portfolio Program contains four forms that deal with the cause of the loss. These are:

1. *Basic Form*—Covers losses from fire, explosion, windstorm, hail, smoke, aircraft or vehicles, civil commotion, vandalism, sprinkler leakage, and several other perils.

2. *Broad Form*—Expands basic form coverage by adding breakage of glass, falling objects, weight of snow, water damage, and some causes of collapse to a building.

3. *Special Form*—Expands broad form coverage to an open-perils basis in the areas of collapse, water damage, and personal property.

4. *Earthquake Form*—Insures against earthquake and volcanic eruption.

Optional Coverages

The ISO Commercial Portfolio Program offers several options for the coverage of buildings and personal property:

1. *Inflation Guard*—A provision that automatically increases the amount of insurance in response to changes in the value or replacement cost of the property.

2. *Replacement Cost Coverage*—Provides for payment on the basis of replacement cost.

3. *Agreed Value Option*—Suspends the coinsurance provision for a specified period of time. It is useful when insurance is carried near the 80 or 90 percent minimum for coinsurance. It ensures that a rapid rise in property value or replacement cost will not reduce the payment for a loss.

4. *Building Ordinance Endorsement*—Provides additional payments if local building codes increase the cost of repairing or replacing a building after a loss.

5. *Manufacturer's Selling Price Clause*—Provides coverage for finished goods at their selling price rather than at their cost. Essentially, this protects the profit on goods that would have been sold.

Miscellaneous Commercial Property Coverages

In addition to the primary property coverage, a number of other forms are available in the ISO Commercial Portfolio Program. These include:

1. *Plate Glass.* The basic and broad forms do not provide adequate coverage for commercial buildings with numerous windows and glass surfaces. It is provided by a separate optional form.

2. *Builder's Risk.* This form is designed for a building under construction, where the value changes each day as improvements are added. Coverage is written for the completed value of the building, with a premium set just above 50 percent of the amount that would be charged for the completed value. The coverage terminates when the building is completed and occupied.

3. *Condominium Forms.* Special forms are needed to cover a condominium, a legal arrangement whereby individuals or organizations own common premises as well as individual living or commercial units.

Business Interruption Insurance

A *consequential loss* refers to any economic loss that occurs as a result of another loss. An example is the loss of profits from not being able to rent a building after a fire.

Business interruption insurance provides coverage against consequential losses, including:

1. *Loss of Income.* The policy can provide funds to meet continuing expenses and replace a portion of the lost income following a property loss. It is designed to assist the organization in meeting its obligations while the property is being repaired. Normally, a coinsurance requirement is imposed.

2. *Extra Expenses.* In addition to continued expenses and lost income, a firm may suffer additional costs following a loss. This form can provide funds for such expenses.

3. *Contingent Interruption or Expenses.* In some cases, business activities are interrupted because of damage to property not owned or controlled by the insured. Business interruption and extra expense insurance are available if a disruption occurs from damage to any of four designated properties:
   a. *Manufacturing Property*—Damaged property of a supplier that provides a large portion of the goods sold by the insured.
   b. *Contributing Property*—Damaged property of a primary supplier of goods sold by the insured.
   c. *Recipient Property*—Damaged property of a customer who purchases a large volume of the goods purchased by the insured.
   d. *Leader Property*—Damaged property of a related business that attracts customers to the insured.

Boiler and Machinery Insurance

Boiler and machinery insurance refers to a specialized area in which engineering and technical knowledge is needed to assess risks, reduce exposures, and design insurance. This form of insurance covers such items as refrigeration units, engines, motors, pressurized systems, and other machinery. The risks in these areas are generally excluded from other commercial property policies.

An important part of this coverage involves the services rendered by companies that specialize in writing the policies. Boiler and machinery insurers provide extensive safety engineering, design, and inspection services that identify potential causes of explosion, rupture, or other loss. Prior to issuing a policy, the insurer makes recommendations on physical layout, system design, and employee practices in the work environment. For most companies, the loss prevention services are as important as the actual insurance coverage.

The basic insurance coverages offered in boiler and machinery policies are:

1. *Insured's Property*—Covers damage to physical property owned by the policyholder. It provides funds to repair or replace mechanical, electrical, pressure, and production machinery in the care, custody, or control of the insured. The policy does not cover wear and tear, corrosion, or other normal deterioration in machinery and equipment when it is being used over time.

2. *Property of Others*—Covers damage to the property of a third party when an insured's property explodes or otherwise causes damage to the property of the third party.

3. *Bodily Injury Liability*—Covers medical expenses and other losses arising from persons injured as a result of damage to the covered property.

4. *Defense Costs and Supplementary Payments*—Covers the legal expenses and other payments needed to defend against lawsuits arising from the covered loss.

With boiler and machinery coverage, it is important to note the exclusions:

1. *Business Interruption.* A separate policy is needed to cover the loss of income and extra expenses that result from boiler and machinery loss. This is available in two forms. A valued form pays a stated amount for each day that an operation is closed down as a result of a covered loss. An actual loss form requires the insured to prove the extent of the loss.

In both cases, a waiting period exists before coverage begins. This works effectively like a deductible.

2. *Consequential Damage.* Indirect damage to other property owned by the insured is not covered in the basic boiler and machinery policy. An example is the spoilage of food as a result of a lack of refrigeration. Consequential damage coverage may be obtained by an endorsement to the policy or a separate insurance contract.

Inland Marine Insurance

Business property not located on the insured premises must be covered with separate insurance. *Inland marine insurance* covers property that may be transported from one place to another within the country. It also covers vehicles or fixed property that may participate in the transporting. Many coverages are available, including:

1. *Transported Goods*—Property designed to be shipped by train, truck, or airplane, normally in the process of moving from manufacturer through suppliers to customers. Examples are raw materials and finished goods.

2. *Mobile Property*—Property that is mobile in nature and may be removed from the insured premises. Examples are overhead projectors and portable generators.

3. *Means of Transportation*—Trains, trucks, and planes that carry goods. Property also includes bridges, tunnels, and pipelines that participate in the movement of goods. As a result of historical practices, it further includes communications equipment that transports words or pictures. Examples are electric power lines and television transmitting equipment.

4. *Dealers Property*—Merchandise that may be transported for display purposes. Examples are jewelry, musical instruments, and furs.

5. *Bailee Property*—Refers to a *bailee,* a person who holds the property of another person and is responsible for its safety and eventual return. An example is an automobile mechanic who must safeguard a vehicle while it is being repaired.

6. *Accounts Receivable*—A right to collect money from another person as a result of the sale of goods or providing of services. The insurance protects against losses when records are destroyed and the receivables can no longer be collected.

7. *Valuable Papers*—Any written documents that are important to the operations of an organization. Insurance can be purchased to protect

these papers, including deeds, mortgages, blueprints, diagrams, and similar items.

8. *Data Processing*—Hardware and software that can be insured against both the value of the loss and the effects of business interruption.

Inland Marine Floaters

A *floater* is an inland marine insurance policy that follows the movement of property that is easily and frequently moved and is of relatively high value. Two categories of floaters are:

1. *Blanket Floater*—Covers a group of articles that are not identified individually but have a relatively large cumulative value. Examples are policies to cover stamp or coin collections, livestock, or salesperson's samples.

2. *Scheduled Floater*—Covers large items that are individually identified and frequently transported. Examples are fur coats, fine art, and generators rented to other companies.

Crime Insurance

An organization can purchase insurance against losses arising from the dishonest acts of employees or third parties. The major coverages are:

1. *Employee Dishonesty*—Insurance against theft, fraud, forgery, and embezzlement of funds, commonly referred to as a *fidelity bond*, which is available in three forms:
   a. *Named Individual.* The insurance covers a single person.
   b. *Position Coverage.* The insurance covers the person appointed to an organizational position, such as the treasurer or corporate secretary.
   c. *Blanket Coverage.* The insurance covers all employees.

2. *Theft, Disappearance, and Destruction*—Covers money and securities that are stolen, disappear, or are destroyed, either on the premises or while being transported.

3. *Robbery and Safe Burglary*—Covers property other than money, securities, and motor vehicles taken by forcible means. This includes taking property from the premises or from an employee or messenger where intimidation or violence occurs. It also covers taking property from a safe or vault where force is used.

4. *Premises Burglary*—Covers property other than money, securities, and motor vehicles stolen from the premises by a third party who unlawfully entered the premises.

5. *Kidnap and Ransom*—Covers payments of a ransom in the event an employee or family member is kidnapped, including employees who travel or work inside or outside the United States in areas where they may be abducted by parties who seek the payment of a ransom. A normal provision when purchasing this insurance instructs the company not to reveal the existence of the coverage, lest it encourage kidnappings.

Surety Bonds

Suretyship is the process of guaranteeing obligations by a third party. A *surety bond* is an insurance policy that achieves such a guaranty.

A variety of surety bonds may be identified, including:

1. *Contract Bond*—An insurance policy that guarantees performance under the terms of a contract. It is sometimes called a *performance bond*. Examples are bonds to guarantee the construction of a building or the providing of supplies to a manufacturer.

2. *Fiduciary Bond*—A guaranty that a person will meet legal obligations to safeguard property. An example is a bond for the administrator of a trust or estate.

3. *Bid Bond*—A guaranty that a bidder for contract work will accept the contract and perform the work if the bid is accepted.

4. *Occupational Bond*—A guaranty that a licensed person will provide honest and faithful performance of duties. It applies to groups such as stockbrokers, undertakers, and collectors of debts.

5. *Tax Bond*—A guaranty that private organizations and individuals will collect taxes and remit them to government agencies. Examples are monies collected in conjunction with liquor, gasoline, and general state sales taxes.

Ocean Marine Insurance

Ocean marine insurance covers property while it is en route on ocean-going vessles. There are four coverages:

1. *Hull Insurance*—Covers the vessel itself.

2. *Protection and Indemnity (P&I)*—Liability insurance for claims by third parties against the owner or operator of the vessel.

3. *Cargo*—Covers damage or loss to the cargo being transported on a vessel.

4. *Freight*—Indemnifies a ship owner or operator for the loss of income when a vessel is lost or damaged.

Commercial Insurance Contracts

The ISO Commercial Portfolio Program has a number of features that affect the specific coverages identified above. In this section, we examine some of the contract provisions and other features of the portfolio approach to providing commercial insurance protection.

Common Policy Conditions

A *common policy condition* is any policy provision that applies to all the ISO commercial coverages. Some common conditions are:

1. *Administrative Provisions*—Clauses that spell out the terms for cancelling, changing, or transferring the policy.

2. *Examination of Books and Records*—Gives the insurance company the right to audit and otherwise inspect the books and records of the insured.

3. *Inspections and Surveys*—Allows the insurance company the right to inspect the property and premises of the insured and suggest changes to unsafe or unhealthy situations.

First-Named Insured

To simplify administration, a *first-named insured* is the party that has the primary rights and responsibilities under a policy. The first-named insured must pay the premiums, can negotiate changes in the policy, can cancel the policy, and is the only party that must be notified by the insurance company if the policy is to be cancelled.

The Commercial Portfolio Program can cover a number of related organizations at different locations. Thus it is important that a first-named insured be designated to facilitate the administration of the policy. This is done in the common policy conditions.

Multiple Coverage

A major advantage of the ISO Commercial Portfolio Program is the coordination of coverages. This reduces the chance of gaps, omissions, and duplication of coverages. Still, it may be possible that a loss is covered under more than one insurance form.

In the event of multiple coverage, the insured is specifically prohibited from collecting more than the actual amount of the loss or damage.

Commercial Policy Forms

Although the above discussion focuses on the property portion of the ISO Commercial Portfolio Program, the risk manager will be exposed to a number of other policy forms in discussions with underwriters and risk managers. Some of the common forms are:

1. *Monoline Policy*—Any insurance against a specific peril or that provides a single type of coverage. Examples are the Standard Fire Policy and flood insurance policies. The trend in commercial insurance is away from such policies.

2. *Multiline Policy*—Covers more than one type of insurance in a single policy. An example is the homeowners policy.

3. *Package Policy*—A multiline insurance contract that coordinates the various coverages. The ISO approach is an example. This kind of policy also provides a simpler approach to risk management since it facilitates identifying the gaps and overlaps in coverage.

4. *Special Multi-Peril* (SMP) *Program*—A package policy that covers property and liability exposures for organizations. Introduced in the 1960s, it was a major step in the direction of packaging and coordinating commercial insurance coverage.

5. *Businessowners Policy*—Similar to the SMP program but designed for smaller organizations.

6. *Business Floater Policies*—Forms of inland marine policies that cover mobile business property. They include a variety of owned goods as well as goods held on consignment.

Exercises

1. A commercial property policy covers seven buildings owned by a company in a single form. It has a policy limit on the basis of each separate claim and requires the company to pay a percentage of each loss. What are three provisions of this policy?
2. A risk manager does not want the special form coverage because it is too restrictive on water damage. Should she take the broad form instead?
3. What is the difference in coverage for earthquake and volcanic damage among the basic, broad, and special forms?
4. A risk manager is concerned that his company will suffer a loss of income if one of his suppliers suffers damages or if a customer suffers damage. Can insurance be purchased to cover these exposures?
5. A large department store attracts customers to a mall where Victoria

Landow operates a fashion store. She wants to purchase insurance against damage to the large store. Is this possible?

6. A company regularly moves portable generators from one construction site to another. In addition, it has two large cranes that work at different locations. Can these be covered in a single property insurance policy?

7. A company has a blanket fidelity bond on all employees. This includes Charlie Thompson, the company treasurer who handles large amounts of cash and negotiable securities. Is this adequate coverage?

8. A company has a contract that requires a subcontractor to deliver goods of a specified quality on time. Once delivered, they are turned over to an individual who safeguards them until they are installed. The company wants guaranties that both individuals will fulfill their obligations. Is this possible?

9. A risk manager has purchased protection and indemnity insurance for the vessel *Ocean Prince*. The policy limit is $2 million. The vessel is involved in a collision at sea that causes $1.5 million of damage to its deck and structure and another $1 million to its cargo. How much coverage is provided by the insurance policy?

10. A risk manager wants to know of any correspondence involving a commercial property policy. To guarantee this, he has requested that he be named the beneficiary of the policy. Will this work?

11. An underwriter tells a risk manager that there really is no difference between monoline, multiline, and package policies. Is this true?

12. A small businessman wants a special multi-peril policy to cover property and liability exposures. Is this possible?

16

Commercial Liability Coverage

We earlier defined *liability* as the exposure to any legal obligation or responsibility to compensate another party for a loss or damages. The possibility of legal liability is as great a threat to organizations as it is to individuals.

In this chapter, we discuss approaches to dealing with the liability exposures facing an organization. The tone is somewhat different than earlier chapters, including Chapter 11 on personal liability. We examine in some detail the changing concepts of liability in the second half of the twentieth century, which have amounted to a virtual revolution in the U.S. legal system. The changes have dramatically expanded the exposures facing businesses and other organizations. As much as any other factor, the need for liability protection has moved the risk manager to the forefront of modern management teams.

Following the discussion of changing liability concepts, we examine methods to provide liability coverage for an organization.

Tort Law and Contract Law

Beginning in the 1950s, a group of legal thinkers and activists undertook a program to fundamentally change the nature of liability in the United States. Their efforts are extensively, and even dramatically, chronicled in a remarkable book, *Liability: The Legal Revolution and Its Consequences*, by Peter W. Huber (New York: Basic Books, 1988). The discussion in this section builds on the concepts outlined in Huber's book.

In the United States, disputes may be resolved between parties in two legal frameworks. *Tort law* covers dealings where no previous understanding has been reached between the parties. *Contract law* covers dealings where parties have agreed in advance to work together.

Prior to the tort changes of the 1950s–1980s, responsibility for most accidents was based on contract law. An individual who purchased an item or service was largely responsible for accepting inherent risks. In this framework, it was difficult to win liability claims.

As a result of new interpretations by the courts, the resolution of disputes has shifted from the realm of contract law to tort law. The development of modern tort law can be traced to a group of individuals who have been named the Founders by Peter Huber. In this section, we cover the goals and motives of these individuals.

The Founders: Role, Concern, Premises, Solution

Peter Huber defines the *Founders* as a group of legal theorists from the 1950s through the 1980s whose ideas, eloquence, and persistence converted common law into the tort law applicable in the United States in the 1980s. The *Followers* were economists and lawyers who provided the tools to argue that changes were needed. They were overwhelmingly effective because some Founders occupied positions as judges in appeals courts and state supreme courts.

The *concern* of the Founders dealt with the consequences of accidents in society. Two aspects of this concern are:

1. *Paying the Cost of Accidents.* The society suffers economic consequences when people are injured or killed. The Founders sought an effective and reliable mechanism to cover these costs. In their view, the courts could develop such a system to play this social role.

2. *Increasing Safety.* The number and severity of accidents can be reduced in a society. The Founders sought a system that would have the ancillary benefit of encouraging greater care and safety consciousness in the design of goods and provision of services.

The Founders and Followers sought to change the legal system and thus to reduce accidents and deal with their costs. They based their ideas on two important *premises:*

1. *Consumer Limitations.* Individuals who purchase goods or services do not assess accident risk prior to making purchases. Hence, they do not demand safety.

2. *Producer Limitations.* Manufacturers and other suppliers are concerned about many things but not safety. Hence, they are careless when designing and providing products and services.

There is considerable disagreement in our society as to the validity of these premises. Aside from this issue, many of the legal interpretations of the past 40 years have been based on either or both premises.

The *solution* developed and implemented by the Founders was to change the law of torts so that producers of goods and providers of services would pay for the cost of accidents. According to their theory, this would have the corollary benefit of encouraging suppliers to be more safety conscious in designing and selling products or providing services.

The new system would have responsibility for accidents settled after the fact by litigation. A buyer and seller would not be allowed to waive any of the rights during the course of a purchase. The acceptable level of safety would be determined in individual court cases, even though this might vary from jury to jury and jurisdiction to jurisdiction.

This movement from a contract- to a tort-based system of dispute resolution was developed through a broad series of changes in the legal system. These changes are discussed in the next sections.

Expansion of Liability Concepts

A major component of the changes to the tort system dealt with the kinds of issues that could be addressed in liability lawsuits. In this section, we examine the expansion of the concept of liability in tort actions.

Modifications to Contract Law

A number of tort law changes from the 1950s through the 1980s affected contracts. The process was evolutionary. Major developments included:

1. *Implied Warranty*—Defined as an unwritten promise that a product is fit for its intended use. The concept has long been recognized under contract law, where warnings must be provided if a product has dangerous features. A first expansion of liability was to hold manufacturers and sellers liable for accidents that occurred when warnings were not present. The absence of adequate warnings was viewed to be negligence.

2. *Express Disclaimers*—Defined as a contract provision where one party is not held responsible for something. For example, a manufacturer and consumer agreed that the manufacturer would not be liable for accidents that result from the use of a product. Suppliers responded to the implied warranty requirements by increasing the length of warnings and adding express disclaimers.

3. *Strict Liability*—Defined as responsibility for an accident or illness even though negligence is not present. If a product is dangerous to use,

the manufacturer may be strictly liable for accidents even though all actions have been taken to minimize the dangers and warnings have been given to the consumer. When this legal concept is applied, it invalidates express disclaimers by holding manufacturers strictly liable for the use of their products.

4. *Contracts of Adhesion*—Defined as a contract drawn up by one party and signed by another. When drawn by a large company and given to an individual, the contract is generally favorable to the large company. As a result, courts have long interpreted such contracts as following the *expectations principle*, defined as interpreting a contract of adhesion to meet the expectations of the individual who did not draw up the contract. In other words, the fine print will not invalidate the main purpose of the agreement. Under the 1950–1980 revisions, express disclaimers in large print were also challengeable in court. The theory was that no consumer was qualified to waive safety features and thus such clauses in contracts of adhesion would not be recognized in the courts.

The result of these modifications to contract law was that contractual arrangements were largely immaterial in torts involving accidents or personal injury. Manufacturers and suppliers of services could be held to strict standards of liability and warnings, disclaimers, or waivers might not be recognized when it came to issues of safety. The final decision would be made after the fact by juries whose verdicts would vary from case to case and jurisdiction to jurisdiction. These changes to tort and contract law were firmly in place in the courtrooms of the 1980s.

Strict Product Liability

A major change in tort law involved the focus of strict liability on the design of the product. It was no longer a question of defects in manufacturing. The product could be delivered exactly as described and fulfill all expectations when used properly. The new focus allowed a jury to consider questions of whether the product could have been designed differently to avoid the accident. If it could, the jury could then find the manufacturer liable for any damages. Several issues did not have to be raised:

1. *Negligence of User*. An accident may be caused largely or partly by the negligence of the user of a product. If the jury determined a design defect, strict liability allowed damages while ignoring user negligence.

2. *Trade-offs Among Safety, Function, and Cost*. Products are always designed by making compromises on safety and cost to achieve specific goals. As an example, heavier cars may be safer but cost more and

consume more fuel. Strict liability allows a jury to ignore conscious trade-offs. If a car is not designed to the maximum safety available in automobiles, the jury could determine that strict liability standards apply in an accident involving the car.

3. *Warning Labels.* Many products carry warning labels. Part of the changing tort system was the inclusion of warning labels in the product design. The warning could be defective. If this was determined to be the case, strict liability for product design could be applied to defects in the label.

Reasonably Foreseeable Consequences

Proximate cause was earlier defined to mean that a person, product, or action must be reasonably linked to the negligence that causes injury or damage. This was the standard prior to the changes to the tort system.

The new standard assumed that most accidents could be seen in advance and avoided. The new standard was *reasonably foreseeable consequences*, defined as the obligation to recognize the possibility of improper use of products or undesirable results of certain actions.

Under this standard, tort lawsuits expanded dramatically. Gun manufacturers could be held liable for the misuse of a gun; a corporation could be held liable for hiring an employee who later did something wrong. The manufacturer or provider of a service could be found negligent by a failure to recognize the possibility of future damage linked indirectly to its product or actions.

Punitive Damages

Punitive damages are dollar awards to a plaintiff as a result of intentional outrageous misconduct by the defendant. They are designed to deter such behavior by punishing wrongdoers. Traditionally, they have been awarded rarely.

The revision to tort law changed the concept entirely. Punitive damages became a way to award large dollar amounts to plaintiffs in pain or who had suffered, whether or not any outrageous conduct occurred. It has even been ruled that such damages can be awarded when the defendant was unaware of the possibility of harm.

Psychic Injuries

Prior to the revision of tort laws, most negligence cases involved physical injuries. The concept of injury has now been expanded to emotional distress. This invites lawsuits alleging damages from a wide range of insults, inconveniences, and annoyances. Bystanders to tragedies can collect damages as a result of the psychological trauma they underwent as witnesses. The concept of psychic injury has greatly increased the number of lawsuits in the courts.

Hypothetical Damages

Still another extension of tort law with respect to time limits involved *hypothetical damages*, defined as the potential for future injury. Prior to the changes, lawsuits were usually filed only after injury had occurred. Afterward, claims could be made in advance of actual damages. Two important developments were:

1. *Enhanced Risk*—Defined as the increased likelihood that a person will incur an injury at a future time as a result of a past action. A person exposed to chemicals is an example. Lawsuits are allowed and damages can be awarded to individuals who had such exposure, even though no injury was yet visible.

2. *Psychological Damage*—An injury that occurs because an individual believes that he or she has been exposed to the possibility of future injury. The fear itself is defined as psychological damage, and a lawsuit can be filed.

Class Action Lawsuits

The term *common question class action* refers to a lawsuit filed on behalf of a group of individuals injured by a common cause. In 1966 rules of procedure in federal courts were amended to allow the filing of such suits. This facilitated the consolidation of damage claims when many individuals were injured by a single action. The final form of this change is that no individual has to allege an injury. A lawyer can file a suit in the name of many people and then contact them to ask if they wish to withdraw from the filing. This procedure is now quite common.

Easier Access to Liability Insurance

An important part of the revision to tort law was to ensure that money, particularly from insurance policies, would be available to pay damages when individuals were injured. A number of changes were made to assure that covered defendants could be named and found liable. In this section, we examine those changes.

Comparative Negligence

We noted earlier that *comparative negligence* means that responsibility for an injury may be apportioned to different parties on the basis of the degree of negligence attributed to each. The rules vary from state to state. As an example of comparative negligence, assume an individual injures himself using a product. The damages are determined to be $100,000 and a jury finds that a defective product was 40 percent of the cause of the accident. The manufacturer would pay damages of $40,000.

This concept allows damages when an individual is the primary cause of his own accident. By arguing that a product or other person's behavior was partly responsible, the plaintiff may be able to collect some damages. If the individual was badly hurt and the other party was insured, juries can award substantial damages.

Group Liability

In many cases, the individual who is the direct cause of an injury may lack sufficient assets to pay the damages from her negligence. Part of the revision of tort law dealt with the degree of liability of defendants. Two expanded concepts are:

1. *Joint and Several Liability*—The right to collect damages from any of the defendants found to be negligent in a lawsuit. This is an old principle of the law that has been extended into new areas as indirect parties are named in lawsuits. Whoever has assets or insurance can be held liable for the full judgment.

2. *Proportional Liability*—The right to collect from parties involved in damages when no one party can be determined to be negligent. If a person is injured by a known chemical sold by an unknown source, all manufacturers of that chemical can be liable in proportion to their share of the market.

Extended Statutes of Limitations

An important revision to tort laws involved new definitions of the time allowed for filing lawsuits. A *statute of limitation* is a law limiting the time period between the commission of an illegal or tortious act and the filing of a lawsuit. The length of such period is determined by two factors:

1. *Is there adequate time to file?* An injured party needs sufficient time to identify the wrong, determine the party responsible for it, calculate the dollar amount of damages, and file the suit.

2. *Is there timely notice to defend?* The defendant needs to know about the lawsuit on a timely basis so evidence can be saved and memories are relatively clear on the circumstances of the action.

The problem with some tort claims is that they have a *long tail*, defined as a lengthy period of time between the injury and its discovery. Chemicals seeping into the ground may take 20 years to cause cancer in an unsuspecting homeowner.

Prior to the revisions, the statute of limitations began when the tortious act occurred. The changing rule involved the concept of *discovery of the injury*, defined as the moment in time when a symptom appears. A state may still have a two-year statute of limitations, but the two-year period does not begin until the symptoms of the injury are noticeable. In effect, this extended concept allows lawsuits many years after the negligence occurs. Any damages remain the responsibility of the organization.

Statistical Cause and Effect

To be liable for negligence, one party must cause an injury and another party must experience it. This involves a relationship of cause and effect. In some cases, this is difficult to prove. As an example, consider a pollution injury. For tort liability, three tests must be met:

1. *Toxicity*. The alleged source must possess a poisonous or otherwise damaging quality that can be transmitted by water, air, or other means.

2. *Exposure*. One or more individuals must be exposed to the alleged source of the injury.

3. *Injury*. One or more individuals must suffer actual injury.

Now assume that chemicals have seeped into the ground and some years later a person is diagnosed with cancer. How can a cause-and-effect relationship be established? The answer is with statistics. If it can be shown that a community experienced a higher incidence of cancer than other communities, the cause-effect relationship can be argued. Allowing such evidence represents an expansion of traditional cause-and-effect linkages.

Shifting the Burden of Proof

In some cases, cause and effect cannot be proved statistically or otherwise. Chemicals are in the ground and an individual who lives nearby has cancer. One of the most dramatic revisions to tort laws produced a shifting burden of proof in cases such as this. Once a damage was alleged with toxicity, exposure, and injury, the burden of proof shifted to the defendant, who must prove that the cause-and-effect relationship did not exist. If no proof exists, damages may be awarded.

The shifting burden of proof was particularly important in cases of alleged product design defects and medical malpractice. The result has been almost a presumption of defective design and negligent medical practice, unless the manufacturer and doctor could prove that no cause-effect relationship existed.

Regulatory Standards and Product Liability

With respect to product liability, the United States has government agencies and regulations. The primary features of the interaction between liability and regulation are:

1. *Violation of regulatory standard is negligence.* The government prescribes standards for many products. Violation of these standards is generally treated as being proof of negligence. This is true even though the manufacturer may not know of the regulation.

2. *Conformity to regulatory standard is not protection against liability.* In the United States, it is not enough to comply with the government regulations. Negligence may still exist. Juries examine the design of the product and may decide that it is defective. Under the changed tort laws, strict liability may apply.

Programs to provide adequate liability protection become difficult when compliance with government regulations is not sufficient to overcome a charge of negligence. If a drug is approved for issue by the appropriate government agency, the manufacturer may still face extensive legal battles and large judgments at a later time.

Abuses of Legal Authority

We have so far covered an expansion of legal concepts that met the social goals of the Founders. Aside from the merits of these expansions, the courts have taken some actions that may be abusive of their powers. In this section, we examine some of the interpretations that undermine the risk manager's efforts to protect the organization against tort claims.

Rewriting Insurance Contracts

One of the major revisions to tort law was essentially a rewriting of insurance contracts after the fact. The most dramatic example occurred in New Jersey with a policy that covered "sudden and accidental" pollution. Although no such pollution occurred, the courts determined that the policy provisions are secondary to the "health, safety and welfare of the people of this State . . ."

The effect of such a ruling is disaster for risk managers. It states, in effect, that contractual arrangements are secondary to social and possibly other causes. When purchasing insurance as part of a comprehensive risk management program, the risk manager faces the prospect that basic contract provisions may later be invalidated by a court. Although this can favor or harm the organization, it adds considerable uncertainty to the process for managing loss exposures.

Multiple Payments From Insurance Companies

The period from 1960 to 1980 showed continuing efforts to ensure that insurance companies were required to pay damages to the maximum extent possible. This was a separate matter from the Founders' goals of paying the cost of accidents and encouraging safety in the society. Two illustrations are:

1. *Triple Trigger*. A *trigger* is an event that activates insurance coverage. Three triggers are possible when a person is exposed to a slow-acting poison such as chemical seepage or asbestos dust. Prior to the 1980s, the period of initial exposure to the dust would be a trigger. In the early 1980s, courts added a second trigger, ruling that the diagnosis of symptoms activates coverage. Shortly thereafter, a third trigger was identified, with a ruling that "exposure in residence" activates coverage. This means that damages could be claimed from all insurance policies in effect from exposure through incubation to diagnosis of damages. A triple trigger thus allows the combining of insurance coverages from different companies at different periods of time. It also means rising insurance premiums since policies must be priced to cover all slow-acting events for the past 30 years.

2. *Collateral Source Rule*. This rule of procedure prohibits informing the jury that an individual has already received money to pay medical and other bills from first-party insurance. Thus a jury may award damages for expenses that have already been covered by other insurance payments. This hits the organization for damages that have already been covered elsewhere in the society.

Impacts on Liability Insurance

The revision to tort laws had a number of impacts in the area of liability protection programs. In this section, we examine these effects.

Nature of Liability Protection

Programs to manage liability exposures must conform to the principles of insurance. The revisions to tort law have produced obstacles to the process, namely:

1. *Law of Large Numbers.* This ability to use statistics to predict occurrences when a large group of events is involved is basically the law of averages. It is the fundamental principle for charging a small premium to offer protection against a large loss. The new tort rules make it difficult to apply historical relationships to liability areas and thus undermine the law of large numbers when determining whether to self-insure or purchase insurance.

2. *Scope of Coverage.* Insurance is provided for specific injuries. Fire insurance does not, for example, cover damage from earthquakes. The amount of the premium is based upon the statistical likelihood of fire, not the higher possibility of either fire or earthquake. The tort revisions have greatly expanded the scope of coverage beyond the pricing of insurance policies. And they have caused uncertainty as to what is covered. This produces an inability to price policies and a reluctance of insurance companies to offer coverage.

3. *Definitions of Perils and Hazards.* The risk manager must identify the perils of the organization and devise ways to reduce hazards. This has become increasingly difficult in the liability area. Perfectly innocent behavior can become a hazard under the relaxed rules and concepts. To some degree, risk managers have thus lost their ability to identify liability hazards and exposures.

Impacts on Insurance Coverage

By the late 1960s, insurance companies realized the changing nature of the market for liability insurance. Since insurance companies pay for large portions of the damages awarded, they had to deal with the uncertainties caused by revisions to the tort laws. Several responses affected liability coverage for individuals and organizations, including:

1. *Increased Premiums.* With higher, more frequent, and unexpected judgments, the companies raised the premiums on most lines of liability insurance. This began in the medical malpractice area in the 1970s and expanded to commercial general liability by the 1980s. These actions produced crises for individuals and organizations because the premium adjustments were large, sudden, and unexpected.

2. *Reduced Coverage.* The companies could not price certain expo-

sures as a result of the uncertainties of the courtroom. A case with major injury might result in no payments other than legal fees, whereas a frivolous claim might produce a multimillion-dollar award. To reduce the exposure from such uncertainty, companies restricted the coverages they offered.

3. *Abandonment of Markets.* In some cases, companies simply withdrew from markets they no longer understood. Some companies no longer would offer automobile insurance; others ceased writing policies in the medical malpractice area. The problems were often compounded by legislatures and regulators, but the real cause of the problems was uncertainty in the area of liability exposure.

Impact on Policy Forms

As part of the changing coverage in the mid-1980s, insurance companies proposed changes to the policy forms. Two kinds of forms are now available:

1. *Occurrence Form*—A policy that obligates the insurance company to cover losses from events that take place during the policy period, even if the claim is made after the policy expired. Prior to 1984, commercial general liability policies were issued using this form.

2. *Claims-Made Form*—A policy that obligates the insurance company to cover only those losses that arise from claims filed during the policy period. In 1984 the Insurance Services Office (ISO) introduced a new form that added the option of providing coverage on a *claims-made* basis.

A major difference between the policy forms involved the "tail" of a policy; that is, the length of time during which an insurance company can expect to receive claims. An occurrence policy has a *long tail*, since claims can be filed many years after the event. A claims-made policy has a *short tail* because coverage applies on the basis of the filing of the claim. If a loss occurs, it is covered by the policy in force when the claim is presented.

The insurer's motivation for the claims-made option can be explained in terms of the changing conditions described above. In all insurance pricing, premiums are based on predicted exposures. Coverages are delineated carefully to ensure that sufficient money is collected to pay subsequent claims. In the liability insurance market, many people felt it was no longer clear that the occurrence form fit this model. Lawsuits were pending on policies issued many years earlier and the courts were making interpretations that far exceeded the original intended coverage of liability policies.

In effect, the claims-made approach passes long-tail risks over to the organization. They become the responsibility of the risk manager, who is less prepared to handle them than the insurance company. If an organization changes from an occurrence to a claims-made form, it immediately faces gaps in coverage.

Changing View of Legal Expenses

Still another development in the liability insurance area is a recognition of the high legal costs involved with claims.

Traditionally, the standard commercial general liability forms have provided coverage for liability losses up to the face value of a policy. Thus a $1 million policy provides $1 million to pay claims. In addition, the insurance company pays the legal costs of defending against a claim.

In the mid-1980s, some insurers sought to change the historical practice. Noting the rise in legal costs in the 1970s and early 1980s, they proposed *defense within limits,* defined as insurance coverage where the face value is the maximum exposure for an insurance company. For a $1 million policy, the insurance company would be obligated to a total payment of $1 million to cover damages and legal costs.

This proposal was a recognition that legal costs had become a substantial portion of the total to be paid when a claim is filed. By incorporating legal costs within the limit of a policy, the insurance company would be reducing its uncertainty with respect to legal expenses.

This, too, has enormous repercussions for the risk manager. Large organizations will retain a portion of liability exposure. They also must retain the high legal costs of defending lawsuits. Frivolous or minor claims commonly involve legal expenses that far exceed any damages that may be awarded.

A Call for Reform

The conclusion to this discussion points in the direction of a need for changes to the current liability exposure situation. Risk managers, regulators, legislators, insurance companies, and others should examine rising liability risks and develop strategies to deal with them. A failure to acknowledge serious exposures is already having consequences for firms and the society. The economic linkage between premiums paid and coverage provided is breaking down with respect to liability insurance coverage. Organizations can afford neither the exposures nor premiums to cover them. As time passes, the likely result will be the failure of businesses and other organizations to cover themselves adequately. Then, legitimate compensation for legitimate losses may not be available.

Commerical Liability Insurance

Because of the large amounts involved, liability insurance is a component of virtually all liability protection programs. In this section, we examine commercial liability insurance.

Three Classes of Insurance Coverage

Liability insurance is divided into three classes:

1. *Automobile Liability.* The organization must cover claims involving vehicles that it owns or uses. These exposures may be covered under the business automobile policies.

2. *Employer Liability.* The organization is responsible for injuries or other losses incurred by employees in the course of their work. These may be covered under workers compensation policies.

3. *General Liability.* The organization faces nonautomobile and non-employee exposures on all sides. These may be covered under commercial general liability policies.

Business Auto Policy

The Business Auto Policy is a standard form under the ISO Commercial Portfolio Program. Some major features of the policy are:

1. *Covered Auto.* The risk manager must be concerned with exposures from vehicles that are owned, leased, used, or otherwise identified with the organization. The standard policy allows wide latitude in selecting categories of vehicles to be covered.

2. *Any Auto.* This is one of the choices of covered auto. Most risk managers seek comprehensive liability coverage, particularly in light of changes in tort law over the past 40 years. Thus they should select this option when purchasing commercial automobile insurance.

3. *Physical Damage.* The Business Auto Policy also provides property damage protection, similar to the Personal Auto Policy.

Workers Compensation Policy

Employers in the United States are basically required to compensate workers for injuries on the job. This is true without regard to fault. That is, even if a worker is negligent and causes his own accident, the employer is liable for the medical and economic consequences of the accident.

A workers compensation policy is the mechanism for meeting the legal responsibilities of the employer toward the work force. Regulations vary by state but most employers are required by law to purchase a policy from either a private or public insurance company. Exceptions may be made in some states for domestic workers, small businesses, or individuals who work occasionally rather than regularly for an employer.

A major feature of workers compensation laws is that the employee loses the right to sue the employer. The worker is indemnified for injury according to the laws of the state. The payments cover medical expenses, rehabilitation benefits, and fixed amounts for partial or total disability. In return for a guaranty of payments, the worker is not allowed to bring suit for pain and suffering or other injuries.

General Liability Exposures

An employer faces a number of exposures that can result in lawsuits alleging negligence that causes injury or property damage. These may be identified:

1. *Premises.* An organization can be sued for accidents that occur in the offices, factories, parking lots, and other facilities that are identified with its name or operations. This is called a premises exposure. An example is a person slipping on an icy sidewalk in front of the building.

2. *Products.* When products are sold, the organization may be held responsible for subsequent accidents resulting from faulty design or defects. This is a product liability exposure. An example is an accident caused by the failure of brakes on a tractor.

3. *Completed Operations.* When services are provided, the organization may be held responsible for future accidents resulting from defective workmanship. This is called a completed operations exposure. An example is the collapse of a wooden deck that injures visitors at a company picnic.

4. *Conduct of Operations.* When employees or representatives are undertaking the organization's day-to-day business, accidents can occur anywhere in the world. The possibility of lawsuits from business activities is a conduct of operations exposure. An example is a person tripping over a temporary electrical cord at a trade fair.

5. *Contracts.* In some cases, organizations agree to be responsible for the actions of others. This is a contractual exposure. An example is a *hold-harmless agreement*, defined as a contract where one party agrees to be responsible for lawsuits against another party. This might be given by a general contractor who hires a subcontractor to perform a task.

6. *Contingencies.* In some cases, organizations will be sued as a result

of the negligence of agents or contractors. This is a contingent exposure. An example is a lawsuit against a contractor for negligent work performed by a subcontractor even though no hold-harmless agreement exists.

Commercial General Liability Policy

The *Commercial General Liability Policy* (CGL) provides an organization's basic coverage for premises, products, and completed operations exposures. It provides a broad coverage for bodily injury and property damage claims. At the same time, it contains a number of exclusions where separate policies would be required. These include:

1. *Employer Responsibilities*—Does not cover claims for bodily injury or damages suffered by employees.

2. *Pollution*—Does not cover injuries, property damage, or clean-up costs from any form of pollution.

3. *Moving Craft*—Does not cover suits arising from the use of automobiles, watercraft, or aircraft.

4. *Owned Property*—Excludes property of the insured.

5. *Custody Property*—Excludes property owned by others but in the care or custody of the insured.

Excess Insurance

Risk managers can provide protection against losses using a variety of means including self-insurance or purchasing insurance. Whatever means is used, it is almost impossible to cover all exposures without insurance. This is true because of the possibility of a catastrophic claim.

Excess insurance affords coverage above the limits provided by underlying risk financing, either primary insurance policies or a self-insured retention. There are several categories of excess insurance, including:

1. *Specific Excess*—Covers insured losses that exceed the underlying policy limit on a per loss, per occurrence, or per claim basis. A company may have automobile liability with a $3 million policy limit and specific excess coverage that covers losses between $3 million and $10 million. An accident with a settlement costing $7 million would be fully covered by the two policies.

2. *Aggregate Excess*—Covers insured losses that exceed a specific dollar amount during a period of time, normally one year. It protects a company against a series of losses that may be individually small but may have a high total cost. This is also known as *stop loss excess insurance*.

3. *Combined Specific/Aggregate Excess*—Covers losses both on a specific and aggregate basis in a single policy.

4. *Umbrella*—A broader policy that applies above a primary coverage. It commonly exists as the first layer above insurance or a self-insured retention. Usually, the coverage begins at a fairly high level of loss.

Characteristics of Excess Insurance

Excess insurance coverages, other than umbrella policies, may be characterized as follows:

1. *Higher Layer.* The underlying risk financing can be viewed as the first layer of protection. Excess insurance can be viewed as a higher layer. For example, a commercial general liability policy provides coverage for a loss up to a limit of $5 million. The excess policy is written to pay for losses between $5 million and $20 million. The CGL policy is the first layer and the excess insurance is the next layer of coverage.

2. *Coverage Follows Form.* The term *to follow form* means that an excess policy contains exactly the same provisions as a lower layer of insurance. To avoid gaps in coverage, the excess policy should begin and end on the same date and define all rights and obligations of the insured and insurer in parallel language. If it follows form, the excess policy provides no broader coverage and no gaps. It just provides a higher limit.

3. *Attachment Point.* Here is the lower limit of the excess insurance coverage. In the example above, the primary CGL policy covers losses below the attachment point of $5 million. The excess policy covers losses above the attachment point.

4. *Property, Liability, or Business Interruption Coverage.* These areas can all have excess insurance coverage above varying structures of underlying risk financing. If the excess coverage has an attachment point based upon aggregate losses in different underlying areas, the insured is said to have a *basket retention*.

Umbrella Insurance

Although a form of excess insurance, umbrella insurance has a number of different characteristics including:

1. *Liability Coverage.* An umbrella policy normally applies only to liability insurance, where the upper limit of loss is problematic. How many lawsuits can be filed following the crash of a jumbo airliner on a crowded city street?

2. *Broader Coverage.* Primary liability insurance covers specific exposures but may have numerous exclusions. An umbrella policy is broader, often covering losses excluded from CGL and other specialized liability coverages. An example occurs with contractual liability, where an insured can be sued over a failure to perform under a legal contract. Primary liability policies are quite restrictive on the contract covered. An umbrella policy can be written to cover all contractual liability (a *blanket coverage*).

3. *Drop-Down Coverage.* Some losses are covered from the first dollar of loss or from some low attachment point. This may be specified for certain liabilities not covered by a primary policy. When an umbrella policy drops down, it in effect is providing primary coverage to an insured.

Issues With Excess Insurance

Several important issues affect the level of protection offered by excess insurance, including:

1. *Gaps in Coverage.* Care must be taken to ensure that the various layers of retention and insurance achieve the organization's goals without gaps in coverage.

2. *Occurrence or Claims-Made Coordination.* The various forms of insurance can be written on an occurrence or claims-made basis. The risk manager must ensure that the various layers are coordinated in order that a loss not be excluded as a result of different forms of insurance policies.

3. *Lack of Uniformity of Excess Contracts.* Because they can achieve so many different goals, excess policies can have a wide variety of clauses and provisions. Considerable time may be needed to ensure that the excess coverage is achieving an organization's goals. Ideally, a comprehensive excess program should follow the form of the primary coverage.

4. *Definitions of Loss.* The term *loss* can have different meanings in different contracts, which can produce disputes when a claim arises. As an example, suppose a large claim involves payment by both a primary and excess insurer. How will the legal fees be divided? The answer depends on how the adjusting expenses are allocated in the contracts. Care must be taken to ensure that both parties define loss in a coordinated manner.

Reinsurance

Reinsurance occurs when an insurance company itself buys insurance to cover a portion or all of the risk it faces under a primary insurance agreement. It is a mechanism that allows insurance companies to achieve a number of goals, including:

1. *Higher Limits.* An insurer may not have the financial strength to accept the full amount of exposure desired by a client. Reinsurance allows the company to write a policy with a high limit and then pass off a portion of the risk to the reinsurer.

2. *Specialized Coverage.* An insurer may not be familiar with the coverage desired by a client. The insurer might get the help of another insurer to assess the risk and then pass on a major portion of it to the second insurer through the mechanism of reinsurance.

3. *Protection Against Catastrophe.* Even though expected losses under a policy are not high, an insurer may have an unlimited liability under the terms of the policy. Some unforeseen catastrophe could exceed the ability of the insurer to cover losses. Reinsurance protects against this possibility.

Reinsurance and Risk Management

Reinsurance plays several roles of interest to a risk manager, including:

1. *Assessment of Primary Insurer Strength.* By knowing the reinsurance practices of the primary insurer, the risk manager can assess whether the insurer follows sound financial strategies. If an insurer does not reinsure in proper amounts and with strong reinsurers, the primary insurer could experience catastrophe problems in the future. Such insurers should be avoided. This is easier said than done in practice. Most brokers do not readily provide specific reinsurance information.

2. *Fronting Insurance.* A risk manager may want or be required to purchase insurance from an admitted insurer who may not be able to handle certain risks. The primary carrier could act as a fronting insurer and reinsure the risk with a company that has the right capabilities. Reinsurance allows such fronting.

3. *Cut-Through Agreement.* An *assumption certificate* is an endorsement to an insurance contract that obligates a reinsurer to assume all obligations of the primary insurer in the event of bankruptcy or other inability to pay claims. The certificate is also known as a *cut-through endorsement.* In effect, such an agreement protects the insured from financial insolvency of the primary insurer.

4. *Captives or Pooling Agreements.* An organization may use a captive or an insurance pooling agreement with other organizations to retain risks. Captives and insurance pools directly purchase reinsurance. A

knowledge of reinsurance allows the captive or pool to make proper retention decisions for its own exposures and thus protects the insured.

Directors and Officers Liability Coverage

A *Directors and Officers and Corporate Reimbursement Policy* (D&O Policy) provides liability coverage to professional managers and others as follows:

1. *Official Capacity.* The coverage applies to actions taken while acting in an official capacity as an officer or director of an organization. It is similar to professional liability insurance purchased by lawyers and accountants.

2. *Wrongful Act.* The coverage is triggered by a claim made against an officer or director alleging a wrongful act committed while functioning in the official capacity.

3. *Varying Terms and Coverage.* D&O policies vary considerably in the coverage provided. A policy may or may not require the insurer to defend against a lawsuit. A loss may be defined to exclude certain items, such as fines, penalties, or punitive damages.

4. *Deductible and Participation.* Most policies contain a relatively small deductible ($5,000–$10,000) and low participation (5 percent) above the deductible.

Specialty Liability Coverages

In addition to the major commercial liability coverages, special policies exist for different purposes. Examples are:

1. *Common Carrier Insurance.* A *common carrier* is a company that transports goods in a scheduled service among designated points. Under the law, the carrier has broad liability for any damage that occurs to the goods entrusted to its care. Special insurance provides liability protection to the carrier.

2. *Bailee Insurance.* A *bailee* is a person or organization that holds the property of another person for a specific purpose. The bailee is responsible for safeguarding the property and returning it in good condition. Special insurance provides liability protection to bailees.

3. *Aviation Insurance.* Special policies are available to aviation companies to pay losses resulting from aircraft crashes or negligent acts of airline companies.

4. *Garage Insurance.* Special policies are available to organizations that sell, repair, service, or store motor vehicles.

Exercises

1. Morris Silver signs an agreement to purchase a car "as is"; that is, with no warranty of performance or safety. As he drives the car home, the brakes fail and he is injured. He sues the seller of the car. Will he collect?

2. Fred Simken and Fenn Putnam are discussing unsafe products. Fred blames consumers; Fenn blames producers. Which position is a premise of the Founders?

3. In the bar, Fred tells Fenn that proximate cause is the most onerous standard possible for linking an act of negligence to a personal injury. Is this true?

4. Four concepts emerge as important to the work of the Founders: (1) implied warranty, (2) express disclaimer, (3) strict liability, and (4) expectations principle. Which concept is the most beneficial to producers of goods?

5. Different juries have returned damage award verdicts using a variety of reasoning techniques. Which of the following are valid?
   a. We award punitive damages to compensate the victim for pain and suffering.
   b. We award general damages for the psychic injuries sustained by the victim.
   c. We award general damages because the plaintiff has suffered psychological damage from witnessing the accident.
   d. We award specific damages because the individual has an enhanced risk of developing cancer at a later time as a result of the exposure to the chemicals.

6. Fenn says to Fred, "I believe in two key principles of tort law—comparative negligence and joint and several liability." Fred replies, "That's stupid. These two concepts are in conflict." Who is right?

7. "Oh yeah?" says Fenn. "Well, I think lawsuits should be filed within 10 days of a personal injury. Otherwise, the statute of limitations should cease suits." Fred replies, "Statutes of limitations serve no purpose at all. They should be eliminated." Who is right?

8. "It seems to me," says Fenn, "that compliance with regulatory standards should protect companies from lawsuits. Failure to comply should be proof of negligence." Fred replies, "I think that is how it is." Is he correct?

9. The indemnity principle is commonly found throughout all insurance contracts and dealings. What are two exceptions in the liability area?

10. What are the three triggers in a triple trigger situation?

11. A lawsuit has been filed against Johnson Industries alleging damages that occurred eight years ago and were recently discovered. The com-

pany believes it had long-tail coverage under its policy at the time and has short-tail coverage under its current policy. Is this correct?

12. A policy states, "We will defend against any lawsuit and pay damages, both to a total of $1 million per occurrence." What kind of liability policy is this?

13. A risk manager has purchased a policy that provides up to $100 million in coverage in the event of a lawsuit alleging personal injury as a result of product defects. The deductible is $10 million. What kind of policy is this?

14. Callie Industries operates a chain of bonded warehouses where goods are safeguarded until claimed by owners. Enterprise Airlines carries high-value goods in regularly scheduled service among 23 cities. It also carries passengers on charter flights. Quick Lube operates a chain of 220 service centers that provide lubrication and oil changes to automobiles and light trucks. What kind of liability coverage might be needed for each company?

17

Workers Compensation

Workers compensation is a system of providing medical, disability, and rehabilitation coverage to employees and their dependents when a worker is injured in connection with a job. Every state has enacted its own system with some major differences. Not all occupations or employees are covered. In some states, negligence can be alleged. In some states, the laws are administered poorly and unevenly.

In this chapter we discuss a number of issues dealing with workers compensation. We begin with the nature of workers compensation and the relationship of the employer to the employee. Then, we examine the categories of benefits covered. Finally, we review the structure of workers compensation in the United States and the problems caused by a myriad of federal and state laws.

Nature of Workers Compensation

Workers compensation is a system of providing medical and disability coverage to employees and their dependents. Health and disability insurance programs must be coordinated with mandatory workers compensation laws and requirements. In this section, we examine the nature of workers compensation as part of the organization's risk management program.

The Beginning of Workers Compensation

The risk manager does not begin a company's program of employer liability after an accident has occurred. Rather, the fundamental role is to view workers compensation as a three-stage process:

1. *Prehire, Preloss.* Before a company hires an employee, it can take steps to reduce the prospect of future injury. New employees should be selected on the basis of safety considerations. If an engineer appears to

be concerned about safety practices during the interview, this is a good sign. If a crane operator has many years of experience without causing injury to fellow employees, this is an indication of safe actions in the future.

2. *Posthire, Preloss.* Individuals should be thoroughly trained in the safety aspects of their jobs and work environment. Dangers should be obvious and safety practices should be stressed. A failure to observe safety rules should not be tolerated at any level of management.

3. *Posthire, Postloss.* In spite of the risk manager's best efforts, accidents happen. The company should implement a rapid response system that starts the process of rehabilitation and handles claims smoothly and properly. The sooner rehabilitation begins, the sooner an employee is returned to a productive role in the organization.

The rest of this chapter builds upon this philosophy of concern for the health and welfare of employees.

Theory of Workers Compensation

Every state administers its own system of workers compensation. Wide variations exist in rules and benefits. However, all systems are based upon a number of principles, including:

1. *No-Fault Benefits.* Workers compensation laws assume that injuries will occur in the workplace and employees should be compensated for medical expenses and loss of income. Fault is not an issue. Neither is negligence on the part of either the employer or employee.

2. *Employer Paid Benefits.* Workers compensation benefits are a cost of doing business. They are the responsibility of the employer and must be covered as an ordinary operational expense.

3. *Limited Benefits.* Workers compensation provides benefits that are limited by law. The amount received varies by state but reflects the salary of the employee, severity of the injury, time period of hospitalization or disability, and other factors. In most cases, the benefits do not fully cover the entire loss of income of the employee.

4. *Final Benefits.* Since negligence is not an issue, no legal recourse is permitted against the employer. Thus workers compensation benefits are final and the employee is barred from suing the employer under most circumstances.

5. *Mandatory Insurance.* The responsibility to make workers compensation payments lies with the employer. To ensure that an employer has sufficient funds to handle claims, state laws require insurance from either

state agencies or private companies. For large employers, self-insurance may be allowed.

Employer's Responsibilities

As a foundation for workers compensation, the law recognizes that an employer has a number of obligations to employees, including:

1. *Safe Workplace.* The employer must provide a reasonably safe place to work and take steps to ensure the absence of unnecessary perils or hazards.

2. *Safe Equipment.* The employer must provide tools, work stations, vehicles, and other equipment that can be safely used by workers.

3. *Sane and Responsible Workers.* The employer must protect employees from the irrational actions of fellow workers.

4. *Safety Rules.* The employer must evaluate the workplace, develop rules to make it safe, and enforce those rules.

5. *Warnings.* Some perils found in a workplace cannot be eliminated entirely. The employer is responsible for identifying these dangers and warning employees to exercise care when exposed to them.

In spite of these obligations to create a safe workplace, accidents occur on the job. Workers compensation systems are designed to handle these situations.

Characteristics of Workers Compensation

States vary in terms of the amount and scope of coverage, but six characteristics are increasingly emerging in workers compensation systems. These are:

1. *Full Coverage of Medical Expenses.* All hospital, medical, surgical, and rehabilitation costs should be paid in full.

2. *Total Period Benefits.* Loss of income payments should be paid for the entire period of disability.

3. *Accident and Occupational Disease Coverage.* The system should cover both workplace accidents and illnesses that arise from the workplace.

4. *Adequate Benefits.* The loss of income payments should be adequate to cover basic bills during the period of disability. This may be expressed as a minimum percentage of the salary, with limits for employees with high salaries.

5. *Dependent Benefits.* The spouse and children of a deceased worker should receive benefits on a periodic basis. A spouse should receive lifetime benefits, unless the spouse remarries. Dependent children benefits should be paid until school is completed.

6. *Coverage of All Workers.* All employees should be covered. This includes farm workers, government workers, and the employees of small firms.

Role of Workers Compensation

Given the above foundation, an organization must incorporate workers compensation laws and requirements into its total health and disability program. The goal is to provide sufficient benefits to meet the needs of employees while avoiding double payments or excessive coverage.

Benefits Covered

Each state and the federal government has its own approach to providing benefits under a system of workers compensation. Some are relatively generous; others are not. In this section we examine the benefits that might be covered under a system of employer liability.

Categories of Benefits

Workers compensation laws generally recognize five categories of benefits:

1. *Medical Expenses*—Cover direct medical costs as a result of a workplace injury.

2. *Death Benefits*—Cover burial costs for a killed worker and survivor's benefits to spouse and dependent children.

3. *Rehabilitation Benefits*—Cover vocational training, therapy, artificial limbs, and other costs involved with returning an employee to the work force as a productive individual.

4. *Temporary Disability Benefits*—Cover loss of income for a worker who is expected to recover and return to the workplace. They cover both total and partial disability.

5. *Permanent Disability Benefits*—Cover loss of income for a worker who is not expected to recover and return to the workplace. They cover both total and partial disability.

Medical Expenses

An injured worker is entitled to payments that cover medical expenses caused by the injury, including medical, surgical, and hospital costs. Some characteristics of this process are:

1. *Providers of Care.* States differ on who may receive payments. All states pay for care rendered by a duly licensed physician or dentist. Others may pay for services performed by a chiropractor or other approved provider.

2. *Selection of Provider.* Some states allow the injured person to choose a doctor and hospital. Others require medical services through physicians provided by the employer.

3. *Level of Payments.* Most states require medical payments without specifying a total dollar limit or without a maximum time period. Some states limit payments either to a time period or total dollar amount.

4. *Nature of Payments.* Most states provide for payments of rehabilitating items. This includes eyeglasses or a glass eye and prosthetic devices such as an artificial leg.

Death Benefit

When an employee dies as a result of a job-related injury or illness, the dependents are entitled to benefits. These vary considerably by state. Some of the benefits are:

1. *Funeral Expenses.* The reasonable value of funeral expenses is paid under workers compensation.

2. *Surviving Spouse.* The surviving spouse will receive compensation in accordance with the state statute. In some states, payments may continue indefinitely until death or remarriage. In other states, the period of time is limited.

3. *Dependent Children.* Any dependent children will receive compensation in accordance with the statute. Benefits are normally paid only until a child reaches a certain age.

4. *Other Beneficiaries.* In some states, other beneficiaries may be entitled to payment in accordance with state law.

Temporary Disability

From a human resources viewpoint, the risk manager is concerned with rehabilitating temporarily disabled workers. This is good business as well as appropriate concern for employees.

Temporary disability may be total or partial. It is total if the injury precludes the employee from doing any work for a limited period of time. In this case, all states require the maximum rate of compensation under the law. Temporary disability is partial when an employee can perform some duties for an employer but cannot work at full capacity. In this case, the individual will receive benefits equal to a portion of the difference between wages currently earned and wages previously earned.

Permanent Total Disability

If an injured person will never be able to return to work, the individual qualifies for permanent total disability. State statutes vary in such a case. Some states require the payment of benefits for the individual's entire lifetime. Others have a limit, in terms of either a time period or a total dollar amount.

Permanent Partial Disability

If an injured person will never fully recover from an injury but will always be partially disabled, the individual qualifies for permanent partial disability. The employee may be able to resume her previous job but may suffer from a lowering of efficiency. The individual may also be limited in terms of competing for other jobs or qualifying for promotion.

Payments for permanent partial disability are difficult to assess. What is the proper compensation for the loss of an eye or a finger? To deal with this problem, most states use two categories of injury:

1. *Scheduled Injury*—Any injury covered specifically under a state's workers compensation schedule. Normally, the law identifies a permanent injury such as the loss of an eye or a finger. The level of disability payments is determined by the specific schedule without regard to how the injury affects the employee's earning capacity. Thus disability payments will follow schedule even though the employee has returned to work.

2. *Nonscheduled Injury*—Not listed on a state's schedule. Benefits are determined differently in each state. Some states require payments based upon an estimated loss of earnings capacity resulting from the injury. The employer and employee work together in some mediation process to determine the appropriate payment. Once the amount is settled and approved by a hearing officer, a lump sum payment is normally paid.

Occupational Disease

Most states identify diseases peculiar to a specific occupation, such as a lung disease that occurs among coal miners. Some states cover all occupational diseases, whereas others cover only those listed under a statute. If an employee contracts a disease that is not covered, he must file a lawsuit in order to obtain benefits.

Laws Affecting Workers Compensation

Workers compensation is largely administered at the state level. At the same time, federal legislation and even a federal system of workers compensation affect the nature of benefits. In this section, we examine the legal framework of workers compensation.

State Statutes

Every state has its own legislation and administrative body responsible for workers compensation activities. Some broad characteristics of workers compensation at the state level are:

1. *Wide Variations in Systems.* Although all systems allow payments without regard to fault or negligence, states vary greatly in their approach to workers compensation. Some states are relatively efficient; others are not. Some states allow negligence lawsuits; some do not. Some states have adequate funding of benefits; some do not.

2. *Uncovered Employees.* A number of occupations and employees are not covered by workers compensation statutes. In some states, farm laborers and domestic employees are examples.

3. *Varying Levels of Compensation.* State statutes differ on the amount of benefits paid to injured workers. Whereas most states cover the bulk of medical expenses, no common standards exist for loss of income payments to disabled workers. States require different percentages of the employee's base salary to be paid. They also require payments for different periods of time. Death benefits for employees killed on the job also vary.

4. *Funding.* State laws approach the issue of funding benefits from different viewpoints. Some states administer workers compensation funds and collect money from covered employers to fund them. Some states require employers to obtain private insurance coverage to guarantee payments to injured workers in accordance with state laws. As an alternative, most states allow employers to self-insure if they meet qualifying standards spelled out in the law and by the state insurance regulatory body.

Federal Workers Compensation Acts

Some workers are covered under workers compensation laws passed by Congress. These include individuals who work in the private or public sector in the maritime industry, civilian employees of the federal government, and other workers under specific circumstances.

Americans With Disabilities Act

In 1992 the Americans With Disabilities Act was enacted by the Congress and signed by President George Bush. The Act prohibits discrimination against disabled individuals. A major goal is to improve the working lives of those who have to overcome obstacles to perform effectively in the work force.

An important goal of the Act is to rehabilitate injured workers and return them to the labor pool as productive employees. As a result, the Act is likely to affect workers compensation in a number of ways. States, particularly those that do not provide significant benefits to rehabilitate injured workers, may be forced to revise their laws.

Third-Party Negligence

Whereas workers compensation laws restrict the rights of the employee with regard to actions against the employer, the restriction does not apply to a third party who causes a work-related injury. An employee may sue a third party for negligence. In some cases, workers compensation laws apply. As an example, the statute may require the filing of the lawsuit within a certain time period as a means of protecting the employer's rights of subrogation. And a portion of the proceeds recovered in a lawsuit may have to be repaid to the party who covered medical or other expenses under the workers compensation statutes.

Overlapping of Laws

Workers compensation laws at the federal and state level are a complex web of obligations and benefits. In some cases, conflicts arise. When an employee is hired and works in one state but is injured while doing a job in another state, the individual can usually make a claim in either state. The same is true if an employee is doing a job that is covered by both state and federal law. In most cases, the employee would make a claim in the jurisdiction that offers the highest level of benefits.

The Future of State Laws

The political pressures that created increased concern for disabled Americans have been operating on state laws for a number of years. Consumer and other reform groups seek more uniform benefits for injured workers as part of a general push for health care benefits for all residents of the United States. In the future, we might expect improvement in those states with weak workers compensation laws, perhaps as a result of federally mandated minimum benefits.

Exercises

1. A worker is injured in a factory that does not follow many of its own safety procedures. He sues for pain and suffering and punitive damages. He also demands his full salary until he returns to work, rather than the 60 percent provided under workers compensation. Can he win his lawsuit?

2. An employer maintains that the company operates a safe work environment and he refuses to purchase workers compensation insurance. He agrees to allow workers to sue for negligence. Is this viable?

3. An individual is injured on the job and incurs $20,000 of hospital bills. His group health plan covers only $15,000 of the bills. He is out of work for 40 days, but the employer only wants to provide loss of income benefits for 36 days. Is the employee out of luck?

4. An employee is killed while working in a factory. She had been living separately from her husband and had filed for divorce. Her husband requests lifetime benefits for himself and the couple's seven-year-old son. Three years after the accident, the man remarries. What is likely to happen with respect to workers compensation benefits?

5. An injured employee returns to work but can no longer perform his previous job. It will cost $22,000 to train him for a similar job at approximately the same annual salary. The company refuses to pay for the training and the employee files a grievance. Is the employee likely to win?

6. An employee suffers a stroke while watching television in his home. He is out of work for three months. He obtains a doctor's certificate indicating that he has fully recovered and is able to perform his job as a teacher in a school. His employer refuses to accept the certificate and tells the employee to report to another physician for an examination prior to resuming his duties. The employee refuses and is fired. He appeals to an arbitrator. Is the employee likely to win?

7. An employee is hired by a company in Wisconsin. She is transferred to a subsidiary in St. Louis. While calling on a customer in East St. Louis, Illinois, she is injured. Which state laws on workers compensation apply in this case?

18

Reinsurance

Reinsurance is widely available as a tool of risk management for corporations and other organizations around the world. An elaborate structure of reinsurance agreements and organizations protects against catastrophic risks. These mechanisms are used by primary insurers and risk managers. To use them effectively, brokers, underwriters, and risk managers must understand the linkages among retention, primary coverage, and reinsurance.

In this chapter, we examine the nature of reinsurance.

Structure

Reinsurance is part of an overall approach to the coverage of pure risk. In this section, we examine the structure of the reinsurance market.

Reinsurance and Risk Transfer

Organizations face large risks that must be transferred via the mechanism of insurance. To ensure that the organization is really covered, the risk manager must know that large exposures are distributed among insurers. Two approaches are commonly used to achieve this goal:

1. *Insurance Exchange*—Refers to a marketplace where multiple insurers can accept portions of a primary risk. The most famous example is Lloyd's of London. With the aid of a broker, an insurance exposure is presented to many underwriters, each of which accepts a portion of the risk. Even very large exposures can be covered if the exchange has enough underwriters with large individual capacities to pay claims.

2. *Reinsurance*—Earlier defined as a contractual arrangement under which an insurer transfers an insurance risk to another insurer. This can be done many times in order to involve numerous insurers with large capacities to pay claims.

Operating Status of Reinsurer

As with the structure for primary insurance, the right of a company to reinsure other policies in any given state is granted under the laws of the state. A number of categories define the operating status of reinsurance companies in the United States, namely:

    1. *Reinsurance Unit of Licensed Insurer.* This unit refers to the reinsurance department or other administrative section of an admitted primary insurance company. Under most state laws, a licensed primary insurer can also participate in reinsurance activities.

    2. *Admitted Professional Reinsurer.* A *professional reinsurer* is an organization whose business is almost exclusively reinsurance and related services. When such an organization obtains a license to operate in a state, it is called an admitted professional reinsurer.

    3. *Reinsurance Pool.* An *insurance pool* refers to an underwriting activity whereby a group of participants agrees to share the risks of writing policies. Generally, each member agrees to accept a fixed percentage share of all profits and losses. When such an agreement is formed to reinsure other risks, it is called a reinsurance pool. The term is synonymous with *reinsurance association* and *reinsurance syndicate*.

    4. *Nonadmitted Authorized Reinsurer.* This reinsurance company has obtained permission to accept reinsurance from licensed primary insurers but itself is not admitted under the state law.

    5. *Nonadmitted Unauthorized Reinsurer.* This reinsurance company has not obtained permission to accept reinsurance from licensed primary insurers. A licensed company is restricted by financial and other regulations as to the amount of business that can be conducted with unauthorized reinsurers.

    6. *Lloyd's of London.* The largest reinsurance market in the world, Lloyd's is a licensed insurer in two states but is authorized to conduct reinsurance business in all states.

Reinsurance Intermediaries

Reinsurance can be placed through a number of channels, including:

    1. *Direct Marketing*—An arrangement whereby the insurer and reinsurer agree to underwrite risks. The arrangements are made by employees of each company.

    2. *Reinsurance Broker*—An individual who arranges for the purchase of reinsurance by a primary insurer. The broker works for the primary

insurance company that is the buyer of reinsurance and seeks the best possible price and terms for the reinsurance agreement.

3. *Reinsurance Management Company*—An agent of the reinsurer who performs marketing and service functions. Also known as a *managing general agent* (MGA), this individual works for one or more insurance or reinsurance companies.

4. *Reinsurance Agent*—An individual who represents the reinsurer in dealings with primary insurers. The agent works for a single reinsurer.

5. *Lloyd's Broker*—An individual authorized to place business with a syndicate of Lloyd's of London. Only a Lloyd's broker can place insurance or reinsurance business at Lloyd's.

Reinsurance Fronting

Fronting may be defined as an arrangement whereby an insurer issues a policy with the knowledge that it will substantially reinsure the risk with a reinsurer selected by the insured. An important aspect of managing risk using reinsurance involves the nature of fronting. This topic is covered in this section.

Seeking Coverage From an Unlicensed Insurer

In some cases, state laws may require an organization to purchase certain types of insurance only from licensed insurers. The same situation exists outside the United States. At the same time, the risk manager would prefer to acquire the coverage from an unlicensed insurance company. This may happen for many reasons, including:

1. *Low Rates.* Unlicensed insurers may offer more competitive rates on the coverage.

2. *Superior Terms.* The terms and conditions of policies offered by nonadmitted insurers may be more desirable than those found in policies offered by admitted insurers.

3. *Better Service.* An unlicensed insurer may be a specialist in the line of insurance desired. As such, it may offer services and capabilities not available from licensed insurers.

Fronting may be used to place a risk with an unlicensed insurer without violating state or government laws. The insurance is initially placed with a licensed company and then immediately reinsured with an authorized but unlicensed company.

Seeking Coverage From Unlicensed Captive

A large organization may have many subsidiaries located in a number of states and countries. Its captive may not be licensed in the domiciles of the subsidiaries. If state or government laws require insurance to be place with a licensed company, fronting allows such placement simultaneously with immediate reinsuring using the parent's captive.

Seeking Local Services

A licensed company may know the local laws and regulations involving the providing of insurance and processing of claims. It also may have a service and support staff to investigate losses, provide loss control services, and facilitate insurance coverage. At the same time, a risk manager may wish to place coverage with a captive or unlicensed insurer lacking these capabilities. Fronting allows the acquisition of local services while passing the coverage through to a captive or unlicensed insurance company.

Maintaining Worldwide Relationships

Some organizations use a single insurance company to provide global coverage in a coordinated master program of risk management. However, local laws or needs for services may require coverages to be placed with licensed insurers. Fronting allows such placement while passing through the risk to the company that provides the worldwide master coverage.

Covering Hard-to-Place Risks

Some exposures are difficult to cover with insurance. Only highly skilled underwriters are willing to assess the likelihood of loss and write policies to cover the risk. These specialty insurers may not be licensed in the country or state of the exposure. Fronting allows local coverage and servicing with backup expertise for hard-to-place exposures.

Cash Flows in Reinsurance Structure

Organizations, primary insurers, and reinsurers exchange cash on the basis of the net interactions among their various business transactions. In this section, we cover the structure of cash flows.

Net Cash Flow

The financial dealings among corporate policyholders, primary insurance companies, and reinsurers involve both cash flows and accounting entries. *Net cash flow* is the difference owed by one party to another. It is determined as follows:

1. *Premiums Due.* A policyholder will owe premiums to its insurance company. The primary insurer will owe premiums to the reinsurer.

2. *Payments Due for Claims.* A reinsurer will owe cash to the primary insurer as a result of claims filed by the policyholder. The primary insurer will owe cash to the policyholder for the same reason.

3. *Net Cash Flow.* The difference between money owed as premiums and money owed for claims must be periodically exchanged in the form of cash. This represents the net cash flow between the two parties.

Net Cash Flow, Policyholder, Insurer, Reinsurer

Figure 18-1 shows the gross cash flows due each party in the reinsurance arrangement and the net cash flow that will occur to settle the balances. In the figure, the policyholder owes $1.7 million in premiums to the primary insurer at a time when the insurer owes the policyholder $2 million to settle claims. The primary insurer has agreed to forward $1.4 million to the reinsurer who owes $1.5 million for coverage on the $2 million in claims. The net cash flow from the reinsurer to the insurer is $100,000. The insurer adds $200,000 to the amount and pays the policyholder.

The cash flow situation is identical with a captive. The policyholder is replaced by the parent and the captive replaces the primary insurer in the diagram.

The diagram would become more complicated if a fronting insurer is used as well as a captive. In this situation, the premiums would flow from the parent to the fronting insurer to the captive to the reinsurer. For payments made against claims, the cash flows in the reverse direction.

Exercises

1. Three companies incorporated in Texas sell reinsurance in Florida. The Southern Reinsurance Company participates in a separate Florida corporation with three other reinsurers who share all risks equally. The Western Reinsurance Company reinsures contracts but only through fronting

Figure 18-1.   Cash flows, policyholder, primary insurer, and reinsurer.

Premium Cash Flows, Period One
Amount Due: $1,700,000

Policyholder
    ↓ $1,700,000
                              $300,000
Primary Insurer —————————————————→ Investments
    ↓ $1,400,000
                            $1,400,000
Reinsurer   —————————————————→ Investments

Claims Cash Flows, Period One
Amount Owed: $2,000,000

                            $1,500,000
Reinsurer   ←—————————————————— Investments
    ↓ $1,500,000
                            $500,000
Primary Insurer ←—————————————————— Investments
    ↓ $2,000,000
Policyholder

Net Cash Flow	Policyholder	Primary Insurer	Reinsurer
Owed:	$2,000,000	$3,200,000	$1,400,000
Owes:	–1,700,000	–3,400,000	–1,500,000
Net Cash Flow:	300,000	–200,000	–100,000

     insurers. The Central Insurance Company has a reinsurance department that sells directly to primary insurers. A fourth company, Oslo Reinsurance Company, also sells directly, even though it is incorporated in Norway. Lloyd's of London also sells reinsurance directly. For each organization, indicate the category of reinsurer from the point of view of the Florida commissioner of insurance.

2. Oklahoma Re sells reinsurance through Raymond and Raymond, a private company whose best-known client is General Machinery Products. Nebraska Re sells through Smith and Smith, a private company whose best-known client is Illinois Re. Colorado Re sells through Chen and Chen, a private company whose only client is Colorado Re. Iowa Re sells reinsurance directly to primary insurers. Lloyd's of London Syndicate #301 sells reinsurance only for marine risks. Identify the reinsurance intermediary, if any, for each organization.

3. An underwriter states that the only factor that should be involved in selecting a reinsurance company is the cost of premiums. Is this correct?

4. Hart Industries owes premiums of $12 million to Standard Insurers. Standard will reinsure $2.5 million of the premiums with Kentucky Re. Standard owes Hart payments on claims of $10 million, of which $1.3 million is the obligation of Kentucky Re. What are the net cash flows in this situation?

19

Global Insurance and Risk Management

Insurance and risk management services are increasingly being provided in a worldwide context. Events during the 1980s broke down many of the barriers that separated nations. The political occurrences were accompanied by a changing approach to commercial activities that are undertaken by large organizations with operations in different countries and small businesses that participate in international trade. As might be expected, the new realities have affected approaches to covering risks in national and international markets.

In this chapter, we examine the providing of insurance in international markets. We also discuss the nature of risk management as it crosses international boundaries.

Managing International Risks

World trade and capital investments across national borders must be accompanied by efforts to understand and manage the exposures that result from the manufacture and sale of goods and the providing of services. The management of risks in an international dimension builds upon the basic principles of insurance and risk management. Allowances are necessary to reflect the diversity and complexity of activities in different national markets.

Another difference with international insurance reflects the range of exposures facing organizations in various areas of the world. Calcutta or Hong Kong are simply not identical to London or Tokyo or New York. Local conditions must be considered in any effort to understand a market for insurance or environment for managing risks.

As a result of national differences, a selection process is necessary when studying international insurance and risk management. From the point of view of the insurance business, not all markets are equally interesting to underwriting companies or brokers. From the point of view of the risk manager, some areas of the world involve greater exposures than others. Decisions on whether to enter markets as a provider of insurance or risk management services hinge on local circumstances and opportunities. Decisions on whether to establish a manufacturing or other subsidiary in a country should be made in the light of risks and exposures.

National Markets

Insurance markets are different. Many of them are isolated by governmental policies and local business practices. Others are relatively open to participation by various insurers and brokers from other nations.

A national insurance market can be studied as an individual entity. In this context, we can identify more than 160 national markets. In doing so, we quickly realize that some markets are more interesting to study than others. This is true for several reasons:

1. *Size of the Market.* Some countries have large and well-developed insurance industries. An industry with a wide range of products and risk management services tends to be more interesting than a small stagnant market.

2. *Economic Level.* Some countries have extensive commercial sectors with many interactions with the world. A high level of economic activity brings with it risks to be managed. Insurance will commonly prosper under such circumstances.

3. *Regulatory Climate.* Some countries have minimal regulation for insurers and brokers. Others are highly regulated with few opportunities for innovation or growth. Still others exclude foreign participation, either directly or through a variety of nontariff or foreign exchange barriers.

4. *Role of the Private Sector.* In many countries, insurance activities are the exclusive domain of the government. This is true for health care and retirement insurance in many nations. It is even true for property and casualty insurance in some countries. If private participation is not extensive in the insurance sector, the country tends to be of limited interest internationally.

Insurance vs. Risk Management

Before beginning a study of international insurance, we should note that international risk management involves a different focus. When the underwriter or broker thinks of foreign markets, the emphasis is on the opportunity to participate as a provider of coverage or risk management services. The focus tends to be on products, providers, and business opportunities.

The situation is different for the risk manager of a multinational company or organization, a partner in a joint venture, or an export/import company. The emphasis for this individual is on the risk of doing business across national boundaries. What are the exposures in the national market? How can they be covered? What are the risks when products or services are provided in other jurisdictions? What are the coverages and, even more importantly, the gaps in coverage as the firm conducts its business?

When we study national markets, we must take the viewpoint of the underwriter or broker. When we study risk management, the risk manager viewpoint should be used.

Context of International Insurance

Insurance in foreign markets can be understood only in economic, political, legal, and cultural contexts, as follows:

1. *Level of Economic Activity*. The level of activity determines the size of the actual and potential market for insurance products or claims and risk management services. In a large market, many opportunities may exist to design and sell various coverages and services. In a small market, limited business may be possible.

2. *Structure of the Economic System*. Nations have different approaches to managing their economies. Some economies are centrally planned with a large bureaucracy providing the planning for state corporations. Some are true market economies with an active private sector and limited government participation. Some are a mixture. Business opportunities, including the ease of market entry, vary considerably with the degree of government control over an economic system.

3. *Political System*. Some countries are representative democracies. Others are characterized by varying degrees of control exercised by individuals, families, or political alliances. Insurance is affected to one degree or another by the way business is done in a country. The local political structure, both visible and behind the scenes, must be understood in order to assess the opportunities and obstacles in a market.

4. *Legal System*. Nations have a wide range of approaches to creating and enforcing personal and commercial relations. The differences are reflected in the laws regulating contracts, torts, and business dealings between individuals and organizations. Differences also exist in dispute resolution. The legal system determines the business and financial risks

of operating in a country. How may insurance contracts be written? How will they be interpreted? What mechanisms exist to settle claims? Reasonable answers to these questions are determined by the existence of reliable and fair laws and dispute resolution systems.

5. *Culture.* The ideas, customs, skills, and arts of a nation are the components of its culture. The national culture affects the insurance market by determining business practices. Will local ethnic groups deal only with other members of their group? Are contracts between strangers acceptable or must all business be done with old friends? Are business dealings completed in an environment of honesty and trust? Local customs must be recognized in any business venture.

Classification of World Markets

The world's 160 or so countries are not equally interesting in terms of their insurance markets. The World Bank classifies countries by income. This is a useful start to studying domestic insurance activities. The categories are:

1. *Organization for Economic Cooperation and Development* (OECD)— Consists of about 25 high-income member countries. A few are more accurately classified as middle income. Essentially, they are developed industrial nations with market economies. They work together through the OECD to coordinate economic policies and activities. They tend to have large and highly developed markets for insurance and risk management services.

2. *Asia Pacific*—Consists of 10 or more middle-income countries grouped regionally along the Pacific Ocean coast of Asia. A few of the countries are low- to middle-income. These nations are characterized by market economies that have both an industrial and agricultural component. Insurance and risk management activities in this area of the world experienced dramatic growth during the 1980s and early 1990s. Such growth is expected to continue in the future.

3. *Latin America*—Consists of about 25 middle- and low-to-middle-income countries geographically located on or near the continent of South America. These countries tend to have market economies with mixed industrial and agricultural sectors. This area of the world is generally characterized by unstable insurance markets and limited linkages to the international insurance market. The various markets also suffer from difficulties in establishing life and casualty markets and processing claims.

4. *Africa and Middle East*—Consists of about 25 geographically

grouped countries. Few similarities exist with respect to their economies or political systems. They include wealthy, oil-producing monarchies and poor democracies and socialist nations. They also vary greatly with respect to customs, religion, and economic structures. Insurance and risk management services vary in this area of the world, ranging from fairly sophisticated activities to a complete absence of insurance availability.

5. *Asian Planned Economies*—Consists of seven or more low-income countries with directed or planned economies. China dominates the category. These countries offer varying opportunities for the conduct of business and trade or other dealings with other nations. Insurance returned to China in 1979 and considerable development has occurred in the national market. The other countries tend to have minimal activity.

6. *Eastern Europe and the Former U.S.S.R.*—Consists of middle-income countries with changing political systems and generally serious economic problems. In this grouping, the term *middle income* covers a wide range of agricultural and industrial systems. Some of the nations are moving rapidly toward market economies. Some may take decades to overcome poor centrally planned economic, political, and legal systems. The countries of Eastern Europe and the nations that were formerly part of the U.S.S.R. represent a large question mark for insurance and risk management.

Largest Insurance Markets

The largest insurance markets in the world can be identified in terms of the volume of insurance premiums. At the same time, population does not necessarily correlate with the size of the insurance market. This is shown in Figure 19-1 where only three of the world's 10 largest countries also rank among the 10 largest insurance markets.

The world's largest insurance markets account for a high percentage of global insurance activity. The 10 largest nonlife markets accounted for almost 90 percent of the world's nonlife insurance activity in 1988. Life insurance is also highly concentrated, with the 10 largest national markets also accounting for almost 90 percent of the world's life insurance activity. These percentages are shown in Figure 19-2.

Health Care Insurance

Consumer spending is a useful indication of the potential for life, health, and personal lines of insurance. Countries with a higher disposable income are generally stronger candidates for insurance products.

The potential for health care markets must be interpreted in terms

Figure 19-1.   Ten largest countries in the world by population and rank of country in terms of insurance premiums.

Country	Population (millions)	Rank Population	Rank Total Premiums
China	1,150	1	
India	820	2	
U.S.S.R.	300	3	6
United States	260	4	1
Indonesia	190	5	
Brazil	160	6	
Japan	130	7	2
Pakistan	120	8	
Nigeria	120	9	
Bangladesh	120	10	

of national health care systems. In some countries, health care is funded by the state indirectly. Although ultimately paid for by individuals, the market is closed to private insurance providers. In other countries, the state funds health care directly. It may be financed by taxes. In still other countries, employers fund health care for large portions of the population. Private insurers may or may not be part of the system.

The relationship of per capita spending and health care paid for by individuals gives an indication of the opportunity for providing health care services. This indication cannot be used without understanding the national system. As an example, health care in Great Britain is largely free at the point of use. By contrast, much of health care expenditures in France are made by individuals and then reimbursed by the government.

Statistics or other figures that compare the percentage of consumer spending that is paid for health care may misrepresent the actual opportunities in a system. A large percentage may indicate a mature market that is already tied up. A small percentage may reflect a frustrated demand that could be freed with the right products and services. At the same time, statistics may be instructive. Figure 19-3 shows the relationship between per capita disposable income and per capita health care spending in selected national markets.

Cost of Living and Market Entry

The cost of living index can be used as an indication of the expenses involved in establishing an insurance operation in a national market. Essentially, a high cost of living may require a costly effort to set up a

Figure 19-2.   Ten largest insurance markets by premiums.

Country	Percentage of World's Premiums	Rank in World
Nonlife Markets		
United States	46.0%	1
Japan	12.0	2
Germany	8.6	3
France	5.5	4
Great Britain	4.5	5
Italy	3.0	6
U.S.S.R.	2.6	7
Canada	2.3	8
Holland	1.6	9
Switzerland	1.3	10
TOTAL	87.3%	
Life Markets		
Japan	32.7%	1
United States	30.3	2
Great Britain	7.4	3
Germany	6.7	4
France	3.9	5
U.S.S.R.	2.9	6
Canada	2.0	7
Switzerland	1.6	8
Holland	1.3	9
Italy	.8	10
TOTAL	89.6%	

business. A low cost of living may allow a small commitment of funds to set up an operation.

The cost of living may point to the form of entry in a market. As an example, licensing or a local partnership venture is usually less costly than establishing a branch office. The local partner already has absorbed the costs of operating in a market. For high-cost markets, such arrangements reduce risks. This is less important in countries where start-up costs are lower.

The cost of living indices in selected countries are shown in Figure 19-4.

Life Expectancy and Insurance Opportunities

Life expectancy is a useful indication of insurance opportunities. Life expectancy statistics reflect opportunities in health care, retirement an-

Figure 19-3. Consumer spending and health care spending, per capita, in selected countries (1990).

Country	Per Capita Annual Disposable Income (in dollars)	Per Capita Health Care Expenditures (in dollars)	Health Care as Percentage of Disposable Income
United States	12,500	1,838	15%
Japan	12,000	1,272	11
European Community			
Germany	10,100	325	3
France	9,800	863	9
Great Britain	7,600	100	1
Italy	8,200	500	6
Holland	9,100	1,120	12
Portugal	2,000	94	5
Pacific Rim			
China	225	5	2
Hong Kong	5,200	350	7
Taiwan	2,900	160	6
Singapore	3,200	141	4
South Korea	1,500	70	5
Eastern Europe/USSR			
Russia	3,000	80	3
Czechoslovakia	5,100	280	6
Poland	1,000	90	9
Yugoslavia	600	22	4
Other			
India	220	4	2
Indonesia	360	NA	
Pakistan	300	10	3
Bangladesh	135	3	2
Nigeria	630	NA	
Brazil	1,600	83	5
Canada	9,500	405	4
Switzerland	15,700	1,700	11%

Figure 19-4. Cost of living indices in selected countries—typical urban prices for an international executive and family (1990).

United States	100*	*Eastern Europe/USSR*	
Japan	186		
		Russia	115
		Czechoslovakia	NA
European Community		Poland	NA
		Yugoslavia	50
Germany	108		
France	111		
Great Britain	104	*Other*	
Italy	109		
Holland	95	India	53
Portugal	76	Indonesia	82
		Pakistan	54
		Bangladesh	73
Pacific Rim		Nigeria	53
China	106	Brazil	42
Hong Kong	89	Canada	102
Taiwan	145	Switzerland	116
Singapore	92		
South Korea	110		

*New York City = 100.

nuities, and other insurance and financial services products. This is true because products can be designed to meet the needs of older residents of a country.

Figure 19-5 shows life expectancy statistics for selected countries.

Economic Activity and Insurance Opportunities

Opportunities for insurance in a national market tend to be closely linked to the level of economic activity. As noted, the world's 10 largest insurance markets account for close to 90 percent of the world's insurance premiums. Yet, they only account for 73 percent of gross domestic product, as shown in Figure 19-6. We might conclude that insurance is more concentrated in industrialized nations than is economic activity. That is, potential opportunities for insurance grow with industrial development.

Admitted Insurers

Insurance coverage may be provided from admitted or nonadmitted insurance companies in national markets. *Admitted insurance* refers to coverage provided by insurance companies authorized to conduct busi-

Figure 19-5. Life expectancy in selected countries (1990).

	Male	Female
United States	72	79
Japan	75	81
European Community		
France	72	80
Great Britain	72	78
Italy	72	79
Holland	74	80
Portugal	70	77
Pacific Rim		
China	68	71
Hong Kong	73	79
Taiwan	NA	NA
Singapore	70	76
South Korea	66	73
Eastern Europe/USSR		
Russia	65	74
Czechoslovakia	68	75
Poland	68	76
Other		
India	58	58
Indonesia	55	57
Pakistan	57	57
Bangladesh	51	50
Nigeria	49	52
Brazil	62	68
Canada	73	80
Switzerland	74	80

ness in a country. Compulsory coverages normally must be placed with admitted insurers. Some common examples are workers compensation and automobile liability.

We can identify some advantages to covering noncompulsory risks with admitted insurance, including:

1. *Legal Requirements.* In some countries, admitted insurance is the

Figure 19-6. Comparison of gross domestic product and insurance activities, percentage of world market, for 10 largest insurance markets (1990).

	World's Gross Domestic Product	World's Nonlife Market	World's Life Market
United States	27.3%	46.0%	30.3%
Japan	16.0	12.0	32.7
Germany	6.8	8.6	6.7
France	5.3	5.5	3.9
United Kingdom	4.6	4.5	7.4
Italy	4.6	3.0	0.8
U.S.S.R.	3.3	2.6	2.9
Canada	2.7	2.3	2.0
Holland	1.3	1.6	1.3
Switzerland	1.0	1.3	1.6
Other	27.1	12.6	10.4
TOTAL	100.0%	100.0%	100.0%

only coverage that is allowed. Penalties can exist for purchasing insurance with nonadmitted insurers.

2. *Payment in Local Currency.* Insurance premiums can be paid using the country's own currency. If coverage is provided by a foreign insurer, payment may be required in another currency.

3. *Claims Settlement.* When a loss occurs under a policy, the claim must be settled in the local country. An admitted insurer has operations and claims adjusters to investigate claims and settle them.

4. *Tax Considerations.* Local laws may allow premiums to admitted insurers to be deducted as a tax expense. Premiums to nonadmitted insurance companies may not qualify.

Nonadmitted Insurers

Nonadmitted insurance refers to coverage provided by companies that are not licensed to conduct business in a market. Many countries allow nonadmitted coverage for some or all of the noncompulsory risks facing an individual or organization. A number of advantages are possible with nonadmitted insurance:

1. *English-Language Policies.* Nonadmitted polices may be written in English where insurance terms are highly developed and widely understood in terms of their meaning. This can facilitate the identification of needs, understanding the gaps in coverages, and resolving claims.

2. *Part of Comprehensive Coverage.* A multinational company can work with a broker or insurer to design a comprehensive package of retentions and insurance. A policy placed with the primary insurer of the parent company can coordinate coverages, premium payments, and retentions on a worldwide basis. This may be possible only by including nonadmitted carriers.

3. *Cost.* Some countries have regulated insurance with high premium rates that exceed actuarial requirements. Insurance placed with nonadmitted insurers can meet the local requirements and give an offset on rates in lower-tariff countries. As an example, suppose a premium should be $100,000 in country A, but local regulations require a rate of $120,000. An insurer can reduce the premium by $20,000 for coverage on a company's operations in another country where rates are not regulated.

4. *Economies of Scale.* Separately from the tariff issue, a coordinated worldwide plan may produce economies of scale that result in lower premiums.

5. *Competitive Pressures.* Nonadmitted insurers face competition on a global basis. They may have more attractive rates or coverages than are found in a protected local market.

6. *Tax Considerations.* Insurance premiums are often subject to the equivalent of a sales tax in different countries. The rate can vary from 2 percent to more than 30 percent. Thus insurance coverage is more costly in some countries than in others. Nonadmitted policies may allow a company to avoid high taxes.

Varied Coverages in Different Markets

Insurance policy provisions may vary widely in different national markets.

1. Coverages will not be identical from one country to another. Time and money must be expended to determine what is covered and whether gaps exist.

2. Policies will normally be written in the local language. The meanings of words may not be explicit. Local customs may affect the interpretation of a policy. This, too, can create questions as to the nature of the coverage.

3. The duties required of the insured under policies will differ from country to country. In order for coverage to be effective, it is essential that the insured perform all duties prior to and following a loss. This requires an understanding of local policy provisions and their meanings.

Employee Benefits

Employee benefits pose a number of issues in different countries.

1. Certain benefits may be required by local laws or administrative regulations. Thus each foreign operation must have a customized approach to employee benefits.

2. Certain benefits may be desirable as a result of local customs. If workers expect certain benefits, the failure to provide them may harm morale or the effectiveness of operations.

3. Certain benefits may be provided by the local social insurance systems. A company must compare local benefits with those offered to its employees in other countries. Then, decisions are needed either to withhold local benefits or integrate them with added benefits that the company wishes to provide to all employees worldwide.

Exercises

1. Select a country and prepare a report on its insurance market as follows:
   a. Structure of the market, including the role of public and private providers of insurance coverage
   b. Availability of life insurance and annuity products
   c. Characteristics of the property and liability market
   d. Opportunities for entry by foreign underwriters and brokers into the market
2. Interview a risk manager of a multinational corporation and ask how the company handles one of the following areas in a worldwide context:
   a. Health care benefits
   b. Risks affecting property
   c. Liabilities exposures
   d. Loss control

Glossary

accidental bodily injury   A broad definition of disability where a person is injured, whether by accident or otherwise.

actual cash value of the loss   The replacement cost minus depreciation on the damaged portion of the house.

actuary   A mathematician trained in probability theory, calculus, and other areas of mathematics and who determines the rates for insurance coverage.

adjusting   The process of investigating an alleged loss and determining whether a claim should be paid.

admitted insurer   An insurance company that is licensed to do business in a state. In some cases, a state law may require companies to take out insurance only with an admitted insurer.

aggregate excess insurance   A form of excess insurance that covers insured losses that exceed a specific dollar amount during a period of time, normally one year. It protects a company against a series of losses that may be individually small but may have a high total cost. Also known as **stop loss excess insurance.**

agreed value option   A provision in an insurance policy that suspends the coinsurance provision for a specified period of time. It is useful when insurance is carried near the 80 or 90 percent minimum for coinsurance. It ensures that a rapid rise in property value or replacement cost will not reduce the payment for a loss.

all-risk agreement   An insurance policy that covers all losses to property except for losses that are specifically excluded.

Americans With Disabilities Act   A 1992 federal law that prohibits discrimination against disabled individuals.

annuity contract   An agreement that provides for a periodic payment to be paid over a period of time and/or for the duration of a life or lives.

assignment clause   A provision in an insurance policy allowing an assignment, or the transfer of contract rights, to another party.

association   An underwriting activity whereby a group of participants agrees to share the risks of writing policies. Generally, each member agrees to accept a fixed percentage share of all profits and losses. Also called an **insurance association, insurance pool,** or **insurance syndicate.**

association captive   An insurance company that provides coverage to a group of companies, frequently in the same line of business.

assumption certificate   An endorsement to an insurance contract that obligates a reinsurer to assume all obligations of the primary insurer in the event of bankruptcy or other inability to pay claims. Also called a **cut-through endorsement.**

attachment point   The lower limit of the excess insurance coverage.

basic premium   The portion of a premium that reflects expenses and profit but not losses and adjusting expenses. It is used in paid retrospectively rated plans.

beneficiary   The individual who will receive the death benefit under a life insurance policy when it is paid.

bid bond   A guaranty that a bidder for contract work will accept the contract and perform the work if the bid is accepted.

blanket coverage   A single insurance amount to cover multiple units of property. It differs from specific coverage, where a stated policy limit applies to an individual property. It is also a situation where an umbrella policy is written to cover all contractual liability.

blanket floater   An inland marine policy that covers a group of articles that are not identified individually but have a relatively large cumulative value. Examples are policies to cover stamp or coin collections, livestock, or salesperson's samples.

bodily injury by accidental means   A narrow definition of disability where an accident must occur and be the source of the injury.

boiler and machinery insurance   A specialized insurance policy covering such items as refrigeration units, engines, motors, pressurized systems, and other machinery. The risks in these areas are generally excluded from other commercial property policies because engineering and technical knowledge is needed to assess risks, reduce exposures, and design insurance.

broad captive   An insurance company that was created to provide insurance for a parent but that will also offer coverage to other companies.

broker   A person who arranges for the purchase of insurance by a customer. Brokers are commonly involved in purchasing insurance for large companies or where specialized knowledge is needed by the insured. The broker works for the buyer of insurance.

builder's risk form   A standardized property form designed for a building under construction, where the value changes each day as improvements are added. Coverage is written for the completed value of the building, with a premium set just above 50 percent of the amount that would be charged for the completed value. The coverage terminates when the building is completed and occupied.

building and personal property coverage form   A standardized ISO business coverage form similar to the homeowners policy for individuals.

building ordinance endorsement   A provision attached to an insurance policy that provides additional payments if local building codes increase the cost of repairing or replacing a building after a loss.

Business Auto Policy   A standard ISO form that provides commercial automobile insurance.

business floater policies   Forms of inland marine policies that cover mobile business property. They include a variety of owned goods as well as goods held on consignment.

business interruption insurance An insurance policy that provides funds to meet continuing expenses and replace a portion of the lost income following a property loss. It is designed to assist the organization in meeting its obligations while the property is being repaired.

businessowners policy A package policy that covers property and liability exposures for small businesses in a coordinated single program of insurance.

captive insurer An insurance company owned by another organization primarily to provide insurance coverage for the owning entity. In effect, it involves the creation of a wholly owned subsidiary to provide self-insurance for a parent.

cargo insurance Ocean marine insurance that covers damage or loss to the cargo being transported on a vessel.

casualty insurance A term that has developed historically and is defined by exclusion. It refers to insurance against losses or liabilities arising from accidents or mishaps that are not defined by law or custom as noncasualty lines.

cause of loss form A standardized form in the ISO Commercial Portfolio Program that deals with the cause of a loss. Four forms are the basic, broad, special, and earthquake forms.

claim A statement that a loss has occurred and a demand for the payment of benefits under an insurance policy.

claims-made form A liability insurance policy that obligates the insurance company to cover only those losses that arise from claims filed during the policy period.

class action lawsuit A court action filed on behalf of a group of individuals injured by a common cause.

class rating Applying a single rate to all applicants possessing a given set of characteristics. It is generally based on historical loss data and is the most common method of establishing the price of insurance products.

coinsurance clause A provision in an insurance policy whereby the insured is required to maintain insurance equal to some percentage of the replacement cost or actual cash value of the property, normally, at least 80 percent. Failure to maintain the percentage will lower the benefit if a loss occurs.

collateral source rule Under the law, a rule of procedure that prohibits informing the jury that an individual has already received money to pay medical and other bills from first-party insurance. Thus a jury may award damages for expenses that have already been covered by other insurance payments.

commercial general liability (CGL) insurance Covers an organization from exposures that can result in lawsuits alleging negligence that causes injury or property damage as a result of its premises, products, or completed operations. It provides a broad coverage but contains a number of exclusions requiring policies.

commercial lines A category of insurance purchased by businesses and other organizations to cover exposures faced by employers, companies, other private institutions, and governments. Commercial coverages indemnify organizations against personal, property, liability, and performance losses.

comparative negligence   Under the law, a situation where responsibility for an injury may be apportioned to different parties on the basis of the degree of negligence attributed to each.

completed buildings form   A standardized commercial ISO property form that covers property damage to completed buildings listed in the declarations.

completed operations liability   An exposure created when services are provided and the organization may be held responsible for future accidents resulting from defective workmanship. An example is the collapse of a wooden deck that injures visitors to a company picnic.

concealment   The failure to voluntarily disclose material facts that may affect the terms and availability of an insurance policy.

condition   A provision of an insurance policy that changes the scope of coverage.

condominium form   A special form needed to cover a condominium, which is a legal arrangement whereby individuals or organizations own common premises as well as individual living or commercial units.

conduct of operations liability   An exposure created when employees or representatives undertake day-to-day business and accidents occur anywhere in the world. An example is a person tripping over a temporary electrical cord at a trade fair.

contingent interruption or expenses form   An insurance policy that reimburses losses caused by the interruption of business activities resulting from damage to property not owned or controlled by the insured.

contract bond   An insurance policy that guarantees performance under the terms of a contract; sometimes called a **performance bond.** Examples are bonds to guarantee the construction of a building or the providing of supplies to a manufacturer.

contract of adhesion   Any agreement prepared by one party and accepted or rejected by another without modification. Insurance contracts are almost always contracts of adhesion.

coverage follows form   A situation where an excess policy contains exactly the same provisions as a lower layer of insurance.

coverage gap   Any exposure not covered by insurance or another risk financing method.

crime insurance   Covers losses arising from the dishonest acts of employees or third parties.

crisis management   Active efforts to meet the organization's responsibilities to its employees, community, and others after a major loss has occurred.

crisis planning   Coordinated actions to minimize direct and indirect consequences of a major loss.

cross-purchase plan   An agreement whereby each owner or partner in a business purchases sufficient life insurance on the other owners or partners to permit a purchase of each other's assets. If a person dies, money is available to buy out the person's interests and continue the business.

cut-through endorsement   *See* **assumption certificate.**

declarations   The first part of an insurance policy containing statements that provide information about the covered person or property.

deductible   An insurance policy provision that requires the insured to pay for losses up to a specified sum. If a policy contains a $5,000 deductible, the insurance company is responsible only for losses above $5,000.

defined benefit plan   A pension plan that specifies retirement benefits according to formulas known to all participants. The formulas may link benefits to salary, years of service, or other factors.

defined contribution plan   A pension plan that specifies no retirement benefits, but provides for employer and possibly employee contributions and grants retirement benefits based upon the money available at retirement.

deposit premium   A charge that covers the actuarial likelihood of losses and adjusting expenses as well as acquisition and administrative expenses of the insurer paid at the start of a policy and later adjusted to reflect actual losses.

directors and officers (D&O) liability coverage   Insurance that provides liability coverage to professional managers and others with respect to actions taken while acting in an official capacity as an officer or director of an organization. The coverage is similar to professional liability insurance.

disability insurance   Any insurance that provides an income to a person who is no longer able to work as a result of an accident, injury, or illness.

drop-down coverage   A situation where excess insurance covers some losses from the first dollar of loss or from some low attachment point. This may be specified for certain liabilities not covered by a primary policy.

earthquake endorsement   A provision in a homeowners policy that provides coverage against losses from earthquakes, landslides, and volcanic eruptions. The earthquake endorsement is designed to cover major rather than minor losses. It achieves this goal mainly through deductibles.

employee dishonesty insurance   Covers losses from the dishonest actions of employees, including theft, fraud, forgery, and embezzlement of funds. Such coverage is commonly referred to as a **fidelity bond.**

endorsement   A written provision that expands, reduces, or otherwise modifies the coverage under a basic property insurance policy.

endowment insurance   A form of life insurance that pays a benefit whether or not an insured individual dies during the period of the policy. It is really a combination of term insurance and a savings program.

errors and omissions insurance   A form of professional liability insurance that covers property loss or damage. It is purchased by lawyers, accountants, insurance adjusters, engineers, and similar professionals.

estoppel   The prevention of a person from making an affirmation or denial because it is contrary to a previous action that he or she has taken. An example is when an insurance company knows of misrepresentation when a policy is issued. Estoppel will prevent a later voiding of the policy as a result of the misrepresentation when a claim is filed.

excess insurance   Insurance that affords coverage above the limits provided by underlying risk financing, either primary insurance policies or a self-insured retention.

exclusion   Any loss or cause of loss not covered under an insurance policy.

expanded first-party coverage   An automobile insurance system with some characteristics of a no-fault system.

expectations principle   Under the law, interpreting a contract of adhesion to meet the expectations of the individual who did not draw up the contract. In other words, the fine print will not invalidate the main purpose of the agreement.

experience rating   Using the prior accident history of the insured to be considered in the rate paid for insurance coverage.

exposure   A condition where risk could cause a loss. Alternatively, it is a situation where an individual or organization is vulnerable to loss.

express disclaimers   A contract provision where one party is not held responsible for something. An example is a manufacturer and consumer who agree that the manufacturer will not be liable for accidents that result from the use of a product.

extra expenses form   An insurance policy that reimburses additional costs following a loss.

fidelity bond   *See* **employee dishonesty insurance.**

fiduciary bond   A guaranty that a person will meet legal obligations to safeguard property. An example is a bond for the administrator of a trust or estate.

financial responsibility law   This requires the owner or driver of a car to demonstrate the ability to pay damages resulting from an automobile accident. Failure to meet a minimum level of financial responsibility may result in a suspension of an individual's right to drive an automobile.

first-named insured   The party that has the primary rights and responsibilities under a policy. The first-named insured must pay the premiums, can negotiate changes in the policy, can cancel the policy, and is the only party that must be notified by the insurance company if the policy is to be cancelled.

floater   An inland marine insurance policy that covers property that is easily and frequently moved and is of relatively high value.

flood insurance   A program administered in the United States under the guidelines of the federal government to provide flood insurance.

fraud   An intentional deception to cause a person to give up property or some lawful right. With respect to an insurance policy, it is a willful false representation, concealment, or deliberate action that is relied upon by the insurer and causes the insurance company economic injury. It is more serious than concealment and may carry the possibility of civil or criminal penalties.

freight insurance   Ocean marine insurance that indemnifies a ship owner or operator for the loss of income when a vessel is lost or damaged.

fronting program   A situation where a company buys coverage from an admitted insurer who immediately reinsures the exposure with a captive of the parent that is not licensed to do business in the jurisdiction. Such a program is needed to avoid the costs of licensing a captive in every state where a parent has business.

funded loss reserve   A liability matched by specific liquid assets that are set aside and invested until needed to pay losses. They may be placed in a specific account of the company or may be held by an insurance company or other external party.

group life insurance An insurance plan covering a number of employees under a single policy issued to the employer.

guaranteed cost insurance Exists when a fixed premium is paid in advance to cover a loss, with no provision to adjust the size of the premium as a result of the level of losses.

hazard Any condition that increases the likelihood of a loss from a peril. An example is a can of gasoline stored in a garage, which increases the chance of a fire.

health maintenance organization (HMO) A health care provider that covers hospital, surgical, medical, and other services in a single comprehensive policy.

hold-harmless agreement A written contract whereby one party accepts legal liability for damages. A common example involves construction. An injured party on a construction site may sue the owner or the contractor. Under a hold-harmless agreement, the contractor agrees to pay for damages awarded if he or she is negligent.

homeowners policy A package insurance policy designed to protect individuals who own or rent residences.

hull insurance Ocean marine insurance that covers the vessel itself.

human engineering Any efforts to reduce accidents that result from careless or unthinking actions of employees or customers. Examples include providing warning labels on products, enforcing safety rules, and avoiding situations of fatigue or inattention.

implied warranty Under the law, an unwritten promise that a product is fit for its intended use.

incontestable clause A provision in a life insurance policy that states that the contract's validity cannot be challenged after it has been in force for a stated period of time, normally two years, provided the insured lives for the two years.

incurred loss retrospectively rated plan A funded insurance plan where the final level of the premium varies with losses. In this sense, it contains both a transfer and retention component.

indemnity A reimbursement that compensates exactly for a loss. It is, in effect, the payment of an amount of money that restores an individual or organization to the same position as existed prior to the loss.

indemnity principle A legal concept stating that payments of claims under an insurance policy must be limited to the actual loss suffered by the insured.

inflation guard endorsement A provision in an insurance policy that automatically increases the amount of insurance in response to changes in the value or replacement cost of the property.

inland marine insurance Covers property that may be transported from one place to another within the country. It also covers vehicles or fixed property that may participate in the transporting.

insurable risk   A pure risk that meets two tests, namely, a loss is not certain to occur and the loss involves a decrease in money or the disappearance of monetary value.

insurance   A financial device that redistributes the costs of unexpected losses from pure risks.

insurance association   *See* **association.**

insurance capacity   The ability of the carrier to provide the kinds and amounts of coverage desired by an organization. A small insurer may lack the financial strength to accept large exposures, even when allowing for the fact that reinsurance can be purchased to cover exposures.

insurance exchange   A marketplace where multiple insurers can accept portions of a primary risk. The most famous example is Lloyd's of London.

insurance pool   *See* **association.**

Insurance Services Office (ISO) Commercial Portfolio Program   A package of insurance forms to standardize business insurance. In addition to eliminating overlap and gaps in coverage, the forms simplify the language of the various coverages.

insurance syndicate   *See* **association.**

insuring agreement   A section of an insurance policy containing a summary of the major requirements imposed on the insurance company by the policy.

joint and several liability   Under the law, the right to collect damages from any of the defendants found to be negligent in a lawsuit.

joint and survivor annuity   An annuity agreement that makes payments when two or more individuals are named as annuitants and continues as long as one is still alive.

key person life insurance   A policy owned by the employer and purchased to cover a key person in the organization.

kidnap and ransom   Insurance that covers payment of a ransom in the event an employee is kidnapped. It covers employees who travel or work outside the United States in areas where they may be abducted by parties who seek the payment of a ransom.

law of large numbers   A statistical theorem stating that as a sample becomes larger, the outcome will be closer to the predicted probability.

legal liability   Any obligation of an individual or organization that is enforceable in a court of law.

liability   The exposure to any legal obligation and the accompanying responsibility to compensate another party for a loss or damage.

liability risk   The economic losses that could occur if someone accuses another person or organization of causing a loss or damage and then pursues reimbursement through various legal means.

Lloyd's broker   An individual authorized to place insurance or reinsurance business with a syndicate of Lloyd's of London.

loss control   Any activities that reduce, prevent, or minimize the economic or social losses from accidents.

loss exposure survey   A form or checklist that categorizes risks and quantifies possible losses. The forms can be developed in the areas of personnel, property, and casualty exposures.

loss prevention   Any effort to avert a loss before it occurs. Removing oily rags from a manufacturing premises may prevent the start of a fire.

loss reduction   Any effort to reduce the severity of a possible loss. Placing fire extinguishers in the workplace facilitates a rapid response to small fires and may limit the damage they inflict.

malpractice insurance   A form of professional liability insurance that covers bodily injury. It is purchased by doctors, dentists, hospitals, and similar entities.

manufacturer's selling price clause   A provision in an insurance policy that provides coverage for finished goods at their selling price rather than at their cost. Essentially, this protects the profit on goods that would have been sold.

material fact   An aspect of the risk that significantly affects the terms of a policy. It can even be sufficient to cause an insurer to deny coverage.

maximum premium   A multiple of the standard premium and represents an additional charge that can be made if losses exceed expectations in a retrospectively rated insurance plan.

minimum premium   A minimum premium that must be paid even though losses do not equal the actuarial forecast.

misrepresentation   A statement that is false with respect to a fact. If it is intentional and deals with a material fact, it can provide the basis for the insurer to void the policy at a future time.

misstatement of age clause   A provision in a life insurance policy that provides for a change in benefits if the age of the insured is incorrect. Although telling an incorrect age is a misrepresentation, the insurance company may not use it to void the policy. The benefits are simply recalculated to the correct age and paid to the beneficiary.

modified no-fault   An automobile insurance system where a pure no-fault system has been modified in one way or another.

monoline policy   Any insurance against a specific peril or that provides a single type of coverage. Examples are the Standard Fire Policy and flood insurance policies. The trend in commercial insurance is away from such policies.

moral hazard   Any tendency of an individual to be dishonest or otherwise lack integrity. An automobile mechanic who installs faulty parts in an automobile increases the chance of an accident. A dishonest employee might steal office supplies, take kickbacks from suppliers, or file a fraudulent accident claim.

morale or behavioral hazard   Any tendency of individuals to be careless. A driver may improperly load his truck, increasing the chance of an accident.

multiline policy   Any policy that provides more than one type of insurance in a single policy. An example is the homeowners policy.

named-perils agreement   An insurance policy that covers only losses from causes specifically listed.

negligence   The failure of a person or organization to exercise a proper degree of care in a given situation. Alternatively, it is the failure to behave as a reasonably prudent individual when faced with certain circumstances.

no-fault automobile insurance   A policy where a person's financial losses from an automobile accident are paid by the policyholder's own insurance policy without regard to any issue of negligence.

nonscheduled injury   Any injury not listed on a state's workers compensation schedule. Benefits are determined differently in each state.

occupational bond   A guaranty that a licensed person will provide honest and faithful performance of duties. It applies to groups such as stockbrokers, undertakers, and collectors of debts.

occupational disease   A disease peculiar to a specific occupation, as a lung disease that occurs among coal miners.

occurrence form   A liability insurance policy that obligates the insurance company to cover losses from events that take place during the policy period, even if the claim is made after the policy expired.

ocean marine insurance   Covers property while it is en route on ocean-going vessels.

organizational practices survey   A form or checklist that examines the policies and procedures of the organization with a view to identifying practices that cause unnecessary financial, legal, or physical exposures.

package policy   A multiline insurance contract that coordinates various coverages in a single policy.

paid loss retrospectively rated plan   An unfunded insurance plan where the final level of the premium varies with losses. It contains both a transfer and retention component.

parole   Oral evidence offered to vary the terms of a written contract. Normally, parole is not permitted to modify an insurance contract.

participation clause   Any requirement in an insurance policy for the insured to pay a specified percentage of any loss.

pension plan   A plan by an employer to provide funds to assist employees when they retire. A qualified pension plan conforms to the requirements of federal laws and receives tax benefits.

per occurrence policy limit   A provision in an insurance policy whereby each separate loss is covered up to the limit of the policy.

performance bond   *See* **contract bond.**

performance risk   The possible economic loss that would occur if a person or organization failed to provide goods or services as promised.

peril   The immediate cause of a loss. Examples are death, fire, an accident, a flood, and theft.

Personal Auto Policy   The most widely used insurance form for the coverage of individual and family automobiles.

personal lines   A category of insurance purchased by individuals and families and covers nonbusiness exposures. Examples are life, health, automobile, homeowners, and boat insurance.

personal property floater   An insurance policy that provides specific protection for individual items, such as jewelry, furs, silverware, cameras, musical instruments, and stamp collections.

personal property form   A standardized commercial ISO property form that covers personal property either owned by or in the custody of the insured.

personal property replacement cost endorsement   A provision that can be added to a homeowners policy that changes coverage from an actual cash value to a replacement cost.

Personal Protection Policy   An automobile insurance policy that combines no-fault and litigation solutions to resolving liability questions.

personal risk   The possibility of economic or emotional losses that might be suffered by individuals as they live their daily lives.

physical engineering   Any efforts to reduce the physical dangers of the workplace or environment of the employee or customer. Examples include eliminating slippery surfaces, improving lighting, reducing noxious vapors, and installing protective devices on machinery.

physical hazard   Physical conditions or behaviors that increase the chance of loss. A company that manufactures chemicals has physical hazards that may increase the chance of cancer.

plate glass form   A standardized property form used for commercial buildings with numerous windows and glass surfaces when the basic form does not provide adequate coverage.

posthire, postloss activities   Risk management steps taken after a loss to return conditions to normal.

posthire, preloss activities   Risk management steps taken to train employees in the safety aspects of their jobs and work environment with a goal of reducing future losses.

postloss service   The assistance provided by an insurance company after a loss has occurred. The insurer can assess the level of damage, make recommendations to minimize further losses, and pay claims promptly.

preferred provider organization (PPO)   A health care provider that charges the individual or employer at a discounted rate each time a service is provided.

prehire, preloss activities   Risk management steps taken before an employee is hired to reduce losses at a future time. An example is the hiring of a worker with a good safety record at previous employers.

premises burglary insurance   Covers property other than money, securities, and motor vehicles stolen from the premises by a third party who unlawfully entered the premises.

premium   The money paid by the insured in order to obtain coverage against a loss.

product liability   An exposure created when products are sold and the organization may be held responsible for subsequent accidents resulting from faulty design or defects. An example is an accident caused by the failure of brakes on a tractor.

professional liability insurance   Coverage for liability arising from a failure to use due care and the degree of skill expected of a person in a particular profession, such as medicine, law, accounting, or architecture.

profit sharing plan   A pension plan where an employer contributes a portion of its profits to a retirement fund for employees.

property risk   The possibility of economic losses that would result if tangible property were to be damaged, destroyed, or stolen. Such losses can be direct, as when a building is destroyed by a hurricane. Or they can be indirect, as when a company loses sales because its factory has been shut down by a fire.

proportional liability   Under the law, the right to collect from parties involved in damages when no one party can be determined to be negligent. If a person is injured by a known chemical sold by an unknown source, all manufacturers of that chemical can be liable in proportion to their share of the market.

protection and indemnity (P&I) insurance   Ocean marine liability insurance for claims by third parties against the owner or operator of the vessel.

punitive damages   Dollar awards to a plaintiff as a result of intentional outrageous misconduct by the defendant. They are designed to deter such behavior by punishing wrongdoers.

pure captive   An insurance company that provides insurance to a parent company and its affiliates or subsidiaries.

pure no-fault   An automobile insurance system where an accident victim collects for damages according to the coverage in his or her insurance policy. Negligence is not a factor.

pure risk   The chance of an unexpected or unplanned loss without the accompanying chance of a gain. These are the risks that are properly the domain of insurance and risk management.

ratemaking   The task of establishing the rate price charged for each unit of insurance protection.

reasonably foreseeable consequences   Under the law, the obligation to recognize the possibility of improper use of products or undesirable results of certain actions.

reinstatement clause   A provision in a life insurance policy that allows a lapsed policy to be made valid again without an increase in the premium.

reinsurance   A situation where an insurance company itself buys insurance to cover a portion or all of the risk it faces under a primary insurance agreement.

reinsurance pool   An underwriting activity whereby a group of participants agree to share the risks of reinsuring insurance policies. The term is synonymous with *reinsurance association* and *reinsurance syndicate*.

replacement cost   The amount of money required to construct a new and similar house on the site of a house that is totally destroyed.

replacement cost coverage   A provision in an insurance policy that provides for payment on the basis of replacement cost.

representation   A statement of fact made by an applicant in the process of obtaining an insurance policy. It concerns the risk and is made to induce the underwriter to provide insurance coverage.

retention   An approach to pure risk when an individual retains the exposure. Involuntary retention occurs when the organization is not aware of the existence of the pure risk. Voluntary retention occurs when the organization is aware of the pure risk and decides to assume the financial impact of any future losses.

retrospective rating   (a) Allowing the actual losses during a policy period to be the basis for the rate. (b) A process of determining the cost of an insurance policy after expiration of the policy, based upon the loss experience during the policy period. In effect, this is also a form of partial self-insurance since the organization and its insurer share losses up to a certain point.

rider   A written provision that expands, reduces, or otherwise modifies the coverage under a life or health insurance policy.

risk avoidance   A strategy where an individual or organization refuses to accept the exposure that can cause a future loss.

risk control   Any technique to reduce the likelihood of loss.

risk financing   The process of managing funds used to pay the costs of property, liability, and personnel losses. It is an integral part of the overall financial management of an organization.

risk management   A systematic approach to dealing with insurable and non-insurable risks facing an organization. An alternate definition is that risk management is a decision-making process that identifies exposures and creates programs to deal with them.

risk management program   A systematic effort to manage the loss exposures facing an organization. It seeks to deal with potential losses by identifying and measuring pure risks facing the firm. Then, it involves the development of a comprehensive approach to reducing the impact of personnel, property, and liability losses.

risk retention   Any conscious effort by an organization to bear the loss from any known sources. It can occur in a number of formal or informal ways.

risk retention group   An organized effort by a number of companies, often in the same industry, to retain a portion of their losses through a formal agreement. By joining together, the companies can enlarge their capacity to retain risk and gain a better use of the law of large numbers.

robbery and safe burglary insurance   Covers property other than money, securities, and motor vehicles taken by forcible means. This includes taking property from the premises or from an employee or messenger where intimidation or violence occurs. It also covers taking property from a safe or vault where force is used.

schedule rating   Using a list of adjustments to a class rating system. If an individual exposure is less risky than the average, the premium is adjusted downward. Higher-risk situations have increases to the class rate.

scheduled floater   An inland marine policy that covers large items that are individually identified and frequently transported. Examples are fur coats, fine art, and generators rented to other companies.

scheduled injury   Any injury covered specifically under a state's workers compensation schedule. Normally, the law identifies a permanent injury, such as the loss of an eye or a finger. The level of disability payments is determined by the specific schedule without regard to how the injury affects the employee's earning capacity.

scheduled personal property endorsement   A provision that can be added to a homeowners policy that provides additional coverage on personal property items that are listed individually. It improves the coverage.

self-insurance   A deliberate plan to meet certain and unplanned losses without insurance or other transfer mechanisms. The term is a misnomer, since it deals with retention, not insurance.

self-insured retention   A conscious risk management decision to retain the first portion of a risk.

single life annuity   An annuity agreement that makes payments for an uncertain liquidation period, namely, the duration of a person's life.

special multi-peril (SMP) program   A package policy that covers property and liability exposures for organizations in a coordinated single program of insurance.

specific excess insurance   A form of excess insurance that covers insured losses that exceed the underlying policy limit on a per loss, per occurrence, or per claim basis.

standard premium   A charge that covers the actuarial likelihood of losses and adjusting expenses as well as acquisition and administrative expenses of the insurer. It normally also includes a profit. It is normally paid as an initial or deposit premium.

stop loss excess insurance   *See* **aggregate excess insurance.**

strict compliance rule   A legal concept stating that a contract is enforced in accordance with its terms. If the terms are clear, the meaning may not be distorted by interpretations. Insurance policies are generally covered by this rule.

strict liability   Under the law, a situation where a party is liable for the consequences of an accident or illness even though negligence is not present. If a product is dangerous to use, the manufacturer may be strictly liable for accidents even though all actions have been taken to minimize the dangers and warnings have been given to the consumer.

subrogation   The right of an insurance company to be reimbursed for payments when a loss is caused by a third party.

suicide clause   A provision in a life insurance policy that provides for only a refund of premiums if the insured commits suicide within a certain period of time, normally one year.

surety bond   An insurance policy guaranteeing obligations by a third party.

surety insurance   Coverage that indemnifies losses when one party defaults on an obligation and thus causes damage to another party. An example is coverage to pay for losses if a contractor fails to construct a building in time for sales during the busy Christmas season.

tail of the policy   The length of time during which an insurance company can expect to receive claims. An occurrence policy has a long tail, since claims can be filed many years after the event. A claims-made policy has a short tail because coverage applies on the basis of the filing of the claim.

tax bond A guaranty that private organizations and individuals will collect taxes and remit them to government agencies. Examples are monies collected in conjunction with liquor, gasoline, and general state sales taxes.

term insurance A form of life insurance where a death benefit is paid only if the insured dies during a specified period of time.

theft, disappearance, and destruction insurance Covers money and securities that are stolen, disappear, or are destroyed, either on the premises or while being transported.

title insurance An insurance contract agreeing to indemnify the insured for any loss arising out of undiscovered defects in the title to real property.

transfer The shifting of pure risk from one individual or organization to another, either through insurance or contractual transfer.

trigger An event that activates insurance coverage.

umbrella insurance A form of excess insurance that often provides broad coverage above other primary and excess policies, usually at a high minimum level of loss.

underwriting The process of determining whether to issue an insurance policy. An underwriter is the person who makes this determination.

unfunded loss reserve A liability that is not matched with any specific pool of assets that can be directly used to pay losses. The liability is decreased when losses are paid from the general cash account of the organization.

uninsured motorist coverage This is insurance that compensates for losses caused by negligent parties when the negligent parties are not financially responsible. This coverage is available in the Personal Auto Policy.

universal life insurance A modification to whole life insurance that allows the owner to change premiums and where any excess earnings are credited to the cash value of the policy.

unsatisfied judgment fund This is a pool of money in some states available to compensate accident victims when a negligent party is unable or unavailable to pay for a loss.

U.S. market cycles A historical tendency of insurance premiums in the United States to rise and fall without regard to the level of losses.

utmost good faith A legal requirement that both parties must make a full and fair disclosure of all facts affecting an insurance contract.

variable life insurance A modification to whole life where the death benefit and cash value vary with investments.

variable universal life insurance A modification to whole life that allows a high level of flexibility with regard to premium payments, cash values, and the investments that support the policy.

vesting An employee's right to collect benefits on the basis of the employer's contributions to a pension plan. Federal law requires qualified plans to provide for full vesting within a reasonable period of time.

vicarious liability A situation where one party is deemed responsible for the negligence of another party. As an example, a company is judged liable for damages levied against an employee.

void   A legal term indicating that an agreement has no legal force; *see also* **voidable.**

voidable   An agreement that can be made void at the option of one of the parties under certain circumstances.

waiver   The intentional relinquishing or abandonment of a known right.

warranty   (a) A statement made to secure insurance coverage that must be absolutely and strictly true. Unlike representations, it is not enough that they be made to the best knowledge of the applicant. (b) A written guaranty on the quality of a product or performance of a service. If the product or service is defective, the manufacturer or provider will be responsible for damages.

whole life insurance   A life insurance policy that provides a death benefit in return for a fixed premium. Three forms of whole life are ordinary life, limited payment life, and single payment life.

workers compensation   A system of providing medical, disability, and rehabilitation coverage to employees and their dependents when a worker is injured in connection with a job.

workers compensation policy   Insurance that allows employers in the United States to compensate workers for injuries on the job without regard to fault. That is, even if a worker is negligent and causes his own accident, the employer is liable for the medical and economic consequences of the accident.

Index

273